Believing in Belonging: Belief ⌐⎯⎯⎯⎯⎯⎯⎯⎯ ⎯⎯ in the Modern World

Believing in Belonging draws on empirical research exploring mainstream religious belief and identity in Euro-American countries. Starting from a qualitative study based in northern England, and then broadening the data to include other parts of Europe and North America, Abby Day explores how people 'believe in belonging', choosing religious identifications to complement other social and emotional experiences of 'belongings'. The concept of 'performative belief' helps explain how otherwise non-religious people can bring into being a Christian identity related to social belongings.

What is often dismissed as 'nominal' religious affiliation is far from an empty category, but one loaded with cultural 'stuff' and meaning. Day introduces an original typology of natal, ethnic and aspirational nominalism that challenges established disciplinary theory in both the European and North American schools of the sociology of religion that assert that most people are 'unchurched' or 'believe without belonging' while privately maintaining beliefs in God and other 'spiritual' phenomena.

This study provides a unique analysis and synthesis of anthropological and sociological understandings of belief and proposes a holistic, organic, multidimensional analytical framework to allow rich cross cultural comparisons. Chapters focus in particular on: the genealogies of 'belief' in anthropology and sociology, methods for researching belief without asking religious questions, the acts of claiming cultural identity, youth, gender, the 'social' supernatural, fate and agency, morality and a development of anthropocentric and theocentric orientations that provides a richer understanding of belief than conventional religious/secular distinctions.

Abby Day is a Research Fellow in the Department of Anthropology at the University of Sussex.

Believing in Belonging

Belief and Social Identity in the Modern World

Abby Day

OXFORD
UNIVERSITY PRESS

OXFORD
UNIVERSITY PRESS

Great Clarendon Street, Oxford, OX2 6DP,
United Kingdom

Oxford University Press is a department of the University of Oxford.
It furthers the University's objective of excellence in research, scholarship,
and education by publishing worldwide.

Oxford is a registered trade mark of Oxford University Press
in the UK and in certain other countries

British Library Cataloguing in Publication Data

Data available

Library of Congress Cataloging in Publication Data

Data available

ISBN 978-0-19-957787-3 (hbk)
ISBN 978-0-19-967355-1 (pbk)

Preface

This book begins to answer a question that has largely remained unspoken in the study of religion: what do people mean by belief? Debates surrounding religion and its relationship to identity, practice, and society are often based on apparently straightforward evidence concerning the big 'Bs' of religion: belonging, belief, and behaviour. We may measure 'behaviour' taking narrow definitions, such as attendance at religious services, participation in rites, or involvement in other apparently religious activities. As every student of religion knows, however, such measurements are crude and need to be developed further by deeper understandings of what is meant by 'attendance' and what is really involved in apparently religious ceremonies such as weddings and funerals. The line between party and piety is sometimes blurred.

We may also measure 'belonging' by taking self-identification statistics or membership data. Once again, we know that people 'belong' to their religious organizations for a variety of reasons, some of which are unrelated to relationships with God. In several European countries, for example, belonging to the national church is automatic; in the UK, many families decide to 'belong' to their local Church of England to ensure their child's place at a religious school; in the USA, scholars have intensely studied why people switch in and out of various churches and denominations. While this book will, I hope, add to those already rich and lively conversations, the central issue here is with the rarely deconstructed and analysed third 'B': belief.

Our lack of knowledge about what people 'believe' raises important questions. The 'genealogy of belief' outlined in Chapter 1 is possibly contentious and undoubtedly partial, but it is an attempt to chart how the term belief has been employed and changed in the two disciplines of anthropology and sociology. As such, it will be the beginning, I hope, of increased dialogue between two distinct groups of scholars, with markedly different approaches to belief.[1]

---

[1] Some preliminary ideas now developed in Chapter 1 were initially published in *Culture and Religion* in my introduction to a larger work on performative belief: see Day 2010b.

Having been discouraged by the sparse academic work on belief, I decided to turn the question back to the people whose beliefs seemed to be, for the most part, either ignored or taken for granted. That approach is outlined in detail in Chapter 2.[2]

The interpretative framework for the book is discussed in detail in Chapter 8. Readers wanting to engage with the ethnographic material (Chapters 3 through 7) principally through an analytical lens may want to read Chapter 8 first.

The book then draws on empirical research exploring mainstream religious belief and identity in Euro American countries. Starting from a qualitative study based in northern England, and then broadening the data to include Europe and North America, I argue that many people 'believe in belonging', choosing religious identifications to complement other social and emotional experiences of 'belongings'.[3]

As every author knows, the act of thanking people who have contributed to one's work is daunting: there are hundreds of people who have helped shape this book in a variety of ways, from occasional conversations to more lengthy interchanges. I am grateful to the organizations to which I belong that have held conferences and seminars to facilitate such exchanges: the American Anthropology Association; the British Association for the Study of Religion; the British Sociological Association, and in particular its Sociology of Religion Study Group; International Society for the Sociology of Religion; and the Society for the Scientific Study of Religion.

While there have been many people who have taught me and shared ideas with me over the years, there are some in particular who have provided significant support and encouragement on this project and to whom I extend my deepest gratitude: Simon Coleman, Jay Demerath, Hiroko Kawanami, Gordon Lynch, David Voas, and Linda Woodhead. I am indebted to all my research participants, who will remain anonymous but who have informed, confused, delighted, and inspired me. Thank you also to the team at Oxford University Press, particularly Tom Perridge, Lizzie Robottom, Tessa Eaton, and Malcolm Todd. Finally, without funding and the other resources from the Arts and Humanities Research Council and the Economic and Social Research Council this work would not have been possible.

---

[2] Some material in Chapter 2 appeared in my *Fieldwork in Religion* paper centring on methodological issues: see Day 2009a.

[3] Some preliminary ideas now developed in Chapter 4 were initially published in Day 2009b and Day 2010a.

My wonderful children Jake and Alex have been a constant source of love and support throughout this project, as has my mother, Gwen. Sadly, my father Stockwell died before he could see the finished book, but he always believed in it, and in me. It is to his memory that I dedicate this work.

Contents

Section 1
Methods and Theoretical Frameworks

In this section I present two chapters, beginning with a genealogy of belief, followed by a summary of the research journey, including key aspects of the book's theoretical background and methodology.

1

Genealogies of Belief in Sociology and Anthropology: Transcending Disciplinary Boundaries

Christians who belong to mainstream churches rise together each
Sunday to recite jointly their creeds as collective statements of their
church's and – one assumes – their own beliefs. As they begin 'I believe'
in their God who made heaven and earth, and in Jesus Christ, one
could wonder if they mean that as a truth claim or a statement of faith
and trust. It could be one, or both. So ingrained is *belief* to their
tradition they may never consider what, exactly, they mean by that
word. Like those everyday Christians, scholars in academic disciplines
of anthropology, sociology, theology, religious studies, and psychology
often use the term 'belief' in their work without analysing or theorizing
what they, or the people they study, mean. In this chapter, I propose
charting genealogies of belief, tracing its movement through time and
spaces, noting how it acquires the assumptions and hues of the people
who use it. Sometimes it remains an unspoken, implicit assumption
within scholars' work; sometimes, but rarely, it is explicitly examined
and, if not theorized, at least uncovered. Where scholars locate and
understand belief is an epistemological choice, but an often unexam-
ined reflection of how they produce knowledge about those they study
and about their discipline. Although that production may be invisible,
it exists nonetheless and influences their interpretations and therefore
our understanding about belief. Ideas about belief do not simply arise
neutrally from either 'the field' or philosophical analyses: they are
deeply embedded in, and not always abstracted from, other overarching themes and disciplinary preoccupations such as meaning, experience, emotion, order, individuality, thought, action, identity, sociality,
rationality, symbolism, and power, for example. How it is conceived

and located reflects the context of the scholar and, therefore, the conclusions those scholars reach about the people they study. Few scholars explicitly trace how they have created their concept of belief; least of all do those scholars talk to each other. Why do we have, for example, near silence within the sociology of religion about individuals' beliefs and yet a near-obsession with societal secularization? Part of the answer lies in choices about scale, but also in disciplinary history, in what Foucault (1972) conceived as sedimentary layers of knowledge.

Before turning to my own case study and related other studies, I will situate myself within that long history and genealogy of belief and, most importantly, begin a conversation amongst scholars who, separated by disciplinary context and time, have rarely spoken to each other. My goal is to synthesize the major works in this area for the sake of a dialogue between disciplines that generates interesting theoretical and empirical advances. In this chapter, I propose charting 'genealogies of belief' with implicit reference to Talal Asad (1993), whose 'genealogies of religion' demonstrated that neither religion nor belief is vacuously produced. Although Asad was principally concerned with how temporally located social and religious groups legitimize certain forms of religious belief, my concern in this chapter is more disciplinary-specific: how did certain scholars conceive of belief and how has their work influenced others? What were their implicit assumptions and locations and what can we, working in the social scientific field of religion, learn from each other? Following Foucault, this chapter will therefore be a mix of archaeology and epistemology: through uncovering various layers I hope to reveal how disciplinary knowledge about belief has been created and how an interdisciplinary approach can loosen some of those structures and promote dialogue.

A brief overview

The genealogy probably rightly begins with Tylor's classic definition of religion where he put 'a belief in spirits' at the heart of it (1958 [1871]). As Lambeck (2002, 21) noted: Tylor's theories 'remain congenial to many contemporary thinkers and [are] indeed almost a part of western "common sense" on the subject'. Robertson Smith (1912, 110) claimed that belief is the core of religion, and takes precedence over theological or historical interpretations: 'it will no longer be the results of theology that we are required to defend, but something prior to theology. What we shall have to defend is not our Christian knowledge but our Christian belief.' The centrality of belief to religion was shaken by Durkheim, who placed 'practice' next to belief on an equal footing and argued that the most important part of religion was not the beliefs, nor even the deities, but the way in which those sharing common beliefs and practices performed together to protect a greater entity, such as society. From the Durkheimian legacy the disciplines of anthropology and sociology began to diverge and follow different paths through the greater part of the twentieth century. Anthropology tended to explain religion in functional rather than substantive terms, shaped by boundaries of time and space. Belief was thus whatever worked best at the time for the specific collective. The sociology of religion, alternatively, tended to favour substantive definitions, adopting a Weberian, meaning-centred adaptation of Durkheim. Belief was therefore whatever worked best for individuals to give meaning and cohesion to an otherwise chaotic universe. The place of belief in anthropology has tended to be localized, specific, and typically small-scale and domestic. Debates have concerned whether enquiries were sufficiently localized, as opposed to universalized, and historicized. The trend was to move from what informants 'believe' to how anthropologists construct belief, with awareness that the subdisciplinary preference of the scholar is likely to determine the interpretation. Durkheim's enormous sociological contribution to the recognition of social structure as a source for belief and other concepts needed to be tempered by the anthropologist Malinowksi's recognition of sociality and individual agency; both those functionalist orientations needed to be corrected by the kind of contribution the cultural anthropologist Geertz made about symbolism, with his incorporation of a Weberian meaning-centred universe, which in turn was rightly criticized for being ahistorical and essentially Christian by Asad, who in turn essentialized power, and so on. (For a wider discussion of how anthropologists have treated secularism and belief, see Day and Coleman 2013a)

A sociological approach to belief has tended to focus on the institutional and societal, asking whether or not secularization is occurring in Euro American countries, with the main emphasis on measures of affiliation and practice, rather than belief. The theoretical grounding in the sociology of religion is largely Tylorian and Weberian, with assumptions about beliefs in spiritual beings and a search for meaning being somehow inherent and irreducibly both human and religious. Having accepted a Weberian analysis about a search for meaning, many sociologists of religion largely ignored the most important part of Weber's analysis – social action, against a background of a decline in the Protestant Ethic. They dismissed the large-scale decline in religious action, measured by church attendance and participation in every significant Christian rite, from baptism to funerals. This would be anathema to a social anthropologist, who would explore varieties of social action as expressions of significance and social structure. Rather than enquiring too deeply about why people choose not to participate in Christian activities, sociologists of religion from Davie to Voas based their arguments on quantitative data that ask questions using religious vocabulary, such as 'do you believe in God?', and deploying Christian-centred values, such as 'do you think homosexuality is wrong?' The results are mixed depending on the survey but tend to reflect proposi-tional forms of belief only, focusing primarily on only one dimension of belief, its content, rather than on its dimensions.[1] I will return later to this problem as I propose a holistic, organic, heuristic model explor-ing seven dimensions of belief.

A conclusion that beliefs are propositional may, therefore, reflect the research method more than the beliefs or experiences of research par-ticipants. In practice, as I will discuss in this book, belief will be propo-sitional, affective, embodied, and performed.[2] I will now turn to revisit in more detail some of the themes highlighted above by exploring where belief has been located in social scientific enquiry. It is central to the theme of this book that 'belief' can be relocated from the individual to the social and from the transcendent to the mundane.

Locating belief: the locus of the individual

Edward Burnett Tylor defined religion (1958 [1871]) in terms of animism, or faith in the soul, stemming from an individual's mis-taken belief in spiritual beings. Religious belief resulted from the need to explain uncanny events and would therefore eventually, he argued, be replaced with the benefit of scientific knowledge and other civilizing influences as societies evolved through a linear series of predictable phases. Tylor came from a Quaker background that may have had two significant impacts on his understanding of belief. His reli-gious upbringing may have predisposed him to accepting a wider, non-theistic view of religion while his religious status as a Quaker barred him from being accepted into university. He first learned about other cultures while travelling in Central America, and returned to England determined to understand more about what became known as 'cultural anthropology'. In several senses therefore, Tylor was a nonconformist.

---

[1] Zinnbauer et al. (1997) report that people identify as religious in terms of belief and spirituality in terms of experience.

[2] For recent reviews of that complexity in practice, see Mitchell, J.P. and Mitchell, H. (2008) on Mormons and Elisha (2008) on American Evangelicals.

Many theorists today, such as those advocating 'rational choice' and evolutionary social science, can trace their intellectual lineage to Tylor. Like Durkheim, and in common with other anthropologists of the nineteenth and early twentieth centuries (see, for example, Frazer 1996 [1922]), Tylor gained his knowledge from reading the accounts of other people, largely missionaries and colonials, and then tended to universalize their findings into general theories. Unlike Durkheim, his account of belief was wholly propositional, rooted in an individual's coherent system of ideas, rather than in collective beliefs and practices. While Tylor's view of belief could be described as intellectualistic, psychological, universal, evolutionary, and explanatory, the point of distinction I would like to raise here is that it is profoundly individualistic. The idea that belief serves to explain uncanny events and gives meaning to life is a strong theme that arises frequently within the sociology of religion.

Although he is usually associated primarily with sociology, the anthropological genealogy of belief needs here to account for Max Weber whose work began to influence anthropology in the mid twentieth century. Although he said he was not personally religious (he described himself as religiously 'unmusical'), through being raised by a Calvinist mother and having visited his Baptist relatives in the United States,[3] Weber would have been intimately familiar with the beliefs and sentiments of those who were. Weber's main academic interest was to explain *social action*. Action, he argued, is subjectively understood by the actor; it is social when the meaning of that subjective action relates to others.

Weber introduced a notion that people everywhere, and throughout time, have searched for meaning and, often, are seeking to resolve the problem of meaning created when their belief in a good god is threatened by bad events. He used the term *verstehen* to express the need for the scholar to understand, from informants' perspectives, the meaning of their actions. His assumption that people are searching for meaning, while central to his work, is rarely problematized: most scholars in both the anthropology and sociology of religion follow implicitly, and sometimes explicitly, a Weberian assumption of

> the metaphysical needs of the human mind as it is driven to reflect on ethical and religious questions, driven not by material need but by an inner compulsion to understand the world as a meaningful cosmos and to take up a position toward it. (1922, 117)

---

[3] Weber's visit to his relatives, members of the Primitive Baptists of the Mountain District Association, was one of his few forays into fieldwork. See Peacock and Tyson (1989) for a fuller account of his visit and their follow-up research.

The process of taking up such a 'position' might otherwise be understood as a propositional, individualized form of 'belief'. Further, Weber distinguishes (1978, 4) meaning as understood subjectively, as it is in the social sciences, from meaning that is attached to something that purports to be true, as represented in the more 'dogmatic disciplines in that area, such as jurisprudence, logic, ethics and esthetics', and, I will add, theology. The distinction between subjective forms of meaning and propositional forms can be applied to the study of belief and anticipates how future scholars, such as Ruel and Robbins (discussed later in this chapter) would make distinctions between 'believing in' and 'believing that'.

That propositional, individualistic, and universalizing way of looking at belief shaped the sociology of religion, particularly through the work of Peter Berger, a sociologist and theologian, who wrote that there exists 'a human craving for meaning that appears to have the force of instinct. Men [sic] are congenitally compelled to impose a meaningful order upon reality' (1967, 22). Berger (1967) and Luckmann (1967) followed a Weberian tradition of locating belief within an individually based, and socially mediated, search for meaning, where subjective realities were the primary framework. For Weber, Berger, Geertz, Luckmann, and others, the focus on making meaning was a universal, and individually driven, human need. The social construction of reality and the maintenance of a sacred canopy depend on social consensus, Berger argued, and therefore the threat to such a shared belief system is pluralism. Mary Douglas, as I will discuss below, was writing at the same time as Berger about similar themes of coherence.

Grace Davie's 'believing without belonging' thesis (1994) rests on a similar propositional, individualized idea of belief in suggesting that people maintain a private belief in God or other Christian-associated ideals, without church attendance or other forms of Christian participation. Drawing mainly on European Values Survey data, Davie argued that the majority of British people persist in believing in God but 'see no need to participate with even minimal regularity in their religious institutions' (1994, 2) and therefore should be described as 'unchurched' rather than secular (1994, 12–13). Her term 'unchurched' reflects a Christian-centric idea that a natural state is one of being 'churched'. Nowhere in her book does Davie discuss what she means by 'belief', although she notes that 'some sort of belief persists' (1994, 107). By omitting certain words she is creating an elision, conveying the meaning of 'belief' as 'belief in God' or 'belief in Christianity'.

Her explanation is footnoted: 'The term "belief" is, of course, a wide one, it does not imply the acceptance of particular credal statements' (1994, 115). In a later work, Davie (2007) suggested that an 'unchurched' European public believes 'vicariously' through others, such as church leaders, who believe on their behalf.[4]

Those beliefs are being performed by an active minority on behalf of a much larger majority who both understand and approve – if only, she adds, implicitly – of what that minority is doing. She notes that the least controversial aspect of her proposition is the church's provision of life cycle rituals. As well as public rituals, the public also expects church leaders to believe and behave in accordance with church teachings: bishops are rebuked if they air their doubts publicly and clergy and their families are expected to behave appropriately. Davie adds that 'Failure leads to accusations of hypocrisy but also to expressions of disappointment' (ibid., 24). Thus far, she suggests, such propositions for vicarious religion are straightforward. The contentious, and yet the most critical point for her argument, is that churches retain symbolic importance for the public as both places of cultural significance and as spaces for the 'vicarious debate of unresolved issues in modern societies' (ibid., 23). That is an intriguing idea, deserving further exploration in light of my research on the institutional importance of institutional Christianity.[5]

Locating belief: the turn to culture

From Durkheim we can clearly trace two main developments that diverged by disciplinary focus: most of early-to-mid-twentieth-century social anthropology of religion adopted a Durkheimian approach where religion was explained in functional, rather than substantive terms, shaped by boundaries of time and space. Belief was thus whatever worked best at the time for the specific collective. The sociology of religion, alternatively, tended to favour substantive definitions, adopting a Weberian, meaning-centred adaptation of Durkheim. Belief was therefore whatever worked best for the individual and, as a result, for the greater good, generally throughout time and in all places.

---

[4] Davie adds that she does not think the concept of vicarious religion is as readily applied to the American religious landscape, where ideas of active membership and participation prevail, but notes that in times of public tragedy there is an expectation that religious buildings and leaders will provide a focus for expressions of public grief.

[5] A rather counter-intuitive finding, but one elaborated in more detail in Chapters 9 and 10 where I discuss how the 'institution' of Christianity becomes more important to some people than its practices, beliefs, or canon.

Within those broad generalizations lie variations that will be briefly summarized here and then revisited during the rest of this book.

Durkheim's analysis of religion needs to be understood within his larger lifetime project to explore and expound upon sociality as the key to understanding human behaviour. One of the problems he sought to resolve related to the origins of categories of understanding: were they, as Kant argued, a priori categories or did they arise through experience and interaction? Individual belief, according to Durkheim and Mauss' theory of social classifications, was not possible. Anticipating what I theorize later as 'performative' belief, they argued that concepts and classifications arose from social relations: 'The first logical categories were social categories; the first classes of things were classes of men into which these things were integrated' (1963 [1902], 93).

Durkheim was not personally religious, but as the son of a rabbi he was raised both to respect and to critically evaluate religion. Durkheim's well-known definition of religion as 'a unified system of beliefs and practices relative to sacred things' takes propositional belief as a starting point but moves it into the realm of performance 'that is to say, things set apart and forbidden – beliefs and practice which unite into one single moral community called a Church, all those who adhere to them' (1915, 47). Beliefs were unrelated to supernatural beings but were created through collective, intellectual effort classifying that which was sacred and profane so that people could practise socially cohesive behaviours. By reducing gods to the place of interesting but unnecessary accessories, Durkheim disrupted forces of power, authority, and legitimacy by relocating belief in the social. Belief was therefore not something one acquired through accepting the pre-formed ideas of society, but rather something that was produced through the performative engagement with others. Within anthropology and sociology there would emerge two important and different understandings of belief, discussed in this book as the 'pre-formed' and 'performed'. The Durkheimian approach was to argue that beliefs were produced (what I would describe as 'performatively') through rituals of belonging rather than interpreting ritual as a mirror or mere performance of already-existing beliefs. Further, what was being worshipped or celebrated was not the entity of 'society' but, I suggest, the embodied, emotional experience of belonging.

A turning point in the Durkheimian understanding of belief came when Bronislaw Malinowksi took a Tylorian and Freudian appreciation of the psychological, individual source of belief and a Durkheimian appreciation of the collective bonding nature of belief. Malinowski proposed that belief was one of several interlocking, interdependent parts of a social system that 'worked' to support both basic individual biological needs and the functioning of society. In showing that the so-called primitive mind was no different or less rational than other supposedly 'advanced' societies, Malinowski refuted a Tylorian, evolutionist and universalistic, perspective and anticipated a performative understanding of belief. For a more detailed explanation of the legacy of that argument see, for example, Tambiah (1990) and Wilson (1974).

E.E. Evans-Pritchard initially followed the example of his teacher, Malinowski, by adopting an intensive fieldwork approach, and was critical of anthropologists who did not root their theories in fieldwork. Although he did not adopt Malinowski's strictly functionalist approach, he theorized that people's beliefs were, as Durkheim described them, 'social facts'. He rejected the ahistorical approach of Durkheim, and dismissed the latter's search for the origins of religion as 'just-so' stories but much of Evans-Pritchard's work draws implicitly on Durkheimian theories about the function of belief, its collective nature, and the segmentary structure of relations. In his study of the Nuer (1940) concepts of time and space, he argued (without, oddly, reference to Durkheim) that their beliefs and social structure were tied to economic and social values and from there to structural relations. Evans-Pritchard therefore contextualized the nature of belief and belonging, arguing that people's sense of 'tribal' belonging was based on their social relations and not the inherent differences in physical characteristics or customs.

In his study of Azande witchcraft belief (1976 [1937]), Evans-Pritchard demonstrated that while an 'intellectualist' outsider may perceive some of their witchcraft beliefs as contradictory, when understood in terms of the function that belief performed there was no contradiction. The Azande had a sophisticated view of how witchcraft worked, but were prepared to ignore some of their basic beliefs to preserve social order. For example, commoners could not accuse rulers of witchcraft; if a close relation was found to be a witch then their blood bond was disputed; if someone behaved immorally, they could not defend themselves by claiming they were bewitched. He wrote that 'there is a vague belief, hardly precise enough to be called a doctrine' (1976 [1937], 2), thus positioning belief as propositional and cognitive, but not individual. The Azande sustain what we may theoretically see as a contradiction because the theory is of no use to them in practice. What matters to them is the preservation of social and kin relations.[6]

---

[6] Evans-Pritchard's own religious orientation changed through his life and may have affected his theories. See, for example, Engelke (2002, 4) and Kuper (1973, 124–5).

Lucien Lévy-Bruhl picked up a Durkheimian theme, coming to anthropology from philosophy, where he departed from universalistic theories about morality by arguing that morals and ethics are pluralistic and relativistic. Lévy-Bruhl followed Durkheim in departing from Tylor and his explanatory, evolutionary interpretation of people's beliefs, arguing (1926) that people's beliefs, particularly organized into myths and rituals, responded to collective needs and sentiments. He provided a direct antithesis to Tylor and the individualist tendency in Malinowski by treating belief as wholly collective, leading to what he described as the 'law of participation' (ibid., 76), itself a form of what I will discuss later as performative belief. For Lévy-Bruhl the 'primitive reality' was a mystical state that did not recognize two separate orders of material and spiritual reality, but one, where all interactions are experienced emotionally and perceived as relational. This 'pre-logical' mind is different from the modern mind where 'laws of contradiction' are taught with the assumption that reasoning must be linear. Even today, he concluded, 'we' are also at times pre-logical and sometimes irrational as, through religions and similar institutions, we seek the ecstasy experienced through a sense of total participation.

Although such terms as 'pre-logical' and the concept of a primitive 'mind' forced much criticism of his work, he later adopted a more sceptical position and expanded on the concluding feature of his earlier work: the difference between people who believe in participation and people who adopt the laws of contradiction is not a matter of their minds being different, but their modes of thinking.[7]

Mary Douglas later criticized (2004 [1970]) Evans-Pritchard for adhering to a functionalist, homeostatic view that depended on accepting certain norms and became entrenched even when unverifiable. She extended her criticism beyond Evans-Pritchard to other colonial anthropologists of the era who felt they had a duty to protect 'primitives' and extended to them a benign tolerance unthinkable in their home societies. Showing that witchcraft had positive, constructive purposes was part of that rationale, she argued. Functionalist analysis,

---

[7] In a reprise of Lévy-Bruhl, Luhrmann (2007) points out that the idea of interconnection, participation, and relatedness lies at the heart of contemporary American evangelical practice (and, by inference, of other forms of contemporary religion and spirituality). She argues that Lévy-Bruhl, and by extension, Durkheim, was correct to suggest that perception was a social process, particularly as Lévy-Bruhl added the variations of different social groups to the Durkheimian universalistic formulation, and anticipated what is now known as cultural psychology. Luhrmann further argues that what is now known as cognitive anthropology often neglects the emotive or bodily processes involved in religious experience and transmission. E.E. Evans-Pritchard also defended Lévy-Bruhl's explanation that individual beliefs were socially determined.

while overly systematic and rigid, was sometimes analytically useful and should not be completely dismissed, she said.

Douglas argued that belief in witchcraft relates to insiders and outsiders, or, as she discussed more fully in a separate work (1966, following a Durkheimian binary classification of sacred and profane) the pure and polluted. She argued, reflecting a Durkheimian orientation to both an understanding of 'sacred' and to associated social structuring, that beliefs are how societies order themselves.[8] All beliefs, for Douglas, were about the varieties of powers and dangers that a society recognizes. While admitting a charge that she may over-systematize, she defends her use of exaggeration as necessary to make her point that beliefs about purifying, demarcation, and punishment all 'have as their main function to impose system on an inherently untidy experience' (ibid., 5). This means that beliefs are not static or universal, but are formed collectively to respond to changing circumstances. Belief arises not as a philosophy or creed, but as a pragmatic (I would add 'performative') means for the 'believer' to impose order and achieve a sense of coherence (as Weber and Berger argued). She was influenced here not only by Durkheim and Evans-Pritchard, but by Raymond Firth and Max Weber.

Firth explored how individuals created and manipulated beliefs. In an interesting anticipation of Bourdieu's (1991) reconciliation of structure and agency through 'strategy', and later theories on performativity, Firth argued that individuals made adjustments by using their beliefs as modes of action, as 'active weapons of adjustment by the person who holds them' (1948, 26–7). These adjustments are necessary, Firth argued, to manage the sometimes contradictory demands and positions between an individual's social and physical context, and her own 'set of impulses, desires, and emotions' (ibid., 26). In so doing, the individual must negotiate a number of motivations, including, perhaps, a search for order and a curiosity about intellectual variety; a desire for self-fulfilment and a desire to be in relationship with others. Such adjustments eventually influence the form that religion takes in society, he argued, thus locating belief firmly, and primarily, in the social, with religion its product and subset. His theory that belief

---

[8] Here, Douglas (writing at the same time as Berger) was influenced by Claude Levi-Strauss, who took Durkheimian and Maussian theories about symbolic classifications but argued that these classifications arose not from society, but from the human mind and represented mental structures that were universal. These classifications were structures often present in myth, and could only be understood through analysis, or 'explication', of both conscious and unconscious thought.

had a pragmatic and flexible quality influenced many anthropologists to come.[9]

Cultural anthropologist Clifford Geertz was influenced by Weber's work on meaning, and explored how ritual provided both a model for and a model of meaning in the world. Here, he imposed a symbolic interpretation of religion in direct opposition to the social functionalism of Malinowski, Radcliffe-Brown, and Evans-Pritchard.[10] He argued that it was a cultural pattern, not individual behaviour or only social interaction, that makes humans what they are: without them they would be merely a 'talented ape' responding creatively to biological impulses, or, worse, 'a kind of formless monster with neither sense of direction nor power of self control, a chaos of spasmodic impulses and vague emotions' (1973, 99).

His specific treatment of 'belief', however, was somewhat tangential, despite his call for anthropologists of religion to stop avoiding the issue by 'relegating it to psychology, that raffish outcast discipline to which social anthropologists are forever consigning phenomena they are unable to deal with within the framework of a denatured Durkheimianism' (ibid., 109). Unlike Tylor and Durkheim, Geertz did not include 'belief' in his definition of religion, but, rather, discussed it *en passant*, chiefly through his exploration of ritual.

Evoking a Tylorian, propositional understanding of belief, Geertz says people turn to a belief in gods, spirits, and other religious forms of authority to explain, following Weber, the 'problem of meaning', reflecting an impulse he claims is 'everywhere the same' (ibid., 110). He then turns at length to discuss what he calls a 'religious perspective' through a thorough treatment of ritual. Here, he points out that belief is not a homogeneous category, such as one's occupation or place of residence, and makes the distinction between belief as a cognitive understanding and belief as a lived experience in ritual. Ritual, I suggest, is understood here as incorporating acts that reproduce pre-formed ideas, values, or beliefs – in contrast to acts that produce ideas, values, or beliefs through performance.

Geertz plots a new course for anthropologists, where belief as an idea gives way to belief as a practice, with ritual symbolizing meaning. Although Geertz and Douglas did not share the Weberian assumption

---

[9] See, for example, Kirsch (2004), who studied how Zambian people often switched their faith in healers, a switch accompanied by a requisite change in belief.

[10] Geertz set a new agenda for much of the anthropology that followed the publication of his seminal essay, 'Religion as a Cultural System' in 1966, later republished with other key works in *The Interpretation of Cultures: Selected Essays* (Geertz 1973).

that everyone searches for meaning, they both consider social action as directed towards making order out of chaos.

Troubling belief

Rodney Needham (1972) began to historicize the way belief has been used by, primarily, anthropologists and philosophers. Needham provided an exhaustive review of 'belief' mainly from the philosophical literature and concluded that it was a mistake to universalize it. He argued that the broadly anthropological literature and, more specifically, ethnographic literature consistently fails to interrogate how scholars are using the term belief. Needham (anticipating Asad's criticism of Geertz, as discussed below) went so far as to say it should be abandoned as a useful concept in research because it could not be universalized. Nevertheless, Needham forced a more careful interrogation about belief and its roots in Christianity. The concern about belief began to shift from concentrating on what other people believed to how scholars were using the concept itself.

Needham was somewhat harshly criticized by Malcolm Ruel (1982), who says Needham's work lacks contextual examples, particularly of the Christian case, which Needham tends to dismiss 'with a few airy waves' (ibid., 24). Ruel was also concerned about how the term 'belief' is used, not because of its instability as a philosophical term, but because it meant different things to different people at different times. Here, he drew on William Cantwell Smith (1977; 1978; 1979), a religious studies scholar, who discusses how the term 'belief' has changed over time in the Christian context, from one of trust, reciprocity, fidelity, and love (a more performative reading of belief, perhaps) to one of membership, proposition, and doubt.

Ruel (1982) describes strong and weak forms of belief where a weak, everyday version of belief generally refers to a sense of expectation or assumption, either of oneself or others, and is therefore not generally misunderstood nor problematic. It is when, Ruel argues, the term arises in a 'strong' sense, as part of a definition, categorization, or problem, that it will usually draw on connotations from its Christian use.

Ruel (1982, 27–9) identified four fallacies common to the treatment of belief: that it is central to all religions, in the same way that it is central to Christianity; that belief guides and therefore explains behaviour; that belief is psychological; that it is the belief, not the object of belief, that is most important. This means that we can separate what people believe about the world from the world itself. As Ruel puts it

(1982, 103): 'A distinction made frequently today is between "belief in" (trust in) and "belief that" (propositional belief).' Ruel concludes it is best to use the term 'belief' as we might use 'faith' if what we mean is 'trust': Ruel says that the original Greek word for faith was *pistis*, expressing the idea of trust, or conduct that honoured an agreement or bond and thus had a *social* orientation. One might, I suggest, elaborate a little if we consider that *pistis* is a noun, meaning a conviction, a persuasion, or acceptance of a truth – what we might call propositional belief. The verb, *pisteuo,* means to entrust, have faith in, and commit to.[11]

Ruel followed Durkheim to some extent by examining religion as a social fact, but chose to accept the object of his study, the *Kuria* religion, as a substantive reality rather than an imagined projection of something else, as Durkheim would have had it: 'Their religion, it seemed to me, was more a matter of knowing than believing' (1997, 5). Ruel follows Robertson Smith, Radcliffe-Brown, and Durkheim in breaking from a Tylorian view of belief as animism and examining instead religious action, principally ritual. Ruel criticizes Durkheim for assuming that 'the sacred', as the object of both belief and action, appears undifferentiated and unrelated to different parts of any society. What occurs in a ritual does not emerge from a well-rehearsed, evolved creed, but from social actions that have occurred over time.

Asad (1993) also pointed out that formulations about belief were Christian, and disrupted the Geertzian (and therefore implicitly Weberian) course of meaning by pointing out that such formulations were essentially universalistic and created without showing how, and under what conditions, meanings are constructed. He further criticized Geertz for arguing that religion brings humans the order they are seeking. Asad said that Geertz makes assertions about belief and ritual without evidence; the phenomenological method Geertz employed was intrinsically flawed through its assumption that religious symbols are *sui generis*.

An important rupture was occurring in the discipline, where we can see shifts in understanding about belief and belonging: the Durkheimian path was to put the belonging into belief, by arguing that beliefs were produced (what I would describe as performatively)

---

[11] Robbins (2007) suggests from his fieldwork amongst the Urapmin in Papua New Guinea that the tok pisin term *'belip'* indicates trust in God to fulfil promises, with the converted coming to 'know' or 'see' God. The term *belip* therefore indicates a commitment to or relationship with God. For a discussion of *belip* as a term denoting relational action, see Street (2010).

through rituals of belonging. Geertz, in contrast, understood ritual as performing already-held 'pre-formed' beliefs.

Asad argued that religion, and belief, were historically contingent and shaped by powerful leaders who authenticated and legitimized certain forms of belief and not others. His main example was medieval Europe where Christianity was practised as a form of knowledge, or what we may now describe as 'propositional belief'. Monks would obey certain disciplines and carry out painstaking tasks such as copying religious texts. When the Enlightenment era, with its emphasis on science and reason, threatened religion, religious leaders responded by stressing the importance of belief which, due to its hidden, invisible nature, could remain private and unverifiable. Asad also traced (1993, 40–1) the privileging of belief in the seventeenth century, when an 'emphasis on belief meant that henceforth religion could be conceived as a set of propositions to which believers gave assent'. Although Asad may have overemphasized and essentialized the role of power, his work radically shifted an anthropological understanding based on unproven ideas about meaning and order to one that would become more temporally and spatially situated.

Asad also considered the work of W.C. Smith and his views about the historicity of belief. Asad's link to Smith was picked up by Joel Robbins, a cultural anthropologist, in his review of the place of 'belief' in the anthropology of religion, and in particular of Christianity. Robbins (2007) discussed how the turn of phrase 'to believe in' represents a cross-culturally acceptable concept of having faith or trust in the object being believed. Alternatively, belief could be used in a pre-formed, propositional sense, where to 'believe that' someone or something exists expresses more uncertainty, as if the statement were open to testing. That form of expressing belief is often not present in non-Protestant cultures, where belief is something more commonly expressed non-verbally. To expect some people to convey their religiosity in terms of 'belief that' or, I might add, 'creedal' statements, ignores the temporal, spatial, and performative dimensions of how belief is being used. As a consequence, Robbins concludes, 'anthropologists have looked for belief in the wrong places' (ibid., 15) when they are looking to people to make 'belief that' assertions rather than explore what people believe in.

What would be more helpful to determine if people are 'really Christian' is to look at what they believe in, Robbins says, manifested by their actions – 'in trying to identify what people are up to culturally' (ibid.). The actions he suggests will be indicative of what they 'believe in' will relate to how they act out the model of salvation intrinsic in

Christian doctrine. This, he says, relates to what Weber describes as systems of value that help organize the relations between ideas. Therefore, Robbins concludes, using the standard of what people 'believe in' should help anthropologists analyse a culture based on how the value statements are organizing the culture. Further, Robbins warns of the tendency to impute or discern 'meaning' when it is perhaps the anthropologist, not the informant, who is seeking it: 'meaninglessness is always something untoward, lobbed in unexpectedly' (2006, 218).

This is a point usefully developed elsewhere in the concept of 'sincerity' by Webb Keane (2002; 2007) where he examines the moral, teleological narrative of modernity that presumes we are now being freed from 'false' beliefs. The semantic differences are not, as he says, in themselves as important as recognizing how the use of 'belief' varies spatially and temporally. The Calvinists he studied, for example, privilege 'belief' because their doctrines taught that when the word of God became 'flesh' in the body (or, as Keane reads, 'materiality') it became degraded. Calvinists thus associated belief 'with immaterial meaning over practices that threatened to subordinate belief to material form' (2007, 67).

Many of the themes discussed thus far concern issues of social organization, individual meaning, and, latterly, sociality. The place of belief in anthropology has tended to be localized, specific, and typically small-scale and domestic. Debates have concerned whether enquiries have been sufficiently localized, as opposed to universalized, and historicized. The trend has been to move from what informants 'believe' to how anthropologists construct belief, with awareness that the subdisciplinary preference of the scholar is likely to determine the interpretation. Durkheim's enormous sociological contribution to the recognition of social structure as a source for belief and other concepts was tempered by the anthropologist Malinowksi's recognition of sociality and individual agency. Both those functionalist orientations needed to be corrected by the kind of contribution the cultural anthropologist Geertz made about symbolism, with his incorporation of a Weberian meaning-centred universe, which in turn was rightly criticized for being ahistorical and essentially Christian by Asad, who in turn essentialized power.

Belief in the sociology of religion

Peter Berger followed a Weberian tradition of locating belief within a social-psychological dimension as a search for meaning. Berger, a sociologist and theologian, wrote that there exists 'a human craving for meaning that appears to have the force of instinct. Men are congenitally compelled to impose a meaningful order upon reality' (1967, 22). That generalization marks Berger as one of many sociologists of religion who assume that religion is an irreducible human phenomenon.

Berger's determination to call on that which is apparently inherent may recall anthropological discussions about the apparently inherent nature of order-seeking, and associated critiques about just who is seeking the order – informants or sociologists? The focus on making meaning was for both Weber and Berger a universal human need. From the apparent need for order we can observe Berger glide effortlessly into 'belief' without explicitly deconstructing how a need for order or meaning would become a belief, and what sort of belief it might become, for whom, in what place and time and under what conditions. What it implies, minimally, is a propositional form of belief that would explain causality, or what Berger sometimes referred to as plausibility, and therefore restore some sort of order to a potentially meaningless world.

Berger and Thomas Luckmann developed a model (1966) that depicted how people create a view of reality through a process of externalization, objectification (or habitualization), and institutionalization. They suggested that people confer legitimacy on the institutions they create by imposing 'symbolic universes' to make plausible both social institutions and individual biography. Berger and Luckmann quickly published individual sequels to their joint work. Berger applied the theory more directly to religion in *The Sacred Canopy: Elements of a Sociological Theory of Religion* (1967) by locating the canopy of a symbolic universe in a specifically 'sacred' realm. Berger's description of the function of the sacred canopy recalls Durkheimian theory that society is created by and worshipped by people: 'The sacred cosmos is confronted by man as an immensely powerful reality other than himself' (1967, 26). Berger breaks with Durkheim, however, in arguing that the most important distinction within a religious framework is not between the sacred and the profane, but between the sacred and chaos. Berger's argument therefore only works if we accept his notion of chaos where Weberian order-centred meaning thus becomes necessary. Further, contrary to the domestic focus adopted in anthropology, Berger defined the profane as synonymous with the everyday.[12]

---

[12] This is a theme to which I will return in the book, when I visit how Robert Wuthnow conceived of the profane as domestic.

The social construction of reality and the maintenance of a sacred canopy depend on social consensus, Berger argued, and therefore the threat to such a shared belief system is pluralism. In his earlier work (1967), Berger argued that pluralism was a by-product of modernity and therefore, he predicted, as a society became more modern it would, inevitably, become more secularized. One definition of secularization he proposed was a state when people and where people regard their world 'without the benefit of religious interpretations' (Berger 1967, 107–8). He suggested this should be known as 'subjective' secularization. He later amended part of that theory by saying that such a secularization process was neither inevitable nor irreversible. Pluralism may undermine plausibility structures with their 'taken-for-granted' certainties, he said, creating a link between meaning and belief, 'but it is possible to hold beliefs and to live by them even if they no longer hold the status of taken-for-granted verities' (2002, 194). Steve Bruce (2002) argued that secularization occurs because people realize that beliefs are relative – as some may be equally true, then some may be equally false. The result is not that they necessarily become atheists, replacing one belief system with another, but rather that they become indifferent. Here, he is conceiving belief in its propositional form. Nevertheless, the Bergerian legacy was to create a model of secularization that set much of the agenda about religion within the sociology of religion for generations.

Berger's collaborator, Thomas Luckmann, also set an agenda through the publication of his work. From his joint work with Peter Berger on the sociology of knowledge (1966), Thomas Luckmann developed a more uniquely religious theory in the *Invisible Religion* (1967). Here, he sought to redress the balance within the sociology of religion, which he argued had shifted too far in the direction of denominational studies with a focus on church-related religion. Nonetheless, like Berger, he assumes there is something essential and universal about humans linking with something that is essentially religious. Luckmann's theory stems from a Weberian assumption that people are engaged in a search for meaning. Further, he asserts, following a Christian-centric assumption, that the search for meaning is religious.

Two strands of theories about religion and belief begin to emerge when Bryan Wilson's theories are added to the Berger and Luckmann theses. The first might be understood as the 'disappearance' thesis: where Berger initially argued that religion would disappear as a result of pluralism, and Luckmann argued that belief would become more 'invisible', Bryan Wilson (1966) added a new strand relating to significance: religion may remain, but become less socially significant. He argued that modernity was undermining the 'social significance' of religion, and that the nature of belief would change as a result. Following a Weberian argument about the link between capitalism and Protestantism, Wilson concluded that the Christian aesthetic ethic became incompatible with a growing desire for personal happiness and gratification through consumerism. Drawing on Weber's theories of rationalization, and Marx's of historic materialism, Wilson argued there was a causal effect involved in the transfer of agency from the supernatural to the secular: religious beliefs would decline as religious practices declined, for they would not be reinforced or integrated into people's lives or consciousness. He assumed this was a global process, 'in which the notion of a world order created by some supernatural agency has given considerable place to an understanding of a man-made and man-centred world' (2001, 40).

David Martin entered the secularization debate with a strongly cautionary note: it would not be correct to assume a process of secularization, particularly as a result of modernity, was inevitable or global. Using an array of international examples, Martin warned against cultural comparisons involving 'almost infinite historical regress' (1978, 13). Secularization is not a linear or uniform process, but relates to degrees of pluralism and differentiation in different societies. By focusing primarily on social differentiation, Martin's work illuminates processes of institutional and societal shifts rather than individual beliefs. The unit of study becomes institutional and societal, rather than individual.

A markedly different approach back to the individual and belief was taken by Bellah (1964), who problematized the concept of belief by acknowledging that although 96 percent of Americans may say they believe in God, those beliefs bear little resemblance to any doctrinal or theological statement of God, which are acceptable only because they can be reinterpreted by individuals. He distinguished belief in 'propositions' from belief as a way for humans to derive comfort and meaning, a distinction reflecting substantive (Weberian) and functional (Durkheimian) views of religion. Bellah (1970, 196–207), referring to the American poet Wallace Stevens, argued that human beings require faith even if they know that faith to be a fiction. He quoted W. C. Smith (1967) in his argument that although the symbolism of 'the sacred' is by definition limited, it gives a coherent meaning to life for those who experience it. Bellah defined religion as consisting of sacred symbols and acts that gave people meaning. An evolutionist, Bellah theorized that religion moved from the primitive to the modern. What he described as 'civil religion' (1967) followed a Durkheimian model whereby the state itself is seen as sacred; this was something he thought would only occur in the 'modern' religious phase.

Like Berger, Luckmann, and Wilson, Bellah was troubled by what he saw was the increasing turn towards individual beliefs and subjective authority. He argued that the important point about modern religion was not about theories of secularization or indifference, but rather about how it had become increasingly acceptable for people to work out their own beliefs in response to changing demands and contexts. A recurring theme for Bellah (and his colleague Steven Tipton; see Bellah et al. 1986 and Tipton 1982) was that of the relationships between expressive individualism and utilitarianism. Although the emotional aspect of expressive individualism served as a useful balance for the cool rationality of utilitarianism, Bellah concluded that the subjective orientation of such beliefs threatened a collective moral consensus. A similar theme of individualization and choice was discussed by Roof and McKinney (1987) as 'the new voluntarism', where people were free to pick and choose, or mix and match different beliefs, identities, and affiliations. The idea of such mixing was described as 'bricolage' by anthropologist Levi-Strauss (1966 [1922]) and later employed in sociology by Hervieu-Léger (2000). The concept of 'fluidity' and narrative may best describe how people construct religious identities today, argued Ammerman (2007).

Thirty years after Berger, Wilson, and Martin had written about religion losing its public, social significance, Casanova (1994) argued that religion had returned to the realm of politics as a medium for ethnic and social conflicts, and has since gained in public visibility. While religion has been pushed from the public sphere and modern bureaucracies act as if God does not exist, Casanova claimed that people continue to believe in God and that religions thrive in different ways.

Grace Davie's 'believing without belonging'[13] thesis argued that people maintain a private belief in God, or other Christian-associated ideals, without church attendance or other forms of Christian participation. Davie wrote her book, she explains (1994, 9), to promote a proactive stance about religion that creates rather than reflects a context. Her evidence is gathered largely from publications on the theme of secularization and the European Values Survey.

Davie argues that the majority of British people persist in believing in God but 'see no need to participate with even minimal regularity in their religious institutions' (1994, 2) and therefore should be described

---

[13] Although popularized by Davie, the term was first coined by Gallup and Jones (1989) to describe a gap between religious belief and practice.

as 'unchurched' rather than secular (ibid., 12–13). She continues that few people have opted out altogether – atheists are rare (ibid., 2). Churches attract an audience that is disproportionately elderly, female, and conservative, and that age contrast, she argued, will affect the future of religion (ibid., 5–6).

Davie then turns to a related theme: the nature of change in British life, where she says, with echoes of Wilson, the 'nature of family life, including the traditional codes of morality, are altering rapidly' (ibid.) and where changes in gender roles have 'for better or for worse, penetrated the churches and influenced theological thinking' (ibid.). Further, an 'influx of immigrants in the post-war period, not all of them from Christian countries, has introduced significant other-faith communities'. This represents a trend towards greater religious diversity and has had a 'lasting effect on many aspects of British religious life' (ibid.).[14]

She notes further that patterns of employment and residence have been changing with large industrial conurbations declining rapidly, thereby reducing those areas of society 'most hostile to religious practice– large cities with high-density working class populations' (ibid., 5). Crucially, Davie identifies a mismatch between those statistics that relate to the measurable religious beliefs and practices that support secularization, and other 'more numinous aspects of religious beliefs' (ibid.).

A major problem in the discipline, she says, is that there are good, but small, studies of 'exotic edges' of religion in Britain, but 'the picture in the middle remains alarmingly blurred' with very little known about 'the beliefs of ordinary British people in everyday life' (1994, 6).

What was therefore emerging in the sociology of religion was a struggle over the hearts and minds of informants. There was little disagreement that public religious participation was in decline, albeit with regional and denominational variation. The struggle became one of territory, where the definition of religion would be stretched by assumptions about beliefs, to encompass what has variously been described as common or implicit religion and to include what Davie describes as 'heterodox ideas', such as 'the paranormal, fortune telling, fate and destiny, life after death, ghosts, spiritual experiences, luck and superstition' (1994, 83).

Steve Bruce (2001, 199–203) objected to the category of religion being expanded, arguing that concerns about life after death, or the meaning of life, or even the experience of transcendence are not

---

[14] Rodney Stark and associates (2005) argued that church-based religion was only one of four main ways of being religious. Further, in contrast to Berger's and Davie's theory that pluralism threatens religion, Stark, and others such as Warner (1993), argued that pluralism stimulates demand and diversity in religion.

necessarily religious. His definition of religion is limited by including only belief in the existence of 'supernatural entities with powers of action' (2001, 200). Voas and Crockett (2005, 14) further criticized Davie's theory by arguing that it was not whether people held certain beliefs but whether they were important to them and influenced their behaviour, that is, whether those beliefs mattered to them.

Here, Voas and Crockett are moving from propositional forms of belief to a practice-centred view of belief as something that influences how people behave because those beliefs are important to them. Pollack (2008) follows that argument by producing data showing that belief in a personal God affects people's behaviours, whereas a more diffuse belief in a vague higher being does not.

Stark and Iannaccone (1993) developed a theory of 'rational choice' that positions belief in a cognitive, economic model. According to this idea, 'firms' like churches do better in competitive environments where they market their services to customers. Customers choose the religion that offers the most benefit for their investment, trying to maximize the benefits and minimize the costs.[15] One of its key assumptions is that such choices are made by individuals, rather than being collectively or sociologically driven.

Contrary to the rational choice model is one that, while constructed by a historian, offers a more culturally sociological account of a discursive nature of belief. Callum Brown (2001) situates belief firmly in a social milieu, where the power of legitimate Christianity is discursive as well as institutional. Brown's main premise is that Britain underwent a massive and profound cultural change post-1960s that changed the way British people believed and behaved. His theoretical claims are based on his adherence to the theories of pre-modernity, modernity, and post-modernity, a position he says divides the academy. Broadly, he asserts that social scientists have mistakenly observed secularization as a feature of post-Enlightenment rationality and relied on structural rather than discursive theories and methods (2001, 195–6). The 1960s were a turning point because 'from the 1960s a suspicion of creeds arose that quickly took the form of a rejection of Christian tradition and all formulaic constructions of the individual' (ibid., 193). Christianity, he argued, was characterized by a gendered discourse that located

---

[15] A problem with such a model is not that choice is unavailable, but that people might not make a cost-benefit analysis in making their choices. According to this model, pluralism is good for religion because it increases the choices. However, as Ammerman (2007, 8) suggests, pluralism may be neither positive nor negative for religion, but 'simply part of the cultural and structural world in which people are living their lives'.

piety in femininity from about 1800 to 1960. Although the majority of churchgoers are women, they are now mainly older women: younger women and girls are missing from mainstream congregations. Brown is thus shifting the location of belief from propositional, faith-based, doctrinal formulations to ones of cultural and individual identity. In a move that recalls Asad, he stresses the importance of what may be authorized as legitimate forms of belief and behaving, and then moves away from institutional forms of power to discursive, cultural forms. Unusually, for the sociology of religion, he privileges female over male agency.

Brown captures a sense of how women view their own sexual identity and how they are viewed by others. Some of his language reflected the tone of many people I interviewed, particularly when they were bemoaning how contemporary femininity is less honourable and respectable than in the past. Brown writes 'Though these things are never instantaneous, the age of discursive Christianity then quite quickly collapsed. It did so, fundamentally, when women cancelled their mass subcription to the discursive domain of Christianity' (ibid., 195). He thus explicitly creates a relationship between the collapse of discursive Christianity and also links this to what he describes as the nature of femininity changing 'fundamentally, shedding its veneer of piety and respectability, and becoming disjoined from the romance which provided women's personal narrative for femininity and piety' (ibid., 195–6). He suggests that female behaviour constructed by an evangelical discourse as promiscuous in 1970 was experienced by the actor as something to which she was indifferent, if not proud. By the 1990s, he says, 'this secular moral aggression of young women had been translated into "girl power"' (ibid., 196). I will turn to this theme later. Brown's work is unusual within the field for not following the dominant orientation towards individualistic, propositional forms of belief. An exception to that trend was Demerath's work on what he described as 'cultural religion', to which I return later in this text, but here will note his distinction between propositional belief and cultural forms of belonging (2001, 221):

> There is an important difference... between intellectual conviction and cultural assent. Many who profess a belief are not expressing a considered opinion that is grounded in reason. Instead, they are aligning themselves with a community and its continuity over time.

In a move that could have been predicted by Asad (1993), Christian leaders moved to minimize the importance of public, and therefore verifiable, manifestations of Christian 'cultural' practice. What has now become sedimented within the sociology of religion is the assumption that religion is not only humanly inherent in a search for meaning, but that belief is individual, invisible, and therefore unverifiable – a little like the circular arguments about witchcraft for which Douglas so soundly criticized Evans-Pritchard.

The most significant neglected group within the sociology of religion is the majority who appear to be not institutionally affiliated but will sometimes claim when asked, and usually only when asked, a subjective self-identification as 'Christian'. These are the people who seem to be the 'unchurched'. The term itself, expressed in the negative form, is passive. One could turn it into something more constructive, even religious, following, for example, Mol (1976, 15) who argued that religion was a 'sacralization' of identity: 'a process by means of which man has pre-eminently safeguarded and reinforced... a complex of orderly interpretations of reality, rules, and legitimations which provides identity'.

The question remains: who are these people who want to claim a religious identity: what do they do and believe? For example, the 2002 European Social Survey probed religious identity by asking respondents about affiliation, practice, and belief and, significantly, how important they rated religion in their lives. A detailed analysis by Voas (see Voas 2009; Voas and Day 2007; 2010) concluded that there were four types: the 'unreligious', who neither participate in religious activities nor rate religion as of any importance to them; the 'privately religious', who may not attend church regularly but may pray alone and rate religion as important to them; the 'actively religious', who attend church, pray, and rate religion as important to them; and then the rest – 50 per cent of those surveyed – who rarely participate in any religious practices, and yet rate religion of having some, although low, importance to them. It is not enough to describe those people as 'unchurched'; rather, we must explore who they are and why religion is neither important nor unimportant to them. This unknown terrain, corresponding to what Davie described as the beliefs of 'ordinary people', has remained virtually unexplored.

Disciplinary orientations

The purpose of this chapter has been to trace the way scholars in the anthropology and sociology of religion have theorized and located belief, stemming from the prime Durkheimian and Weberian legacies.[16] The most obvious differences between the two subdisciplines are those of scale and location. With regard to scale, anthropological research has tended to explore the everyday and domestic, while sociology has focused mainly on the institutional and societal. As for location, anthropology has often defined itself in terms of studying 'the other' through ethnography, involving lengthy periods of fieldwork in colonial or post-colonial settings, and using participant observation rather than interviews; most sociological research in religion has either been large-scale quantitative or interview-based qualitative, with the majority of data collected in Euro American contexts.

Those different orientations will inevitably produce different results. We would expect to see deeper, richer, more located studies emerging from anthropology and broader, more comparative, generalized work arising from sociology. The main implication for the study of belief is that the anthropological record has tended to deconstruct and problematize belief, whereas the sociological tradition leaves it virtually untouched – see, for example, work in the emerging anthropological subdiscipline, the 'anthropology of Christianity' (Bialecki 2008; Cannell 2007).

The task of this book will be to illustrate how and why people today in Euro American modern societies construct, negotiate, and perform beliefs. Using both anthropological and sociological theories and approaches, I will be expanding a single case study through international and interdisciplinary comparisons. The themes that have emerged thus far demonstrate how scholars in those subdisciplines currently understand belief and what, sometimes hidden, assumptions they bring to their work and the data they collect. Following Foucault, I have tried to uncover various layers and reveal how disciplinary knowledge about belief has been created. The themes that will underlie this book are, largely, culled from those disciplines and will therefore centre on questions of relatedness, locality, and temporality. The argument that forms the core of my work is that, in conditions of late modernity, belief to many people is an expression of how they belong to each other.

---

[16] This book is principally focused on sociology and anthropology, but the problem of neglecting how belief can be theorized runs through other disciplines as well. See, for an excellent treatment of problems within psychology, Wulff (1999).

2

A Research Journey Begins

In Chapter 1, summaries of key debates and methodologies about belief showed how the anthropological and sociological disciplinary paths derived and then diverged from a Durkheimian approach to locating belief in the social, a theme to be more fully addressed in the following chapters. That was the gist of Chapter 1, but that is not how the research journey began. Like most important journeys, it was a voyage of discovery. Unlike most journeys, it did not begin with a map and even began with a different destination.

I began my PhD at Lancaster University with Linda Woodhead and Paul Heelas who, with three other researchers,[1] were in the middle stages of the largest study ever conducted in Britain on contemporary religion, the Kendal Project (Heelas and Woodhead 2005). One day, Paul and Linda and I were discussing the findings from the UK 2001 census, where 72 percent of the population identified as Christian. We wondered what those people really meant by 'Christian' and whether the census results undermined, as some were suggesting, the dominant secularization paradigm. Census data are not universally accepted as reliable indicators of population characteristics, in the UK or elsewhere, but what interested me was not simply their statistical categories, but their performative power.[2] Linda, Paul, and I agreed it would be interesting to find out more about the mainstream. What do people really believe in and how would we find out?

---

[1] Bronislaw Szerszynski of the Institute for Environment, Philosophy and Public Policy, was third Co-Investigator, supported by researchers Benjamin Seel and Karin Tusting. The Kendal Project was funded by the Leverhulme Trust.

[2] In a more recent example, as an indication of the need to explore census material and impact, the May 2010 issue of the monthly American Anthropological Association newsletter, *Anthropology News*, focused on research about the census, carrying several pieces interrogating censuses and their impact in North America, South America, and Europe.

And so we began what now becomes the story of this book, in itself an amalgamation and interpretation of other people's stories. They informed me, and they confused me. I will therefore start the story of the journey with my most surprising exchange: one that forced me to drop every map I had ever used to chart the territory of religion and belief. It was my interview with Jordan, 14, that first transformed my idea about belief and caused me to begin theorizing in ways that influenced my work then and since. I knew my opening question – 'What do you believe in?' – was deliberately ambiguous and designed to allow informants to provide their own definitions and vocabulary, but I was completely unprepared for the apparent contradiction that Jordan presented.

I began my interview with Jordan by asking him my first question, to which he replied in Yorkshire dialect, using 'nowt' for nothing and 'owt' for 'anything'.

ABBY: What do you believe in?
JORDAN: Nowt.
ABBY: Sorry?
JORDAN: I don't believe in owt. I don't believe in any religions.
ABBY: You don't believe in any religions.
JORDAN: No. I'm Christian but I don't believe in owt.

As a product of a certain historical era, and one raised in a church-attending family, it was initially difficult for me to account for Jordan and the many other 'anomalies' I was to meet in my research. It was sometimes my own emotional and cognitive response to interviews that showed me I had entered difficult, and therefore potentially fruitful, territory. Blanes (2006) provides an insight into how being aware of our own beliefs can influence our fieldwork and analysis. My questions provoked discussions with atheists who believe in ghosts, agnostics who despise religion and say they are Christian, humanists who believe in life after death, and Christians who prefer praying to their dead relatives rather than to God or Jesus. Many people, for example, reported feeling the presence of their deceased relatives. Although I did not ask people about uncanny or supernatural experiences, experience of the supernatural was very common: a third of my informants reported something of this sort, irrespective of age and social class. Reports varied from feeling the presence of God or deceased relatives to seeing ghosts or hearing inexplicable sounds. It made little difference, however, whether the informant self-described as 'religious' or 'spiritual': most did not and nor did they describe such experiences in religious terms.[3] Making sense of those apparent contradictions became, and remains, at the core of my work.

This book is the result of those initial doctoral and later postdoctoral explorations,[4] beginning in small communities in Yorkshire and widening, through further reading, seminar organization, conference attendance, and international networking, to the industrialized nations of the modern world. Initially set in northern England, the aim was to probe beliefs amongst three generations of people from a wide cross-section of society. I researched religion without asking overtly religious questions or selecting people on the basis of their interest in religion or spirituality. The remainder of this chapter describes the rationale behind the research method, its design and execution. The chapter also discusses how the intellectual and geographical scope was extended beyond sociology to wider disciplines, primarily the anthropology of religion, and to comparisons with other Euro American countries.

Rationale

During 2003 and 2004 I engaged with roughly 250 informants, including children at three schools. I interviewed sixty-eight of those people,[5] aged 14–83 and living in towns and villages in northern England, recording[6] the interviews and transcribing them verbatim

---

[3] In my study more women than men reported supernatural experiences (39 percent vs 25 percent) and discussed those experiences differently. I reflect more fully on those gender differences in Chapters 8, 10, and elsewhere (Day 2008a; Day 2013c). For discussion of other theories about women's religiosity, see also Walter and Davie 1998.

[4] Doctoral work was funded by the AHRB (as was, now the AHRC: Arts and Humanities Research Council). Postdoctoral work was funded by the ESRC and situated at the University of Sussex, mentored by Simon Coleman.

[5] With the important exception of school students, I asked interviewees to choose where they would like to be interviewed. The options I suggested were their home, my home, their place of work, or any other venue they might like. The only option I had for interviewing students was in the school itself. I tried to engineer some 'choice' by asking them to choose where to sit. It seems like a minor detail, but I was impressed by work stressing the importance of allowing children choice to encourage their role as participants in research (Barker and Weller 2003). I underwent all criminal record checks in line with ethical and legal guidelines. The adults varied in their preference for location, including my home, their home, and on two occasions the local pub. I did not detect any major differences in informant behaviour or tendency to disclose which I would associate with the venue itself. People often demonstrated emotional intensity, sometimes with expressions or tears and laughter, which occurred in all of the venues. I conclude that the important factor was that it was their choice.

[6] I agree with Speer and Hutchby (2003) that recording devices in themselves are not necessarily seen by participants as intrusive; indeed, in my study I found the use of the device helped me reinforce the importance of what they as informants were telling me.

(Day, A. 2006). The project was initiated partly in response to what appeared to me as puzzling: the results of the 2001 UK decennial census of population revealed that 72 per cent self-identified as Christian, in a country where all forms of public Christian religious participation have been declining for at least the last fifty years, notwithstanding considerable regional and denominational variations (Brierley 2006; Garnett et al. 2006; Gill et al. 1998; Gill 1999; Gill 2001). The apparent contradiction was neatly articulated by a BBC report announcing that 'while the UK is basically secular, it is also overwhelmingly Christian'.[7]

Some scholars argued that people today are religious in belief but not in practice, that religion may have lost its public social significance but is being pursued privately, and that to understand religion now we should broaden the definition of 'religion' away from a theistic, doctrinal, institutionally based faith (Davie 1994; Hay and Hunt 2000; Hunt 2002; 2005; Stark 1999; Wilson 1966). Others suggested that Britain is now a secular culture with traces of a Christian identity, where secular means a rational worldview without beliefs in supernatural powers (Bruce 1995; 2002) and where people regard their world 'without the benefit of religious interpretations' (Berger 1967, 107–8). Other research argued that new forms of spirituality are growing which are subjective, experiential, and suggest different ways of relating to 'the sacred' (Fenn 2001; Heelas 1996; Wuthnow 2001). Some suggest that religion is transforming, rather than declining (Warner 1993).

Warner (1993) argues that religion in the United States is different from that of Europe and therefore requires what he describes as a new paradigm specific to the United States. Davie (2004a) argues that concepts such as modernity and post modernity in Europe need to be understood as multiple identities particular to Europe. She also (2004b) summarized the sociology of religion as concerned with patterns that analyse how people organize themselves in non-random ways in relation to religion. She argues that there exist different sociologies in the world depending on the religious activity of the culture being studied and the nature of scholars studying, and that a secularization thesis is unsustainable except, perhaps, in Europe (Davie 2002; Halman and Riis 2003; Lambert 2004).[8] Although there is not a

---

[8] Levitt (2007) also points to a richer understanding of 'multiple' identities and multiple belongings, exploring how immigrants to the United Stations often maintain transnational religious connections and identities. That 'globalisation of the sacred' (ibid, 108) has deeper roots in long-standing religious traditions whose identities do not strictly demarcate between church and state.

question on the US census about religion, other data, notably the 2008 American Religious Identification Survey (http://www.americanreligion-survey-aris.org/) revealed that 15 per cent of the US population said they had no religion, a figure in line with most Euro American countries.

A Christian-based research centre, the Barna group, reported in 2004:

> Since 1991, the adult population in the United States has grown by 15%. During that same period the number of adults who do not attend church has nearly doubled, rising from 39 million to 75 million – a 92% increase! (http://www.barna.org/barna-update/article; last accessed 15 September 2010)

Who the people are who do not attend church may overlap with some who specifically claim a 'no religion' identity, but the picture is unclear. I agreed with Davie (1994, 6) that there are several good but small studies of the 'exotic edges' of religion in Britain, but 'the picture in the middle remains alarmingly blurred' with very little known about 'the beliefs of ordinary British people in everyday life'. I will revisit those theories in more detail in Chapter 10 as I reappraise them in light of my data and analysis, but here I will return to the beginning of the research journey when, in conversation with my supervisors, the question was raised by Paul Heelas:[9] 'What do people in the general population believe and how do we find out?' While the nature of case study, small-scale qualitative research renders it impossible to speak on behalf of the 'general population' (see, for example, Burns 2000; Flick 2002; Yin 2003) it was feasible to explore that question, design an appropriate method, and draw out implications for the wider population.

The research design objective was to probe beliefs amongst a broad cross-section of informants without skewing selection processes or questions towards religiosity. This meant I would construct questions without using overtly religious vocabulary and concepts, and would avoid recruiting people who might self-select because of their religiosity. That rationale was driven both by what appeared to be a census question puzzle, as described above, and by what I identified as methodological gaps within the sociology of religion. Large-scale quantitative studies sometimes ask overtly religious questions using religious vocabularies that could force religious, and particularly Christian, answers (Hill and Hood 1999; Kadushin 2007). Survey questions often

---

[9] The PhD began with Paul Heelas and Linda Woodhead, but part-way through the work, mainly due to Paul's overseas commitments, I asked for supervisors to be changed from Paul to Hiroko Kawanami. Koko's own anthropological work in religion gave my focus an important new turn and complemented Linda's expertise in theology and sociology.

demand closed answers to closed questions that could be used to support a variety of arguments but would not reveal nuances of meaning. For example, in asking if someone 'believes in God' it would not be apparent from a survey what people might mean by belief or by God. Abercrombie et al. (1970, 106) tried to qualify the question by asking if respondents believed in a God who could change the events on earth. One woman replied: 'No, just the ordinary one.' As Towler (1974, 145) noted, once researchers start to use empirical measurements, they will be forced to use items drawn from a range of 'conventional orthodoxies':

> the moment a researcher uses the word 'religion' a ready-made set of attitudes will be thrust at him. As a rule these will be attitudes to 'the church', and any attempt to break through to the respondent's own beliefs will be impossibly hampered. (ibid., 157)

The census results may provide a false picture of an enduringly Christian Britain because of the language and form of the questions. It is certainly out of step with other surveys about religious affiliation and beliefs. Most other surveys, such as the British Social Attitudes survey, the BBC's Soul of Britain survey or European Social Surveys, rate the incidence of Christian religious affiliation much lower than did the census. This may be because they measure religiosity more broadly, asking questions not only about affiliation but also about, for example, belief, practice, and belonging (Voas and Day 2007). The England and Wales census question simply asked 'what is your religion?' Although the question was voluntary, and respondents could choose 'None', its affirmative grammatical form nonetheless implies, as Voas and Bruce suggest (2004, 26), that respondents have a religion and therefore may prompt the respondent to select an option from the list.

Having decided that the census question may not provide an accurate sense of people's religious identities or beliefs, I turned to the sociology of religion literature to find alternative approaches to exploring those issues.

Disciplinary methodological gaps

Within the literature of the sociology of religion, I looked for qualitative or quantitative studies where people were not selected based on their involvement or articulated interest in religion or spirituality and where the researchers were not asking overtly religious questions. Examining UK and international journals and books, I could not find any such examples. One method illustrated at a conference in 2003 and later published as a book (Savage et al. 2006) came close to what I was looking for by showing respondents photographic images and exploring in focus group discussions whether or not the images inspired a 'religious' response (most did not). Barker (1989) also tried to avoid forcing religious answers by not introducing the topic of religion until her informants did. While Campbell (1971) approached the concept of 'irreligion' his theoretical treatment did not assist me in developing methodologies.

Scholars within the sociology of religion often use large, quantitative studies to support their arguments, both for enduring religiosity and inevitable secularization of society. Davie's 'believing without belonging' thesis (1990; 1994; 2002), for example, draws on surveys to conclude that the majority of British people believe in God, hell, sin, and heaven but just do not attend church regularly. Other scholars (Bruce 1995, 2001, 2002; Bruce and Glendinning 2003; Field 2001; Voas and Bruce 2004; Voas and Crockett 2005) draw on surveys to defend secularization theories, primarily by analysing the degree of importance people accord to religion, God, or other, primarily Christian, doctrines. Brown (2001) does not use surveys but uses historical data to theorize about the 'death of Christian Britain'.

Further, scholars often define certain paranormal experiences as religious or spiritual, although variously named as, *inter alia*, folk, common, invisible, or implicit (see, for example, Bailey 1990; Davie 1994; Luckmann 1967). Their conclusions, I argue, may be driven by assumptions about religiosity and by religious vocabulary, a theme to which I will return in Chapter 5.

Having found no model for probing the beliefs of people who neither volunteered nor were selected by religiosity or spirituality, or for probing beliefs without asking religious questions, I set out to construct a method. There were four stages and components of my method summarized here:

1. situating the study within social sciences, not religion or theology, when recruiting informants;

2. asking the informants questions to prompt discussion without using overtly religious vocabulary;

3. encouraging informants to digress and elaborate in order to capture conceptual frameworks and vocabulary;

4. interpreting and analysing the data through categories that arose inductively. While I began by exploring the content of informants' beliefs, how their beliefs developed and how they were practised, my data analysis enriched those categories and enabled me to create two more categories exploring how beliefs were important to people

(salience) and what their beliefs did for them (function). Later, through postdoctoral research, I further developed that interpretive model through adding dimensions of place and time.

1. Situating the study and recruiting informants

To further my objective of situating the study sociologically, I chose to select people from young to old, male and female, and from a mix of socio-economic groups. This allowed me to situate the informants in their social milieu and cover a critical time period of 1945 to the present, coincidental with a dramatic decline in church attendance.

I lived in the region throughout my study and had previously researched an aspect of religious life in its main town (Day 2005). It was a suitable location for the research for several reasons. As my research question was provoked by why British people self-identified as Christian, I would not deliberately situate the study in a location predominately populated by people who would be more likely to have affiliated with other religions. In practice, it proved difficult to refuse the participation of an enthusiastic student whose hajib indicated her non-Christian adherence, and, indeed, her observations proved insightful. My focus on Christianity, however, precluded me from actively recruiting people from other faiths. I drew a boundary from where I lived near Skipton south to the comprehensive school from which I would draw most of my informants and east/west by about five miles. I decided I would recruit informants from within that geographical area. A potential disadvantage of any geographic focus would be its possible parochial nature. Census data confirmed that the population of the region generally conformed to England and Wales national averages, particularly related to ethnicity and social class, and to how they answered the religious question. I decided that any supposed urban/rural dichotomy was irrelevant, mainly because decline in church attendance in rural areas matches urban decline (Gill 2001, 282).

Recalling that I did not want to recruit people on the basis of their participation in or withdrawal from or even interest in religious or so-called spiritual activities, I decided to find middle-aged informants more eclectically rather than from a single site and was reassured by reading about a 'gatekeeper' approach (Jackall 1988) whereby I would approach people who had access to certain groups of people. Prospective student interviewees were introduced to me first in their classroom environment. I had agreed with my first teacher-gatekeeper that Year 10 students (14 years old) would be a good year to focus upon. We agreed that I should focus on the Religious Education class as it was a compulsory course for all students to attend and would therefore not reflect self-selection, at least in the introductory phase. I introduced myself to each class as a researcher at Lancaster University looking at what people believed in nowadays. I became a participant-observer through leading classroom-based discussions and exercises, and then I asked for volunteers to be interviewed.

2. *Prompting discussion avoiding religious vocabulary*

My first challenge was to consider what and how to ask people about their beliefs without asking overtly religious questions. The approach I chose was inductive, rather than deductive, whereby I did not begin with a hypothesis or even a definition of religion or belief but adopted a Weberian approach, assuming any definitions would arise from the field, if they arose at all. Drawing on feminist research methods (Reinharz 1992; Skeggs 1995) I wanted to give informants as much control and choice as possible over how they interpreted and answered my questions so that I could capture their conceptual frameworks and vocabulary, in what Yin (2003, 89–90) refers to as 'guided conversations' or Bellah et al. (1986, 305) recommended as the method of 'active interview', where the interviewer and interviewee strike up a dialogue. I therefore decided to conduct semi-structured interviews, while also suggesting to the interviewees at the outset that I would like them to question my vocabulary if it did not make sense to them, and to digress onto related topics if they chose. As my inquiry was about what people believed and how they discussed those beliefs, not only about how they behaved or self-identified as religious or not, I decided to use interviews as my main source of data and deconstruct the narratives that emerged.[10]

Criteria for interview questions were that they should be open-ended and not explicitly suggest anything to do with religion. They were designed to probe what people believe in, where they sourced those beliefs from, and how they practised them. The questions I describe as 'ontological questions' were intended to probe what some people describe as religious, ethical, or metaphysical questions. For example, Weber (1922, 117) described:

> the metaphysical needs of the human mind as it is driven to reflect on ethical and religious questions, driven not by material need but by an inner compulsion to understand the world as a meaningful cosmos and to take up a position toward it.

---

[10] Mitchell (2005) made a similar choice in interviewing thirty-five people about their Protestant or Catholic identities. Although she had other data available, such as participant observation, she chose to focus on her interviews because she was interested in how the participants used their own narratives in the process of identity construction. See also Mitchell and Todd (2007).

I designed questions to begin discussion about what might or might not be an 'inner compulsion' without assuming such questions were 'religious'. Further, following Weber (1922, 20), I wondered 'who is deemed to exert the stronger influence on the individual in his everyday life, the theoretically supreme god or the lower spirits and demons?' Or, perhaps, people would not feel themselves influenced by gods or demons at all. I designed questions to probe where people located power, authority, and meaning. Douglas (1966, 93) describes questions such as, 'Why did it happen to me: why now?' as metaphysical questions entertained by religions. This may render religious institutions anomalous in the modern world, she says, 'For unbelievers may leave such problems aside' (ibid.). She does not state what she means by unbeliever or believer but the contrast with religion within the paragraph implies to me that she is referring to unbelievers as people who do not believe in God or religion. The elision also creates a further omission: why should people who disbelieve in God leave such problems aside? Some of my informants were aware of such omissions and elisions and needed to disentangle themselves from that default position of what they did not believe in before they could discuss what they did believe in.

The questions I designed to probe sources sought to explore how people explained the origins and development of their beliefs. There is an argument within the discipline that suggests people with no religion have no beliefs. Percy (2004, 39), for example, wrote:

> In the absence of religion, people tend to believe anything rather than nothing, and the task of the church must be to engage empathetically with culture and society, offering shape, colour and articulation to the voices of innate and implicit religion.

Unconvinced about that argument, and noting its absence of supporting evidence, I decided to ask people to discuss with me what they believed in and where they thought they formed those beliefs, assuming they might believe in matters that were non-religious. Asking people how they formed beliefs and how those beliefs might have changed would give me their impressions but not, I realized, an exclusive and exhaustive account. People might be unaware of some of the sources of their beliefs. In a similar way, how they practised beliefs would, I assumed, take many forms, from public expressions to more subtle, even unconscious, manifestations. This might include overt actions such as attending church or covert actions such as practising racism. The questions I asked were piloted through two classroom discussions and five separate adult interviews.

All pilot interviewees agreed that the questions were appropriate, with one exception. I had originally asked 'How do you think the universe began?', but the students said this was too exam-like, with respondents perhaps being led to think there was a correct answer. One student suggested some people might not think it began at all, but was eternal. We decided it would be better if I couched the question in uncertainty, beginning 'no one knows for sure'. I further tested my questions by saying at the beginning of each interview that my questions were broad and designed to explore what they believed in. There may be, I continued, a question that did not really make sense to them or there might be a way I was phrasing something that did not seem right. I said it was important for my research to understand how people express their beliefs and values and therefore would appreciate it if they stopped me or asked for a question to be rephrased if that seemed appropriate for them. They agreed to this. In practice, the only change anyone suggested during the interview was the question about happiness. Antony, 14, a grammar school student whose mother owns a catering business and father is a warehouse supervisor, paused when I asked him what makes him happiest. He said he thought my question presumed happiness was an ideal state, whereas for him his 'ideal state' was not happiness but somewhere in between happiness and unhappiness.

In each interview I tried to ask each question in the same order. The informant sometimes answered a question without being asked and I therefore did not repeat it. On other occasions, we became so absorbed in one question that others were either truncated or omitted. I feel confident, however, that most of the time most of the questions were covered.

1. *Opening question (testing ideas of belief, beginning dialogue)*

   - What do you believe in?

2. *Questions about morality (probing content, sources, and practice)*

   - What are rights and wrongs for you? Examples?
   - Have they changed for you?
   - How do you know those things?
   - How do you put that into practice?

3. *Questions about meaning and transcendence (probing content, sources, and practice)*

   - Has there ever been an inspirational figure to you, real or fictional?

- Are there any books, movies, TV programmes which have significance for you and influenced you?
- How much influence or control do you think you have over your life?
- Do you ever think about the purpose or meaning in life? If so, what?
- No one can say for certain how it all began, but I wonder what your thoughts might be on how the universe came into being?
- What happens to you after you die?
- When are you happiest?
- When are you most unhappy?
- What frightens you?
- What do you do to comfort you during those times?
- What, or who, is most important to you in your life?

4. *Final question (religious self-identification)*

- For the first time the census had a question about people's religion, do you remember what you said? [If not—] You could have said 'None; Christian; Buddhist; Hindu; Jewish; Muslim; Sikh' or you could write in something for 'any other religion' or you didn't have to answer it.

3. *Encouraging digression and other vocabularies*

In practice, the open-ended questions and style of interview provoked discussions that surprised me. My opening question served as a useful technique to begin a dialogue about 'belief'. As I discussed in the previous chapter, although a predominant theory in the academic field of the sociology of religion is that people are Christian or at least theistic, although they do not practise in ways conventionally associated with religiosity, it is rare to find the term 'belief' explored. I therefore decided to put that term at the heart of my questions and ask informants what it meant to them.

Below, I will review briefly how they responded initially to my opening question.

I received generally three sorts of immediate responses which I describe below as conditional, stalling, or assertive.

CONDITIONAL RESPONDERS

A conditional response was when the informant wanted to know more about a possible religious nature of the question before answering. They needed to ensure that I did not necessarily want a discussion about religious beliefs. What emerged was their desire to create a space where they could talk about their beliefs without relating them to God or any religion. The exchange with Liz, a 55-year-old married mother who owns her own business, began in this way:

> ABBY: My first question I'll ask you is, what do you believe in?
> LIZ: And I'll ask you, what do you mean? What do I believe in? Which area of life, or, death?

This kind of exchange helped me realize that people did not want to know in general what I meant by the term belief; they wanted to know if it would be acceptable for them to talk about their beliefs if those beliefs were not religious. It often seemed as if the interviewees were asking for my permission not to talk about religion, as if the word 'belief' initially triggered that connection but that it was not a connection which the informant really wanted to make. In the same way, Terry, a 49-year-old agricultural contractor, married to Louise with two adult children, needed to check first that he did not need to talk about religion:

> ABBY: What do you believe in?
> TERRY: Believe in?
> ABBY: Yes.
> TERRY: Uh, what do I believe in? Tell you what I don't believe in [laughs]. Are you asking do I believe in God? Is that what you're aiming for?

Terry explicitly ruled out what he did not believe in before creating the space to tell me what he did believe in. This helped me understand how belief appears differently in specific social contexts, times, and places and how people will often talk about their beliefs by way of lengthy, elaborate examples.

The need to rule out religion before telling me about his beliefs was also expressed by Charles, a 16-year-old student at a boys' grammar school. He lives with his school-teacher mother and visits his unemployed father, with whom he is very close, at the weekends. He answered the question slowly, pausing frequently:

CHARLES: As a religion or as a way of life, or... what do you mean? [*pause*]
I don't believe in a god as such. [*pause*]. It's a hard one that. [*pause*] What do
I believe in? [*pause*] what sort of beliefs are we wanting here, just in general?

Once again, it seemed we had to rule religion out before discussing
beliefs in more detail. Charles had coherent beliefs stemming from
his position, he told me later, as an anarcho-communist. He had
a deep respect for history and for political thinkers. Georgia, an
18-year-old A-level student at a large comprehensive school, lives with
her parents on a farm. When I asked her my first question, she said:

Nothing religious at all, anything like that. I believe in things like love
and stuff like that, feelings, more so than religious things. I don't have any
beliefs on that side at all. Happiness, things like that, feelings really. Things
like that.

STALLING RESPONDERS
Sometimes informants demonstrated surprise at the question and
needed a few seconds to gather his or her thoughts. Some physically
drew back and looked at me in shock, as did Barry, a 48-year-old
bookkeeper, living with a partner, who said, 'Oh, dear, that's an interesting question to start with, isn't it?' Responders such as Barry would
then typically pause for a couple of seconds and then answer with a list
of their beliefs. I received a similar response from Paul, a 33-year-old,
single, restaurant manager. When I asked him the question he looked
at me, startled, and asked: 'What do you mean, believe, I don't know,
like—?' He paused and looked at me questioningly. I said I didn't know
what I meant and what really interested me was what he might mean by
it. He nodded, thought for a few seconds and then said, 'I believe in
ghosts. Destiny.' After a few more seconds he shrugged and added,
'God, yes, but there's no proof.' In examples like these I felt the interviewees were taken aback by the enormity and perhaps vagueness of
the question and were stalling for a little more time while they gathered
their thoughts. The stalling response added to my impression that the
word 'belief' is loaded not only with religious implications but potentially other unknown variants that the informant needed to consider.

ASSERTIVE RESPONDERS
People who believed in God or their faith were quick and assertive in
their response. They did not hide or reveal it somewhat tentatively as
an afterthought. For example, when I asked John, a 51-year-old married
teacher and father what he believed in, he answered:

As far as God is concerned, or? I suppose, that's a huge area, but the basic thing I believe is I believe in a God I know and a God that loves me and a God that has a plan and a purpose for the world.

David, for example, a 48-year-old married paramedic with two children, answered my question by saying:

I believe in God and we do, we've not been to church so much recently, because I'm so busy, but we do go to church.

When I asked Jane, a 61-year-old married teacher and mother, she said:

I believe in God, one God, which I define as a spiritual being or a spiritual presence, no gender, all loving, all powerful, all mighty, creator.

The above examples illustrate the immediacy with which some people attested to their belief and how it formed part of many of their answers. Examples like these reinforced for me my assumption that if I began by asking people what they believed in, that they would answer in terms of their faith in God if they had one. It was implausible to me that God-believing Christians would neglect to mention God or their faith. It also seemed to me implausible that people who held strong beliefs in other forms of spirituality or other-than-human influences would fail to mention those during the course of my interviews, particularly when we discussed matters of death, important parts of their lives, and the level of influence they feel they have over their lives.

The different kinds of responses to my opening question helped me stay attuned to what I will describe as the myth of the naive informant: people are constructing what they are saying, reflexively, in far more depth than many people will allow. Converse (1964; 1970) argued that most people answer open-ended questions without really thinking about the issue and their answers, therefore, do not reflect an ideology or belief system. Their responses, Converse concluded, were unstable, and so erratic as not to relate to the instrument or the question. The mood of the respondents, their perceptions about the interviewer (in panel surveys), and desire to please or conform to social norms were major influences on how they answered. Others, a minority of those polled, would have strong and stable opinions. And yet, as Giddens (1991, 5) argued, reflexivity is a mark of modernity:

The reflexive project of the self, which consists in the sustaining of coherent, yet continuously revised, biographical narratives...because of the 'openness' of social life today, the pluralisation of contexts of action and the diversity of' 'authorities', lifestyle choice is increasingly important in the constitution of self-identity and daily activity.

Particularly if they are allowed to recount stories and those stories are deconstructed as holistic, organic belief narratives, as I explain further in Chapter 8, then we may well find that when people are being interviewed by a sociologist about ideas, beliefs, and values they are aware that they are not only informing the researcher but are co-agents, constructors of knowledge. They are collaborators, although unequal in that project. As Bourdieu pointed out, the anthropologist (or, often, sociologist) often painstakingly draws out certain details from informants, reorganizes them, and fits them into certain categories and then claims this is what the 'native' believes. As I discussed in Chapter 1, anthropologists such as Evans-Pritchard, Douglas, Turner, and Ruel have agonized over just these issues.

Having reviewed how people respond to the word belief, it is left for me to conclude what I will make of it. I do this in more detail in Chapter 8, where I propose a way of looking at belief through dimensions, not definitions. This not only allows more detailed considerations of what belief means, but allows the range and mutability of the concept. Above all, informants impressed upon me their desire to have their beliefs understood and respected as being their beliefs, not the beliefs of others imposed on them. This does not, I will argue in this book, arise from an ethical position wherein they respect the rights of all people to hold divergent beliefs. Informants are often critical and dismissive of other people's beliefs, while retaining the conviction that their own beliefs are to be respected. This is not, I suggest, a contradiction or hypocrisy. Belief for many people is a statement of self, a way of saying who they are: 'I believe, therefore I am.' Defending their own beliefs is an important way to enhance their identities; opposing other people's beliefs functions in the same way to the same end.[11]

4. Interpret their responses widely, exploring such areas as content, sources, practice, salience, function, place, and time

As I began to listen more closely to how people discussed their beliefs, I realized that they were not giving me coherent, creed-like statements, but lengthy and sometimes elaborate stories or 'belief narratives' that I only understood as I analysed them multidimensionally, as I discuss in more detail in Chapter 8. I began to understand belief as being

[11] The need to claim reflexivity may point to another possible distinction between belief and faith – one explored by Balzer (2008) in her study of Siberian shamanism in the context of post-Soviet transformations. 'Beliefs' were fairly stable generic concepts, where 'faith' described a personal, more idiosyncratic commitment.

more connected to personal values, trust and emotion than to facts, propositions or creeds. Although many informants pointedly distanced themselves from institutionalized religion, they did not evoke more 'individualized' narratives but, rather, the opposite. What I was witnessing was sociality, not individuality, with a common theme of belonging to adherent, reciprocal, emotional relationships. From there, I developed my thesis of 'believing in belonging', a deliberate inversion of 'believing without belonging'.

Finally, interpreting belief narratives multidimensionally helped me resolve what appeared to be the 'census question' puzzle, as I describe in more detail in Chapter 8, and identify two belief orientations: anthropocentric and theocentric. This finding helped elaborate the previously undifferentiated category of Christian 'nominalism', as I identified three types of nominalist Christian: natal, ethnic, and aspirational. I discuss this in more detail in Chapter 9.

Section 2
Cosmologies of the Mainstream

The five chapters in this section present the core empirical data gathered initially in northern England and then compared cross-culturally. The first chapter introduces a key theme that will reappear and resonate throughout the book: the intersection of belief, culture, and identity. Through exploring belief with young people, discussion is focused on how they reject religious impositions and creeds as they struggle together to find where they belong in an ever-expanding universe of alternatives. Analysing people's experiences of the 'sensuous social supernatural' it becomes evident that belief narratives that describe the experience of sensing deceased relatives suggest a self-conscious desire to continue belongings. Further, fate-belief has a provisional quality as people act to 'cover the cracks in belonging'. When describing their moral beliefs, most people do not seek to 'do unto others', but rather to mark clear boundaries between those to whom they do or do not want to belong.

3

Believing in Belonging: The Cultural Act of Claiming Identity

The small village where I lived has one pub that is frequented by only a fraction of the population; indeed, during the three years of the course of this research it was closed once temporarily on the edge of financial disaster and subsequently changed ownership. It is not a quaint, attractive, *olde-worlde* style pub that might be the subject of a BBC mini-series or a Merchant Ivory film: it is fairly stark, simply furnished, and frequented mainly by locals, who themselves are largely white and working class. Before smoking was banned in pubs it was filled with fumes produced by a large proportion of the clientele. The food is simple and unaffected by recent forays into organic or fusion cuisine. Until recently the wine list consisted of what was available through the bar tap. The pub is well-known for hosting local events and it was one of those that I now want to describe: a Halloween 'fancy dress' party for adults (several of whom were my direct informants) held to raise money for the annual village children's Christmas party. One man came dressed as a 'golliwog' caricature with black face and long black braids. Although I was shocked and offended at what I perceived as blatant racism, I said nothing about it but remained in the group he had just joined. A few minutes later, to my horror, I watched as one of the few non-white residents of the village, a black man in his 20s, strolled over and showed mock surprise at the 'golliwog'. He said, in a deliberately exaggerated tone, 'hey, man, you taking the mick?' (an English expression for 'poking fun at me'). Everyone had a good laugh and continued their evening together. When I asked someone else if they thought any offence had been taken, he laughed and said 'course not. We all get on – he plays on our football team'. Such warmth and inclusiveness is completely absent from the language acts I will now describe as constituting cultural performativity. While that may be puzzling it is perhaps the constant problem that anthropologists explore: 'the central problem of anthropology is the diversity of social human life' (Carrithers 1992, 2).

The process by which people claim a cultural identity is sometimes obscured by theorizing on the widest, societal level of, for example, the discursive production of ideologies (see, in particular, Asad 1993; Foucault 1980; Lukes 2005). I intend to make some, albeit modest, contributions to that wider theory presently, but first I will explore how I observed many of my informants engaging in claiming a cultural identity and how those engagements can be understood as strategies to reinforce their sense of collective belonging. I will argue that such claiming acts are often the product of specific social interactions, rendering an understanding of cultural identity and belonging impossible unless tightly secured to a specific time and place.

Cultural performativity

My informants typically did not discuss culture as do anthropologists or sociologists, who largely agree that culture is learned. Most of my informants seem to assume that culture is acquired at birth and that what they believe is about facts, not symbols. They are who they are collectively and what they know is, initially at least, inherent and then developed and transmitted. To therefore claim a cultural identity in the sense I am using it is not, for many of my informants, to acquire or to learn one but to attest to it and strengthen boundaries around it to prevent entry. As Jenkins (1997) described, identity formation and development involves a dialectical process requiring both an individual sense of belonging to a social group and awareness that people external to the individual also recognize that distinction. Swidler (1986) drew on the metaphors of tool kits and different recipes to argue that culture is not a homogeneous whole, but rather a set of social resources. Hall (1996) stressed the importance of the subject both 'being' and 'becoming' in a process of identity formation and change. While my informants were aware that they had the freedom to choose many aspects of their lives, it was striking that in matters of wanting to belong to a particular people defined by culture, religion, birth, or geography they were sometimes intransigent and sought to claim a right to that particular identity as something that was ascribed. The point of ascription, I will argue, is that it forms a barrier to entry.

My informants discuss such matters as belief, law, morality, history, religion, education, custom, and politics in terms that most often convey an inherent view of culture. For them, it is not, as social scientists would argue, learned, flexible, and changing but static, or 'traditional' in their terms. It can, and should, be reinforced and transmitted through the family and through schools. Transmission failure is a serious threat to the continuity of the culture and therefore those who fail to transmit, being specifically mothers,[1] were severely excoriated by many of my informants. Reasons why people do not transmit religious values are complex and may reflect anything from laziness, forgetfulness, ignorance, indifference, or deliberate suppression.[2]

Believing in belonging to a particular culture is, nevertheless, actively demonstrated and the claims vigorously supported by demonstrating adherence to certain social truths, or facts, that are presented as self-evident. The 'facts', offered in evidence of membership in the culture, help strengthen impermeable boundaries that define who has the right to belong. The act of claiming that identity is what I describe, following and adapting Austin (1962) and Butler (1990; 1993) as performative: it brings into being a social reality for the informant and provides a comforting sense of cultural homogeneity. It may do so by relying both on already-held beliefs and on assumptions that are pre-formed, adjusting them to particular circumstances through performing them. In that case, it does not depend on the number of times a particular act is performed, but upon what Butler referred to as the 'binding power' (Butler 1993, 225) of the act and thus, I will argue, helps reproduce a certain idea of a certain 'culture'. Tambiah (1985, 128) argued as well that performativity entails more than repetition and stage-like performance, but also reinforces certain values.

For example, when Fortier (2000) studied Italian migrants in London, she focused largely on what she described as 'performative belongings' with performativity and belonging explored as constitutive of cultural identities that are both and at once deterritorialized and reterritorialized. Fortier complicates a theme of the transnational subject that supposes a postmodern condition of uprootedness and mobility. She shows, markedly through her ethnography at St Peter's Italian Church, that cultural identities are created (not simply reproduced), performed, and embedded through socially 'binding' linguistic acts and events such as processions, weddings, newsletters, and first communions.

---

[1] See Warner and Williams (2010) for a summary of their research into religious transmission in Christian, Hindu, and Muslim families. They stressed the importance of adult-supervised religious activities in and amongst families.

[2] See Carsten's (2007) edited volume for cross-cultural examples of 'remembrance and relatedness'.

The pragmatic, binding nature of performative belief can also be seen as a 'rhetorical' strategy to help people belong to their social groups. Demircioğlu (2010) argues that, for infertile women, religious beliefs may also exist as rhetorical strategies both to allay their insecurities and to help forge social identities. Through ethnographic research on infertile women in Turkey, she concluded that childless women use the rhetoric of God's will to create meaning from their experience of childlessness.[3] Demircioğlu elaborates on the instrumental use of identity and belief by arguing that when such concepts become instruments for persuasion and overcoming division it is more accurate to refer to them as 'rhetoric'.

I sketch out below how my informants discuss apparently divergent themes and bind them in ways that help them perform a certain social identity. I interpret those processes as a means of marking the boundaries that, for them, define cultural identity by providing evidence of exclusive membership to a specific group. Following Barth (1969), I paid particular attention to observing how boundary-marking constructed an identity. I was not assuming a pre-existing cultural or ethnic group; indeed, following Weber (1978), my use of the term 'ethnic' here does not presume an inherent identity, but rather one constructed and reinforced in different social contexts and at different times: 'ethnic membership does not constitute a group, it only facilitates group formation of any kind' (ibid., 389). Ethnic identity can thus serve as an identity marker, what Gans (1979) described as 'symbolic ethnicity' consisting of a 'nostalgic allegiance' not necessarily accompanied by practice in everyday life (ibid., 9). It is also worth noting, as Chong (1998) did in his study of second-generation Koreans in Chicago, that not only does ethnic identity help to bolster the identity of people who see themselves as a subculture, but it is possible for them to do so because 'ethnicity' itself has become more acceptable as a cultural resource.

I also note the flexible, malleable, and agent-directed nature of belief, as mentioned in Chapter 1 with reference in particular to Bourdieu (1991) and Firth (1948). Kirsch (2004), in his study of spiritual healing practices in Zambia, explored how people switched their loyalty to healers depending on the perceived efficacy of the healer. Their ability to stop believing in one healer and start believing in another illustrated belief as 'wilful acts and were governed by pragmatism' (ibid., 708).

---

[3] She explicitly connects her work to that of Rudiak-Gould (2010), who argues that his informants in the Marshall Islands bring forth certain identities to legitimate their sometimes contradictory beliefs.

An unusual finding in my work is the prevalence of what I will call ethnic nominalism, or ethnic Christianity, to describe white mainstream populations. This runs contrary to how 'ethnic Christian' is usually presented. For example, a website titled 'Ethnic Christian Church Directory' (http://www.ethnicchurch.com/info/About.aspx) describes it as follows:

> This directory includes Christian church congregations that focus on a particular ethnic people group, or groups. Usually the congregation will have a primary emphasis on first or second-generation immigrants throughout the year. Many of the nations have come to America and Canada. We can participate in the mission to have representatives from all nations (ethnic people groups, tribes) worshiping the Lord Jesus Christ before the throne.

I will return to the theme of 'ethnic' identity in later chapters, particularly Chapter 9.

Claim to a single collective identity

The view of a flexible, contingent nature of collective identity was not shared by my informants. Language is a tool people use to claim a cultural identity, as if in speaking in a certain way they are bringing into being the very ideas they believe in. People who discussed with me their views about those who belong and those who do not often went to the trouble to explain that they were not racist, or opposed to the right of other people to exist – only that they were out of place in 'our country'. I found it notable that they employed the term 'our' as an inclusive term in conversation with me, knowing that I am a Canadian immigrant. It did not appear that I was, at least in the context of immigration, 'other'. The terms they used to describe the 'others' slipped unproblematically but usually synonymously between designations of religion, ethnicity, or national status. The term 'outlier' therefore best describes for me the sense that some people do not belong, not because they are of a particular religion or perceived ethnicity but because they are 'out of place', anomalous, and somehow dangerous. I suggest, following Douglas (1966) that their very presence is considered to be a threat that may pollute the existing pure and indigenous culture. How boundaries are erected between the members and outliers will be summarized briefly below and then returned to in more depth in the following chapters.

Imposing the possessive plural pronoun was a common technique used by some of my informants to present an unproblematic, un-nuanced view of membership in a static, common culture, while simultaneously identifying outliers. The possessive plural claims the territory beyond one individual to imply whatever is being said is being shared by others. When, for example, I asked Chris, a 43-year-old manufacturing supervisor, whether he thought Christian moral beliefs were different from those of other religions, he answered:

> Well, I don't know. I don't really know any. I don't have anything to do with, um, any other religion's people. No doubt Pakistanis, and Hindus and Muslims and whatever have their own thoughts on it. Probably very nice people, I just think there's too many of them in our country.

It is notable how he distances himself and, with a stress on separation and dismissal, falters before he can name the people with whom he does not belong. The phrase 'don't have anything to do with' is one usually used when conveying disapproval and censure. He then further distances himself by classifying religion as an entity, perhaps similar to a nation or an institution that has 'people'. The people are then further classified as a single category of impersonalized 'people' irrespective of whether they are identified by religion or nation of origin. Finally, they are completely dehumanized by dropping any personal pronoun and using the impersonal 'whatever' instead of 'whoever'. This contrasts with his recovery of personalized language when referring to 'our' country.

Another informant, Rick, 20, a painter-decorator who lives in the same village as Chris, used similar language construction. He said:

> I probably say, I'm not racist, like, but your Asians, stuff like that. I disagree with them, stuff like that. Not with them being in country, but with way they live when they are in the country. Asylum, immigration, stuff like that. I have my beliefs on that.

By saying 'your' Asians, Rick was dissociating himself from Asians. By saying he disagreed 'with' them, Rick was not suggesting he was engaged in a particular discussion or point of disagreement with Asians, but rather that he disagreed about them. What he thinks and feels about that are described as his 'beliefs', those matters that he thinks are true. He was using 'belief' not only in a propositional sense, as a truth statement that could or could not be true, but he was claiming his particular orientation to it through locating it in a particular time and place. Rick also distances himself from cultural outliers through his use of possessive pronouns: they are 'your' Asians. He inverts the use of the possessive pronoun from how Chris used it by explicitly using the second person.

Terry, a 49-year-old agricultural contractor, also distinguishes between those who belong and those who are, in his term, 'aliens'.

He told me that he thought where he lived 'there's a bit of anti-Muslim feeling as anywhere else'. When I asked if he meant 'around here' he replied:

Oh, aye. But that's because they read bloody stupid newspapers like [the] Sun and all that. Which stir it up, don't they? I mean, I wouldn't go shoot somebody just because he was a Muslim, but that is an alien culture to our culture, isn't it? Or is it? Am I just taking the same fears up as other people?

Terry assumes a position of restraint and superiority by suggesting he would not shoot a Muslim, without apparently noticing that the idea itself might be shocking. He also seems unaware that he is not defining what is meant by 'our culture' nor that he includes by inference me, a Canadian immigrant, as part of his culture while simultaneously excluding a Muslim immigrant as alien. I will return to this point below.

The discussion thus far shows how culture is often portrayed in terms of a common country, but distinctions within the 'country' are sometimes made to mark other differences, such as social class. George, 60, a semi-retired bookkeeper, spoke at length about 'political correctness', which, when I asked him, he defined as:

Political correctness means it's, where people say we have to behave in a certain way, it's like we have the, the uh, ban Noddy, Enid Blyton books from libraries, stuff like that.

He refers to 'we' as a category including him that is different from 'people' who appear to be others imposing their will on him. These impositions took the form of, particularly, anti-drinking and anti-smoking restrictions. The 'people' to whom he was referring were identified with his comment that such restrictions were 'to do with being a middle class situation as far as I could see'.

Boundaries are also drawn by using the term 'community' to reflect a common culture different from others. Graham, 34, a technical analyst, talked in our interview about how he believed his beliefs were derived from the family and life experience. When we discussed how society was changing, he said he did not think it was changing in the small village where he was raised:

Not in a small community which I lived in, but if you look out to the outside world, to television, newspapers, I think the world, I think it's being displayed more in those things than when I was a child.

The word 'community' is evoked to declare a boundary around the people Graham grew up with and those in the outside world. Graham described Britain today as 'massively multicultural', saying 'with them come their beliefs and I don't know whether their beliefs filter out to the rest of us, I don't know'.

Chris, cited earlier, had defined himself as strongly anti-religion and anti-church, yet urged me to read the biblical book of Revelations to understand, as he described it, how: 'god will fight god and we are fighting against our religious beliefs as regards the Pakistani point in the local community'.

Thus, 'community' serves as a reference group, a real or imagined entity used to distinguish between one group and others and to provide apparent external validation for one group's beliefs. I suggest the word 'community' is a marker being used to denote boundaries and claim a cultural identity. Gilroy (1987, 235) argues that community 'is as much about difference as it is about similarity and identity'. It is a relational word, he says, which is laden with different symbols and meanings, most of which serve to create boundaries. Cohen's classic definition (1985, 9) mirrors this by defining community as symbolically constructed as 'a system of values, norms, and moral codes which provides a sense of identity within a bounded whole to its members' and calls for a more Wittgensteinian emphasis on meaning-in-use: 'on the element which embodies this sense of discrimination – the boundary' (ibid., 11).

If the boundary encapsulates the identity of the community and is brought into being through social interaction, then beliefs about community are, I suggest, performative. While some boundaries might be physically marked, such as the boundaries of a country, others are conceived in people's minds and therefore, Cohen notes, might be 'perceived in rather different terms, not only by people on opposite sides of it, but also by people on the same side' (ibid., 12).

It is also, of course, a word that for many people might mean multiple and diverse relationships. Reimer et al. (2008) studied the practices and beliefs of Muslims and Christians involved in peacemaking activities in many different countries. By analysing their qualitative interviews, the researchers were able to identity a number of themes, including 'community'. Some of the interviews reflected community as a source of social support, others as a symbol of civic identity, but what they all shared was that relationality in communities was 'a core religious precept embodied in their view of the world and divinity' (ibid., 92–3). I will return to this theme in, particularly, Chapter 7.[4]

---

[4] For wider discussion on the various understandings of 'community' see, for example, Day, G. (2006); Delanty (2010 [2003]).

My discussions with my informants also emphasized the counter-intuitive finding that Barth (1969) presented: it is through the interaction with others that ethnic identity is formed on the boundary. Besides using language to claim a cultural identity, informants often strategized their beliefs by producing what appeared to be evidence of their cultural claim. I will discuss below several of these relating to birth claims, entitlement claims, and moral claims.

The birth claim – natal membership

Membership of a culture is apparently automatically conferred by being born into a family of that culture. It is not enough to be born in the country: second-generation Asians, for example, are not accepted as members. It is therefore the idea of an indigenous, inherent character that is important, not nationhood. For example, immigration laws that permit entry into the country and even acquisition of nationality do not make someone a member of the culture. Jordan, 14, attends a large comprehensive school and lives with both parents, both factory workers. When he wanted to convince me that he was a Christian, despite not believing in 'God and Jesus and Bible and stuff' he said, 'on my birth certificate it says I'm Christian, so'. It is not practice for a UK birth certificate, or passport, or indeed any other state-produced document to have a religion stated on it. I did not challenge Jordan, tell him he was wrong, or ask him to meet me the following week and produce his birth certificate. I assumed he either had confused his birth certificate with his baptismal certificate or had otherwise received the impression that Christianity is something that comes from birth.

When I asked Graham, cited above, what he had said on the census, he replied: 'I probably would have put Christian, actually, because that's how, what I was raised as. Not that I'm a practising one, but, I was born and raised that, so if I were to mark a religion that would be it.' Gary, 52, said he would have ticked Christian because: 'How I was brought up. I don't believe, but I don't disbelieve either.' Barry, 48, explained, 'I suppose it was instilled into me from an early age that I was a Christian.'

Natal membership therefore creates an impermeable boundary as it is understood to be inherent, not acquired. That already-held, inherent identity is inscribed through certain acts performed by the national church, particularly baptisms. The claim to a Christian cultural identity was often made by people who had otherwise described themselves as non-religious. Graham, cited above, said 'I've been baptized and confirmed as a Christian so in effect I was, I am a Christian but I'm not a practising Christian believer.' Harriet, 14, a student at the

55

grammar school, said she would answer the census question with 'Christian. Don't know why. Because I was baptized. I'd just answer Christian without thinking.' Penny said, 'Because I was christened Church of England.' The above examples may be a form of 'belonging without believing'.

Entitlement claim

Claims to cultural identity are sometimes expressed as claims about resources or other material benefits, but on closer examination it appears the 'entitlement claim' is another way to mark boundaries. Rick, cited above, continued our conversation by defining who is entitled to benefits, such as pensions. How he moves amongst the pronouns, from the plural possessive to the distance of the third person, reinforces his sense of belonging and difference:

> Yeah, like we pay our tax, our national insurance, and like you see people, old people now, complaining about their pensions, and what have and this and that, when we pay a lot of taxes to keep these immigrants and that in our country, you know.

Atypically, I decided at that point to intervene by calling attention to myself, a white, female Canadian. I wanted to see whether I would be classed as one of 'these immigrants'. I asked him directly: 'What about me? I'm an immigrant.' Rick looked genuinely surprised and slightly embarrassed and replied: 'Yeah but you, you work. You're doing something with your life, aren't you?' The question was phrased rhetorically and while I could have reinforced the fact that I was a student and therefore in principle unemployed, I decided not to argue: 'Right,' I said. Rick continued: 'You don't claim off me all your life, do you?' I did not respond to that direct question but returned to the general point by asking, 'So, immigrants who claim off you?'

A long silence fell between us. I sensed he was uncomfortable and wanted to see how he would reconcile his opposition to 'immigrants' with his obvious ease with me. I waited to see how our social interaction might produce an amended view of his beliefs. After a moment or two he continued:

> I don't know if I'm racist, I probably am. Don't think I am racist, but I might be. Don't know how you're classed as a racist. All I know if people come in my country, into our country, if they work and so on I've got not a real problem with it. It's when they sit on their asses and don't do owt.

It was the first time he had used the personal pronoun 'my' to describe the country, and I noticed how he looked at me directly and corrected himself quickly to include me in 'our' country. I was not an outlier, but, at least temporarily, a member. He may have been responding to social norms to be polite, but I would conclude more safely that a white, female, middle-class Canadian was more, in his mind, a member than an outlier. The boundary was being stretched a little.

The contrast between outliers and pensioners was one made by Veronica, 48, who owns a village shop. When I asked her if she was involved in anything because of her beliefs, she said no, not like a political party or anything. I asked if she was ever concerned about wider issues she might see on the news, either nationally or internationally. She said not really, apart from the asylum seekers. She was not racist, she said, and she has 'no problem with the ones who are genuine', but she doesn't think it is right that 'some people should come into this country and have everything they want made easy for them and yet there are old people living just down the road who will be cold this winter'.

Claim to unique culturally-derived morality

Rick, cited above, raised the idea of 'Asians' when talking about morality. I had asked him about his beliefs on rights and wrongs and he answered:

> I don't know, when I do them. Many things are right and wrong but I never really know til I do them. You think in hindsight, oh, if only, but you've done it. I don't know what makes your mind up. It's like when you might tell a white lie or something. You never know why you're doing it. Well, you are, you're doing it to gain something. When you're lying, you're doing it to gain something, aren't you?[5]

He then spoke for a moment about lying and telling the truth before saying, as if changing the subject: 'Yeah, I have ideas about what things I'd like to be different'. When I asked him what that might be he said 'uh, I don't know if this is right to say'. I encouraged him to say it anyway, and then he went directly to the point cited earlier about 'disagreeing' about Asians. Interpretations of morality are discussed in

---

[5] Rick is positioning 'lying' in a social context, as something that is not absolutely or inherently wrong but something that is wrong because it involves deception and gain. I will discuss morality in more detail in Chapter 7.

a later chapter, but the salient point here is how the idea of right and wrong triggered his thoughts about belonging.

Robert and May described themselves as Christian by way of an example of morality. Robert, 73, is a retired printer-manager, married to May, 68, who described herself as a housewife. They had said they were not sure if God existed and they never went to church, but would describe themselves as Christian because they had 'a Christian outlook'. I asked them if they thought that outlook was different from those who were not Christian. Robert said:

> In some cases, yes, yeah. I don't want to bring racism into it, but it's difficult not to in certain cases. But I'd class the treatment of females by the Muslims, and I'm afraid this is the Kilroy Silk situation coming out, but I think it's always been my belief that the women are trodden into the ground in the Muslim world, entirely.

He went on to explain that his view was not formed only from the media, but from a friend who used to stay with Muslim families in north Africa. He said the boys in the household:

> would go into the bathroom and would shave and just throw all the shaving gear into the washbasin and leave it, and then the girls would, his sisters had to come in and clean it all up, and that is the sort of attitude I'm afraid that does prevail to this day.

May, who was usually silent in the interview or talked over by Robert, was nodding to herself. I decided to draw her into the conversation:

ABBY: Is that what you think, May, you talked about –
MAY: Yes, yes, yes.
ABBY: Right and wrong, you –
MAY: Yes, yes, yes.
ROBERT: Yes.
MAY: Like I said, we both really have the same outlook. Yes, yes, I –
ROBERT: I'm not saying that Muslims are bad, in every sense of the word, they're not all terrorists.

Robert identified himself as Christian by referring to the treatment of women, apparently unaware that he discourages his wife to speak and that in her role of housewife she was specifically charged with cleaning up after him. I suggest this shows how certain norms, in this case, white patriarchy, are held unconsciously while moral superiority becomes a cultural marker. Colley (1992) argued that a feeling of British superiority has been a feature of British culture for at least the past three centuries, nurtured by successive series of military victories and domination of other countries. Her analysis resonated with

Robert's comments above as she described how Britons compare their laws, their treatment of women, and other parts of their societies with other societies they do not understand yet consider inferior. The act of claiming moral superiority over others is often analysed as non-religious attempts to reinforce the status of one social class over another, particularly in times of social change. In their discussion of American 'crusades' against pornography Zurcher and Kirkpatrick (1970) argued that much of the battle was to consolidate social hierarchies – a point also made in Gusfield's (1963) study of American campaigns against alcohol.

Sometimes, that need to claim superiority results in socio-religious responses often positioned, as Nussbaum (1999) pointed out, as defences of 'culture' or 'tradition'. Both terms, she argues, often serve to mask inequalities and reflect the views of a dominant, typically male, group who see themselves not only as more powerful, but as better than others. Many sociological and political commentators have examined a general upsurge in American conservatism in both politics and religion, in the 1970s and 1980s, described as the 'New Right' and 'New Christian Right', and in particular the rise of the Moral Majority, a well-organized network of mainly fundamentalist Christians credited with helping Ronald Reagan become president. This has been seen as a response to the liberalism of the 1960s counter-culture, the rise of feminism, a perception of 'secular humanism', the economic recession caused by the 1972 oil crisis, and perception of a threat to the United States' world standing (see, for example, Beyer 1994; Bruce 1988; Carter 1997; Fackre 1982; Liebman and Wuthnow 1983). Those anxieties were represented by the 'New Right's' social traditionalism, concerned with 'the breakdown of family, community, religion, and traditional morality in American life' (Himmelstein 1983, 16). Those concerns then formed a political agenda:

> In political terms, the conservative response is to pursue legislation against the Equal Rights Amendment, the Gay Rights Bill, abortion, gun control, and sex education in public schools. (Hunter 1983, 152)

To take just one example, in the United States, pro-gun groups have successfully influenced legislation through well-funded professional lobbying, though groups on both sides of the divide argue about each other's polls and statistics: some studies say that a majority of Americans consistently favour stronger regulations and nearly a third favour a complete ban on all handguns (Carter 1997, 48–63). Broadly, the American pro-gun lobby consists of two categories: single-issue groups which exist only to campaign against gun control, and groups which argue against gun control as part of a wider agenda. The single-issue category consists of organizations such as the National Rifle Association (NRA), Gun Owners of America, and the Second Amendment Foundation. The wider-agenda category ranges from evangelical Christian churches (predominantly Baptist and Assembly of God churches) to militia-style racist groups (such as the Aryan Nation and Stormfront) and the Christian Identity movement, which views the United States as the promised land and Jews as the 'seeds of Satan' (see Quarles 2004 for a fuller account).

The NRA firmly positions itself as defending what it sees as indivisibly 'American' and 'God-given'. The following was extracted from their website:

> This nation was founded on a set of fundamental freedoms. Our Constitution does not give us those freedoms – it guarantees and protects them. The right to defend ourselves and our loved ones is one of those. The individual right to keep and bear arms is another. These truths are what define us as Americans...
>
> We believe any individual who does not agree that the Second Amendment guarantees a fundamental right and who does not respect our God-given right of self-defense should not serve on any court, much less the highest court in the land. (http://home.nra.org/#/home, accessed 7 September 2010)

Partly in response to organizations like the NRA, the Democratic Leadership Council organized a conference in 2003 under the title 'God, Guns, and Guts':

> What we want to do here is have a nuts-and-bolts discussion on how to seize the cultural center in three critical areas: national security, role of religion in public life, and responsible gun ownership. (http://www.dlc.org/ndol_ci. cfm?contentid=252171&kaid=126&subid=189, accessed 7 September 2010)

Claiming the high moral ground and conflating that with cultural, religious, or national identity is, as Weber (1922) observed, one way that groups seek to create and maintain their power. He (ibid., 56) pointed to the link between morality and culture when he argued that monotheism was produced by monarchs who wanted to consolidate power and then, by so doing, to control the population further through guides to behaviour:

> [T]he personal, transcendental and ethical god is a Near-Eastern concept.
> It corresponds so closely to that of an all-powerful mundane king with his rational bureaucratic regime that a causal connection can scarcely be overlooked.

Bloch's (1986) analysis of circumcision rites amongst the Merina of Madagascar traced the changing nature and meaning of that ritual through history, showing how it was not just a family or religious ceremony but also, at times, a way for the state to reinforce the 'culture' (and monarchic power) in response to advancing colonialism. In another example, Buckser (2008) explored how influential Danish Jews shaped the understanding of Judaism in Copenhagen in two different periods to achieve two separate goals; one of integration in the early 1800s and another of distinctiveness in the late twentieth century. The nineteenth-century form of Danish Judaism had emphasized the performance of distinctive ritual in obedience to Law, whereas it became important for the purpose of assimilation for Jews to adopt a more intellectualist (one might say, with reference to Chapter 1's discussion, 'propositionalist') approach to their religion in line with other religions at the time. Later, in the late twentieth century, an understanding of being Jewish shifted to become more located in cultural identity. Those turns, in response to changing cultural contexts, show how dimensions of content, practice, salience, and function of Jewish belief and identity changed in specific times and places. In a separate example, Pace (2007) describes how Catholicism in Europe was often framed in opposition to others: in fifteenth-century Spain, it was a way to protect national identity 'based on the idea of purity of bloodstock' (ibid., 40); in later years the Catholic church often opposed national identity when that identity was constituted by socialist or communist movements: 'Catholicism came to be used to mark the boundaries, both symbolic and territorial, of areas of Catholic predominance over against socialist-communist hegemony' (ibid., 41).

In using the terms 'race' and 'ethnicity' I am referring to a system of social interactions, not biological traits. As ethnicity is constructed as a form of group formation it is a powerful form of belonging and is important to people. As Jenkins observed:

> This means that we must also take seriously the fact that ethnicity means something to individuals, and that when it matters, it can *really* matter. (1997, 168; italics are his)

From listening to my informants I conclude that ideas of ethnicity really mattered, even if the word 'ethnic' was often replaced by 'race' or simply 'them'. Following Mason (1995, 1) I agree that both race and ethnicity are 'a matter of how people see themselves and of how they are defined by others'. I also agree with his concern that the term 'white' is under-theorized, but will use it both to reflect the way I argue my informants see themselves and because 'it captures a key feature of the ethnic exclusivism which characterizes much of the life of modern Britain' (ibid., 17).

I will return in Chapter 8 to the effects of time and place on beliefs as I explore how what I identify as seven dimensions of belief interact holistically and organically.

I will turn now to a specific example that prompted much of my fieldwork in the UK, as I briefly described in Chapter 2, the creation and response to the 'religious question' on the 2001 UK census.

The village hall question: the case of the UK 2001 census

Consider a conversation I had with one of my informants, David, 48, a health worker and active member of his local community association. He works hard with other local volunteers to organize events, such as the annual bonfire night, and raise money for various local projects. We were chatting about my research and how I was trying to focus on asking people open questions rather than conduct a questionnaire. He sympathized, he said, because he had some experience with survey methods. The community association had decided to create a questionnaire to assess local needs for community facilities and committee members were, he explained, aware that in surveying people they might inadvertently influence the outcome:

> ... if you're trying to draw things out from people but without putting ideas into their mind. I mean, one of the things we wanted in the village was better village hall facilities, and everybody on the community association wants better village hall facilities. But you can't put 'would you like a new village hall' cuz you're leading, you're feeding them the answer you want them to give you.

That principle of 'leading' and 'feeding' applies to large-scale survey instruments measuring national characteristics just as it does to small-scale surveys about community facilities. The case was no different for the UK census.

One of the first questions to be asked about the 2001 census question was, therefore, why have the religious question at all? Part of the answer was given to me by one of my informants who, although he was an atheist, said he had ticked the Christian box on the census. When I asked him why he had done that, he replied: 'Well, only because they asked us to.' Here, I suggest, we have the census equivalent of 'would you like a new village hall?'

So, who wanted a new village hall? The political impact of having a question about religion placed on the census would have almost been enough, whatever the outcome, to have created an impression that religion was important. As the Bishop of Manchester said in the House of Lords:

> The importance of religion and spirituality was, as noble Lords well know, illustrated by the national census, for which religion was deemed sufficiently important by the Government to have its own section. (Hansard, 22 May 2003)

Such a decision did not, however, arise accidentally. The inclusion of a religious question in the 2001 census marked the first time in the 200 years since the decennial census began in 1801 that questions about people's religious affiliation had been asked in England, Wales, and Scotland. Somewhat confusingly, in 1851, on the same day as the population census was taken, a separate exercise called the *Accommodation and Attendance at Worship* census was carried out. That census, popularly called 'the religious census', asked questions about church attendance, not affiliation. Religion had been covered in the Northern Irish census since 1861. The inclusion in the UK census resulted from intense lobbying by several religious groups affiliated to the Religious Affiliation Sub-Group (see, for example, accounts from two of its members: Francis 2003; Weller 2004; for further detailed examination and historical review, see Avis 2003; Southworth 2005). The final wording and placement of the question was not decided by that group, but by the Office for National Statistics, in consultation with government.

Weller (2004) points out that religious groups wanting a question about religion represented a change from their position ten years earlier. Some had opposed including such a question because it might single some groups out or bring an undesirable amount of focus on some identities. That position softened primarily after several religious/ethnic urban disturbances prompted government to work more closely with religious and other community organizations.

The result was something that would likely not have been acceptable to David's village hall committee, nor to many members of the Religious Affiliation Sub-Group. Its problems can be explained partly by reviewing the census in terms of basic principles of quantitative research relating to the wording of the question, the response options offered, the order of the question and the options offered, and the 'mode effect' – that is, the medium used to ask the questions. Variations in how those principles were followed, or not, means that both the main census results and any direct cross-cultural comparisons are highly problematic.

The census question was asked differently amongst the countries of the UK (and internationally). The England and Wales version of the question 'What is your religion?' implies less of a subjective orientation than a statement of fact. As Voas and Bruce (2004, 26) suggest, its affirmative form implies that respondents have a religion and therefore the phrasing may lead the respondent to answer positively.

The Scottish census question also supposed the existence of an identity aligned to institutional religion, but introduced the subjective element of 'belonging', asking: 'What religion, religious denomination or body do you belong to?' The Northern Irish question was different, first asking 'Do you regard yourself as belonging to any particular religion?' If the answer was yes, the respondent proceeded to the next question: 'What religion, religious denomination or body do you belong to?' The Northern Irish question thus allowed respondents to first consider whether there was a religion to which they belonged, before choosing one from the list. The England/Wales and Scotland questions, in contrast, immediately prompted respondents to choose options amongst forms of institutional religion.

Such wording is incompatible with other surveys about religion that probe issues of belonging and find considerably lower affirmative responses. For example, the UK Christian charity Tearfund (Ashworth and Farthing 2007) asked UK adults, 'Do you regard yourself as belonging to any particular religion?' Their study concluded that just over half (53 per cent) of UK adults 'belong' to the Christian religion, a much lower figure than possibly implied with the census and one more in line with, for example, the British Social Attitudes survey or the European Social Survey.

Returning to the problems of the UK census, the response options and the order of the options were also different on the three different country censuses. For example, the England and Wales version had tick-box options: 'None; Christian (including Church of England, Catholic, Protestant, and all other Christian denominations); Buddhist; Hindu; Jewish; Muslim; Sikh', followed by an option to answer 'any other religion'. The Scottish question did not offer a general category of 'Christian' but three tick-box options of 'Church of Scotland, Roman Catholic and Other Christian (Please write in)'. Other non-Christian religions were then listed as in the England and Wales version. The Northern Irish census did not list non-Christian religions specifically, merely offering the option: 'Other, please write in'. While the Religious Affiliation Sub-Group argued for denominational differences for the English and Wales version, the final question included only the 'Christian' option. Weller (2004, 9) points out that the character of sectarianism in Northern Ireland and Scotland means that the 'differentiation within the category of "Christian" is of public significance in these countries'.

And yet, none of the UK censuses allowed subcategories of other religions, providing a picture of a nuanced, complex form of Christianity but a blanket, if not banal, approach to other religions: ignoring, for example, important varieties in the second largest religion in the UK, Islam.

Another issue relating to options and order was the question's location on the form. On the England and Wales version it immediately followed a question on ethnicity and, as Voas and Bruce (2004, 28) suggested, could have been interpreted as a supplementary question. On the Scottish census it was positioned before the ethnicity question; the percentage who chose Christian in Scotland was significantly lower than England and Wales (65 per cent vs 72 per cent), possibly because of both the wording and the location.

Finally, both the Scottish and Irish, but not the England and Wales census, then ask an additional question: 'What religion, religious denomination or body were you brought up in?' repeating the main question's options. This is potentially helpful in assessing what proportion of people disaffiliates from which religions over time.

If it is difficult to draw comparisons amongst the three countries of the UK, the picture complicates even further when we turn to continental Europe. For example, some countries list a generous choice to Christians of Catholic, Adventist, Lutheran, Free Baptist, Methodist, and so on; the Republic of Ireland not only offers the respondent an array of Christian denominations but also 'Lapsed Roman Catholic'. Continuing their rather optimistic tone, the Irish also offer respondents a choice of agnostic but not atheist (although you can have 'no religion') whereas in Portugal you can be atheist but not agnostic.

Outside of Europe, we find the Canadian data similar to the UK, both with the 2001 census and similar church attendance levels. The Canadian data offer longitudinal comparisons as the questions had been asked in previous years. The percentage of those claiming the Christian identity (72 in 2001) has been decreasing. The Canadian census offers denomination subcategories and the percentage of those who affiliate with the general category 'Christian' rather than a specific denomination has more than doubled between censuses, representing the largest percentage increase among all major religious groups. This tends to support the tendency, as I discuss later, to associate with

65

Christianity as a cultural symbol rather than as a practised religion. Further, also in line with the UK, the percentage of those claiming no religion has increased in Canada from 12 to 16 per cent.

The apparent 'exceptional' case of the US, as discussed at more length in Chapter 2, is partly obscured by its lack of a religious question on the census. The most recent results from the American Religious Identification Survey (http://www.americanreligionsurvey-aris.org/), published in 2008, revealed that 15 per cent of the US population said they had no religion – a figure in line with most Euro American countries. Two years later Putnam and Campbell (2010) suggested the figure might be 17 per cent.

Claiming the Christian identity: the political impact

The above section served to show that the wording and placement of the religious question on the UK 2001 census broke a number of fairly rudimentary rules about questionnaire design. These shortcomings in basic data gathering did not, however, affect the generally positive reaction amongst sociologists of religion and church leaders. For example, the main sources of church attendance figures in the UK, relied upon virtually unquestioningly by sociologists of religion, is an organization called 'Christian Research'. When the census results were announced, its Executive Director wrote that 'Like the Census conducted 2000 years ago under Syrian Governor Quirinius, there is good news for the church!' (Brierley 2003).

That jubilant reaction needs to be understood within its spatial-temporal dimension but also materially and discursively. The purpose of the census is to inform government decisions about spending money on public resources, such as education, health, and welfare, but the discursive element cannot be minimized. Although my specific case deals with the UK census and the religious question, other countries have their own related problems about interpretation and impact. In the United States, for example, the purpose of the census is to gather data to apportion seats in the House of Representatives and equitably allocate money from the federal budget.

This material, political aspect to the census was specifically raised in the UK by the Muslim Council of Great Britain, which issued a statement supporting the census religious question on the grounds of race discrimination. As Muslims define themselves in terms of their religion, not ethnicity, a census religious question would give government necessary information about the Muslim community:

The allocation of resources and the monitoring of discrimination on the basis of ethnicity alone are therefore no longer adequate. An objective of the 2001 census is to provide essential statistics for the more equitable allocation of public services and better planning on matters such as community relations, health care, education, employment and housing. Without a religious affiliation question, the 2001 census will lose a valuable data collection opportunity. (http://www.salaam.co.uk/knowledge/ukcensus.php)

While the Muslims here were in favour of a religious question to combat discrimination, the result has been in some cases to justify discriminatory practices.

The census figures have been used to inform and justify major government decisions, not only affecting how public money is spent, but how major policies affecting a wide range of issues are debated and decided. For example, a leading Christian politician used the census findings to defend discriminatory practices. This particular discursive impact was illustrated during an exchange in the House of Commons between Dr Evan Harris, then Liberal Democrat MP for Oxford West and Abingdon, and Jack Straw, then the Leader of the House, who has described himself as a Christian who regularly attends church. Evans raised the issue of religious groups carrying out publicly funded services when some of them did not comply with human rights legislation, discriminating against certain clients (a reference, presumably, to some organizations' refusal to accord equal rights to women and gay people). In response, Straw said there had already been a debate on the wider issue, and he had agreed that religious groups could be exempt from human rights legislation. He added that:

the hon. Gentleman is a secularist, and I respect his views, but his is not the position of the vast majority of this country, 70 per cent of whom declared themselves to be Christian in the 2001 census, and there are many who subscribe to other religions. (Hansard, 25 January 2007)

The census figures were also quoted in an attempt to influence public broadcasting. The Archbishops' Council of the Church of England suggested that the country's broadcasting company, the BBC, should change its programming policy (Archbishops' Council, 2006), claiming that the 'The 2001 Census finds that a higher proportion, 80%, associates with a faith community.' It is probable that the figure of '80%' refers to the statistic that 78 per cent of respondents identified themselves with a religion. Nonetheless, the same point was made in the House of Lords by the Bishop of Manchester who said the census figures 'support broadcasters who are seeking peak time for high-quality religious and spiritual content' (Hansard, 22 May 2003).

The census did not ask about spirituality, but nonetheless the Bishop's speech indicates the weight the census religious question lends to arguments about the place of religion in the UK today. One Bishop even referred to the census to strengthen his claim that people believed in God. For example, Rev. Barry Morgan, when he was inaugurated as the new archbishop of the Church in Wales on 12 July 2003, commented (Morgan 2003) that he faced challenges with church congregations 'slumping' but he was 'heartened by the 2001 Census results, which show most people in Wales believe in God'. The census questions for England and Wales did not ask about belief or God, only religious affiliation.

Again illustrating how census data are used to affect legislation and how terminology slips between several related terms, the following comment was made during a debate about assisted suicide. Here, the Lord Bishop of St Albans extends the census finding from religious self-identification to include both belief and spirituality.

> ...the most recent census figures would indicate that, yes, of course fewer people attend and practise their belief in specific religious buildings, but the levels of belief and spirituality in our nation are huge. To describe us as secular is simply not accurate. (Hansard, 6 June 2003)

The British Humanist Association campaigned against the inclusion of a religious question on the census and its impacts on public policy, particularly public broadcasting:[6]

> This representation of the data as implying the population in England and Wales as strongly religious and spiritual is used to influence the direction of legislation passing through Parliament (and sometimes with success), despite the fact that the Census 2001 data on religion attempts to measure religious affiliation/identity and does not even attempt to measure feeling, belief or faith. The Census data have been referred to here in the context of resource allocation: that 72 per cent are Christian, and therefore public service broadcasting should be censored along the lines of the church, and that more programmes should be religious. The Census 2001 data on religion does not measure practice, nor does it measure belief or 'faith', but rather attempts to measure affiliation/identity. As the Census 2001 data on religion does not measure religiosity as such, it cannot be inferred from it that the majority of

---

[6] I am grateful to the BHA for providing convenient access to the Hansard excerpts used in this chapter.

people would prefer greater religiosity in, and greater religious ownership of, broadcasting.

Finally, conveying rather neatly the confusion caused by the figures, the BBC announced the results as 'while the UK is basically secular, it is also overwhelmingly Christian'.

The above examples illustrate that one of the main terms being thrown like a weapon is 'secular'. I note how Jack Straw, cited above, not only uses the term Christian to describe the majority of people in the UK, but uses the term 'secularist' to describe Evans. The Lord Bishop of St Albans makes a similar linguistic move. As discussed in Chapters 1 and 2, sociologists of religion have been arguing about secularization for the past thirty years, with many of them now adopting the term *post-secular* to describe the religious landscape in modern Euro America. It is apparent that 'secular', 'religious', 'Christian', 'faith', and 'spirituality' are loaded terms being used to claim the identity of a nation – and sometimes of a discipline. The Chair of the Religious Affiliation Sub-Group, Rev. Prof. Leslie J. Francis, for example, asserted that the census results refuted the secularization thesis. Secularization, he wrote, 'no longer commands general academic consensus' (Francis 2003, 51).

To obtain statistical evidence for a claim about Christian identity was, and remains, an important goal for many. Measured against all the usual metrics of church attendance, participation in rituals, and membership, mainstream Christianity is in steep decline in the UK, Europe, and other Euro American countries. The only problem is, what if those census results are misleading, and do not properly inform us about who is Christian in the UK? Who, precisely, does the census represent, and why would they tick that box? The answer to that question does not require in-depth, nuanced, painstakingly difficult qualitative research: it is available with a few clicks of a mouse and some simple statistical computations.

Introducing the survey Christians: performing Christian identities

Although the census apparently represents every person in the UK, the summary figures such as those quoted above give only a partial, and unrepresentative, picture. To understand in more detail what the numbers represent it is necessary to break down the numbers into smaller groups. When we do that, we find something interesting about the figures that have been ignored by the jubilant voices reported earlier:

the numbers indicate that Christianity is in rapid and overwhelming decline in the UK.

Most people who ticked the Christian box were over 50 years old. In keeping with other data we have about young people and religion, the census figures confirmed that young people are less likely to claim a religious affiliation than older people. A similar pattern exists in other Euro American countries: in Canada, for example, the decline in mainstream Christianity is partly explained because members of the mainstream denominations are aging and fewer young people are identifying with them. Figures from the American Religious Identification Survey 2008 revealed that 22 per cent of Americans aged 18–29 years self-identify as 'Nones'. De Graaf and Grotenhuis (2008, 595–6) concluded from their study in the Netherlands, with comparisons to the UK (see Crockett and Voas 2006), that religious belief will continue to decline due to cohort replacement. They also found that people did not become more religious as they age and therefore concluded that 'in the Netherlands for the years to come, a continuing "silent secularisation revolution" in which both religious belief and religious affiliation decline is the most likely longitudinal trend and not a large-scale religious revival'.

In contrast to the positive response of religious leaders above, analysed by age profile the census tells us what we already knew: Christianity is in decline. We then might wonder who those older people are. Why would they choose the category of Christian? The census Christians are probably not much different from other people who claim a Christian identity when asked in surveys.[7]

For example, among people aged 65 and over surveyed for the British Social Attitudes (BSA) survey in 2004, only 22 per cent say that they regard themselves as belonging to no religion, while 63 per cent of young adults (18–24) so describe themselves. These differences, as argued above, are not explained by life course (i.e. that people become more religious as they grow older), but the evidence suggests that in the main they are generational, produced by a steady decline in religiosity over time (Crockett and Voas 2006; Voas and Crockett 2005). Gender is also associated with religion. Exactly half of white men say that they have no religion (in the BSA 2004), versus 41 per cent of white women. To put it another way, men make up 58 per cent of the secular category using European Social Survey data, but only 36 per cent of the religious groups.

---

[7] I am grateful to Prof. David Voas for much of the following survey material. See also Voas and Day 2007.

Using 2001 census data for England and Wales, however, there is a tendency for those responding 'none' to the question 'what is your religion?' to be in the higher occupational categories. Among men (omitting those not classified) 51 per cent of the Nones were in intermediate, managerial, or professional occupations, as compared with 44 per cent of (nominal) Christians. These findings are consistent with the suggestion that many of those describing themselves as Christian on the census were working-class whites who viewed the term as an ethnonational rather than a religious label (Voas and Bruce 2004; Day, A. 2006).

The overview thus far gives a picture of survey Christians as predominantly older and more conservative than the general population. It is therefore more realistic to interpret such surveys, and in particular, the census, as a reflection of a particular and declining proportion of the population. Further, the nature of a survey is not neutral. It is evident to most people that information will be used to provide a picture of their 'culture' and it may therefore be in their interests to perform a certain kind of identity. I argued above that the wording and location of the census questions for England and Wales and for Scotland 'funnelled' respondents away from a subjective, personal sense of religion that may have received, as the Scotland example suggests, a lower response. To help reveal my informants' practices of self-identification, at the conclusion of each interview I asked them if they remembered what they had said on the UK 2001 decennial census in answer to the question on religious identity. (In asking the question, I did not divulge the information that 72 per cent had selected Christian.) Some said they did recall, but most did not. I explained that choices offered to the question 'what is your religion' were Christian, Hindu, Muslim, Sikh, Jewish, Buddhist; or one could say 'none' or 'other' and write something different or not answer it at all. I was often not allowed to finish reading the list of options as people interrupted me to declare 'Christian' or 'Church of England' (although Church of England was not an option).

Just more than half the people I interviewed answered 'Christian'. My study is small, included people under 18 (who did not complete a census form) and was in a different context from the census and is therefore unsuitable for a direct comparison. Nevertheless, one finding from my small study will have, I argue, implications for how we interpret the census: half of my informants who answered 'Christian' were either agnostics or atheists, who either overtly disavowed religion or at least never incorporated religion, Christianity, God, or Jesus into our discussions. They were, as I will elucidate further during this book, functionally godless[8] and ontologically anthropocentric.

The first time the word 'Christian' arose in most interviews was when I posed it at the end by asking them how they had answered the census question. A notable few could not give me an easy or spontaneous response. Chris, 43, had told me during the interview that he had been born and raised a Catholic and was now an atheist. He rejected religion, although not the transcendent or paranormal; he told me he had once seen a ghost and he believed in aliens. Chris disliked church of any kind, describing the Catholic Church as 'illegal' and saying that he refuses to pray or even sing the hymns when attending church weddings or funerals. Yet, he said he was initially unsure how to respond to the census question: 'I may be very close to being a Christian. I'd help anybody out, things like that.' (The conflation of 'Christian' to 'moral' is a theme I discuss in more detail in Chapter 7.) Eventually he ticked 'none'.

For most, the answer seemed obvious and required little further reflection: they were Christian because they were baptized, they said, or had attended the Church of England when they were younger or had otherwise been 'brought up' Christian. To be a Christian, for them, did not include participating in liturgy or ritual, or engaging with Christian principles such as faith in God, the resurrection, or the life of Jesus. It only required being 'named' or attending church when children or, as I will discuss later, being part of what they described as a Christian 'culture'.

Davie (1990, 1994) conceived of 'belonging' as a private belief in God or other Christian-associated ideals, without church attendance or participation. In contrast, my concept of belonging relocates Christian identity as a public, social act. Today's census Christians can forgo regular church attendance and even Christian propositional beliefs as they align themselves to institutional Christianity and what, for them, it represents. More specifically, why would they be asked to identify a religion – to, as it happened, ask us to align with the institution of Christianity, or, even more implicitly, with the established church? Part of that answer may lie in what Talal Asad (1993) described as the historicity of legitimate Christian belief. Drawing on Foucault (1980) I suggest there is nothing more powerful than to lock people into a process of claiming an identity for themselves, which happens to

---

[8] Unfortunately, the term 'godless' became politically loaded in 2006 with the publication of an eponymous book written by American columnist Ann Coulter. My use of the term preceded hers and is not intended as a criticism or slur on people without faith in gods.

coincide with the desired identity promoted by the powerful. In the political and religious climate of the late 1990s, we witnessed what has been described as 'new nationalisms' driven by religious identities (Juergensmeyer 2006). Although the examples given are generally Islamic and non Euro American, I suggest the predominance of Christian nominalism can be read as such a phenomenon. Nominalists may not believe in God or Jesus, but they, as I will discuss below, believe in what they describe as their Christian roots and their Christian culture. In that endeavour they are supported and welcomed by Christian leaders. Here, institutional affiliation to strengthen the perception of the UK as a Christian country has become more important than subjective belief or belonging.

My case study material and further cross-cultural examples reveal intimacy with such discourses amongst my informants. How we represent people's identities depends on both the method used and the social context in which it is located. Asking people to claim an identity in, for example, a questionnaire or a census presumes a unity of self and nonrelatedness that is not corroborated by my qualitative research. As Demerath noted (2001, 221):

> Mark Twain once observed that 'faith is believing what you know ain't so'. The very phrase 'religious belief' is subject to misinterpretation because it is so often confused with cognitive certainty as opposed to cultural identity. What we actually believe – and with what level of intensity – is fraught with ambiguity and inconsistency, depending upon the social circumstances. It is hardly surprising that questionnaire responses are manipulable.

4

Youth and Belief: Belonging to Connected Selves

Introduction

In the UK and most Euro American countries, successive generations seem to be less religious than their parents, insofar as being religious is measured by church attendance, belief in doctrine, self identification, and personal religious practice, such as prayer (Brierley 1999; Dudley 1999; Pollack 2008; Voas 2010).

In this chapter, that wider notion of generational decline in religiosity is informed through analysing how young people were actively and reflexively locating their beliefs and belongings to kin and friendship relationships shaped by faith and love. Findings in other studies within sociology and anthropology are compared to problematize and enrich theories about the location and legitimacy of beliefs in belonging.

September: chaos in the classroom

The boy was standing by the fire door at the rear of the classroom, waving good-bye to his friends. Two of them stood up and looked like they would join him. I had no idea what to do: I was not a teacher, only a visiting researcher trying desperately to maintain some kind of class-room order. The Religious Studies teacher, Jim Smith, had left me in charge of the class to give them a short talk about religion in Britain, before conducting a short exercise and then asking for volunteers to be interviewed. So far, few had paid much attention to my mini-lecture, and I was about to lose three of them through the fire escape.

'Stop right there!' I commanded. The boys turned to look at me with insolent grins: Tom, Gavin, and Jordan, the three most notorious trouble-makers in a Year 10 class known for trouble. I could not have known then that Tom and his two friends would become three of my most significant informants, helping me build my theories about belief, belonging, and social identity. What they were performing that September day were acts of relocating what they perceived as sites of legitimate authority. The classroom was their space and the relationships within it theirs: I was the transient interloper; the prey to their hunter. Before they would admit me to any kind of equal relationship, I would have to leave, banished to the wilderness as it were, and return to a shared space with a willingness to negotiate claims to authority.

Meanwhile, we were busy performing our beliefs and reinforcing boundaries of belonging. It did not seem at that moment that we would become willing collaborators in the construction of alternative forms of knowledge. My only objective as I stood, powerless, at the front of the classroom was to somehow not lose them and be forced to report to the Head that, under my supervision, three 14-year-olds had gone missing.

It seemed a long time ago that I had sat comfortably, waiting in the reception area of Comprehensive High[1] as arranged. My contact, Jim Smith, had said he would meet me at break time, 10.35, and we could have a coffee in the staff room before the class at 10.55. I had felt relaxed and confident. The ten-minute overview of 'Religion in Britain today' had been well-accepted when I had piloted it at the girls' grammar the previous April in a similar age group. Also, I had taken Jim Smith's advice and created handouts which they would use in groups; I had talked about teaching styles with him and two other teachers I knew; and, above all, I had the recent pilot experience behind me when I had met a group of bright, cooperative 17-year-olds. I was well prepared for this experience today, I reminded myself, as Jim walked into the foyer. Had I thought more about it I would have realized that no two schools, two classrooms, or two experiences with different people would be the same.

'Might as well look like a teacher,' Jim said as he handed me a pile of books while we waited for the security doors to be unlocked. 'I didn't realize until this week that you are having the most difficult class of the year group. Sorry.' I tried to ask him what he meant but by then it was too late. The doors had swung open and we were now in the midst of a

---

[1] Not its real name, but a 'comprehensive' school in Britain is a state, free, non-selective entry school. It is where most UK students are educated. A minority attend the state grammar schools, free but with selective entry.

churning mass of people surging through the narrow hallway between classrooms. Suddenly, Jim was shouting, barking orders at them as we squeezed through the hurrying crowd: 'Get in single file! Don't run on the stairs! Yes, that vending machine is out of order, can't you read? Leave it alone! Make one line on the stairs! Don't walk together!'

A few minutes later we entered the staff room, bustling with teachers coming and going and chatting to each other, but comparatively quiet and calm compared to where we had just been. Yes, Jim was telling me, as term had got underway he had realized that this Year 10 class was the hardest so far. I should expect that some students would pay no attention to me at all, he said, and some might even become disruptive – but not in a threatening, abusive way to me.

'Just misbehaving boy stuff,' he said. I nodded, trying to imagine, and failing, what that might look like. He said he would introduce me, then pop back ten minutes later to see how I was getting on. He had agreed that I could have the class on my own but, he explained, ten minutes would give me time to assess who the troublemakers were, and if they were being too disruptive, Jim would take them out with him. As I accepted a cup of coffee I asked him, nervously, what would happen if somebody did become abusive or threatening – what should I do? He reached into his pocket and withdrew a red plastic credit-card-size card with 'Remove Card' printed on it.

'Just hand this to a responsible-looking student who will take it to the nearest staff member. Someone will arrive immediately and remove the student.' I briefly wondered what effect this might have on the 'responsible student's' reputation, or the likelihood that they would make it safely home after school without being pounced on by 'disruptive student' and friends. And yet, as I put the card in my pocket I felt instantly powerful, as if I had received the mark of authority: this was the Control ticket, the Don't Mess With Me card, the Sheriff badge. Given that it came with no consequences for me, no follow-through with the Head or the parents, no post-expulsion reports or tearful interviews with the contrite offender, I recognized an unfamiliar but strong sense of power without responsibility.

The bell rang and off we went, out through the churning mass of students, outside to a temporary classroom block where the Year 10 class awaited. When we entered, most of the students were there, some sitting in rows, others standing in small groups. It was noisy and few people even looked towards me and Jim. It was very different from my experience in April at the girl's grammar and nothing like my own school days thirty years earlier, when we would have risen when a teacher entered the room and said nothing until spoken to.

Jim called loudly to the class to be quiet. There was a slight ebb in the noise level for a few seconds, but about half the class continued in conversation with friends. Jim raised his voice and explained I would be talking about religious decline in Britain and would be asking them to complete a short exercise. He would leave but return in about ten minutes and would take away anyone who had been disruptive. He nodded to me, left the room, and most of the students immediately turned to their neighbours and started talking. Two boys stood up and looked out the window, waving to someone outside; a group of three boys sitting close together starting taunting a group of three girls sitting behind them. It was chaos.

I raised my voice just as Jim had done a few minutes earlier and asked them to keep quiet. The noise level dropped noticeably as the students looked away from their friends and studied me. Pleased that my stern, no-nonsense demeanour had successfully quelled the uprising, I began to introduce myself as a researcher at Lancaster University, here to discuss matters about religion in society today. I didn't get much beyond the title, 'Religious Decline in Britain since 1945', before the hubbub began again, the boy trio turning their backs on me to continue tormenting the girls, who were too busy talking to each other to really notice.

'Please be quiet!' I implored, catching the eyes of a few attentive-looking girls sitting closer to the front, in the middle, with open notebooks and pens ready. One, Charlotte, was sitting apart from the others and watching me with an almost beseeching look. I was to interview her in a few weeks' time and realize that her plaintive look reflected her sadness about her unpopularity and what I began to fear was bullying.

I noticed that the activity in the classroom was spatially clearly represented: the left side was filled with noisy boys, and a few girls, who were not paying attention to me. The middle section of the classroom was populated with attentive girls who smiled at me, nodded, took notes, and appeared to be engaged. The right side was populated by noisy boys. Front and centre, alone, was Charlotte. The effect was to draw attention constantly from the middle group of quieter girls towards the boys.

Suddenly, the classroom door burst open and two boys strode in, one small and fair, the other tall and dark, grinning at the others who jeered happily in response. They sauntered by me, threw me a cool appraising look and raised their eyebrows as if to say 'who's she?' before taking their seats near a group of boys on the far right side of the room and immediately turning their backs on me to talk to the other boys.

'Excuse me!' I said sharply, causing them to turn around. 'We're having a ten-minute talk about religious decline in Britain and then we'll be having an exercise. Could you please be quiet?' This caused the fair-haired one to smile and begin to sing to himself. I glared at him for a few seconds, willing him to surrender to my self-confident air of authority. He shrugged, got up, walked to the back of the room and opened the fire door as if to leave. Two of his friends joined him, I told them to be seated, and then, right on cue, Jim Smith entered the room.

'Everything ok?' he asked.

'It's ok,' I said.

'Anyone causing any trouble?' he asked, staring hard at Tom and Gavin. With only a minor twinge of regret, I nodded in their direction.

'Just them,' I said.

'I'm not surprised,' Jim replied, grimly. 'Come on you two, you're out with me,' and off they went, grinning and waving as they left. Jordan and some of the other boys waved back; most of the girls in the middle ignored them.

I felt sickened by my behaviour. In less than an hour I had changed from reflexive, feminist, flexible, self-confident, collaborative researcher to authoritarian despot.

I circulated a sheet of paper asking the students to write their names down if they would be willing to be interviewed and was certain it would be returned blank.

'Does it mean we miss some class, Miss?' asked Jordan. When I confirmed that yes, the interview would take place in a private room, during class time, he grinned broadly and wrote his name down on the interview list. As he strode into the interview room a few weeks later, he laughed mischievously and said he had come because it had meant he could then be excused from the regular class. Tom and Gavin told me they had agreed to be interviewed for the same reason. I was pleased, rather than discouraged, by their explanation. At least it demonstrated personal agency and choice.

I left the classroom that morning feeling worn out, a little shaken, and disappointed. As I recounted the event to Jim Smith in the staff room, he just smiled and said it sounded as if I had done very well. At least there had been some order, most people had written something on their sheets, and I had volunteers for interviews.

Locating belief: family matters

In Chapter 2, I described how Jordan had upset my thinking on 'belief' by describing himself as a Christian who did not believe in anything. During that interview, I encouraged him to expand on what he meant by belief, moving beyond an idea of belief as strictly related to creedal or propositional content. He told me he was a Christian but he did not do 'owt Christian' by which he meant he did not go to church. I asked him what the term 'Christian' meant for him, and he replied that it did not mean much apart from being 'someone who believes in God and Jesus and Bible and stuff'. I asked him if he believed in those things and he said he did not, but his grandparents did:

JORDAN: No, I don't, but my Grandma and Granddad do. They're like Irish and really strong Christians.
ABBY: And so they believe in – ?
JORDAN: The whole bible thing.
ABBY: And God, and Jesus?
JORDAN: Yeah.

In explicitly linking religiosity to kin, Jordan embeds belief in kinship, particularly the significance of grandparents in the process of religious identification and definition.[2]

Charlotte, who had sat without friends during my class discussion, also talked about the influence of grandparents during our interview. She had told me that she was not religious, did not go to church other than on 'Poppy Day' and Christmas but that she did believe in God and the resurrection of Jesus.

ABBY: So where did you get these ideas, do you think? You haven't been to church much, but you believe in God and the resurrection.
CHARLOTTE: I read it in books, like I read the Bible in primary school and I believe little paragraphs of that. And I've got a bible at home.
ABBY: Do you read any other religious books besides the Bible? There are books for other religions as well.
CHARLOTTE: Not really. The only religious book I have is the Bible. I have, like, three of them. I have a children's one and like an older one and an adult one.
ABBY: Where did you get those?
CHARLOTTE: They got passed down from my great, great grandma.
ABBY: All three of them?

---

[2] The role of grandparents, and grandmothers in particular, as active agents in the process of religious identification has been insufficiently researched, but see, for example, Copen and Silverstein 2008 for a discussion of a longitudinal study on religious socialization over three generations.

CHARLOTTE: Yeah.
ABBY: Was she religious?
CHARLOTTE: Yes. She was. She was a Christian.

It then transpired that Charlotte not only read her grandmother's bibles, but also her diaries, which gave her more insight into her grandmother's life and beliefs. The mystery of her adherence to certain biblical beliefs begins to be solved through, once again, a lens not of religiosity but sociality and kinship,[3] just as it had with Jordan.

After he had described his grandparents as Christian because they believed in that 'stuff', I continued to probe in what I now hear as a slightly inquisitional tone:

So, those people are Christians and they believe in all that stuff, and you're a Christian – but you don't believe in that stuff?

He replied, simply: 'No'.

ABBY: What makes you think or say, or describe yourself as Christian?
JORDAN: Well, on my birth certificate it says I'm Christian, so.

As I discussed in Chapter 3, what Jordan was conveying was not bureaucratic accuracies but the sense of where he was locating his belonging, in kin. The idea of 'kin', while present in many of my interviews, was neither monolithic nor uncomplicated. I found amongst most of my young informants an acute awareness and desire to articulate their sense of 'belonging'. While most adults spoke about their families being most important to them, the young people I interviewed were selective and self-referential about who, in their views, would count as 'family', most often with regard to their feelings about their present mothers and often absent fathers.

When I asked young people about what was most important to them in their lives, or who they thought they got their beliefs from, 'mother' was mentioned most often. Grandmothers also featured strongly amongst young people, particularly as someone who would listen to them and support them unequivocally. The importance of parents to young people became particularly clear when we discussed their worst

---

[3] Sammet (2009) discovered grandmotherly influences arose in her research project into contemporary belief in East Germany. The young unmarried mothers she interviewed were atheistic, connecting the Christian religion to childish beliefs, such as Santa Claus. One mother discussed how particularly as a child, she frequently spoke to her deceased grandmother, but now believes that was a means of recovering from her loss. Whether or not young people 'grow out of' such beliefs and behaviours remains to be seen. Carsten (2007, 24) observed how accepting and incorporating loss into one's biography is 'an integral part of adulthood, and of creating new kinds of relatedness in the present and the future'.

fears: young people did not often express fears of dying, but rather a fear of losing a parent.

For some, their biggest fear was the return of their absent fathers. For example Jeff, 17, was in his final year at the comprehensive school when I interviewed him. When I asked him what he believed in he said:

> I believe, I believe that like, in your family, 'cuz I'm quite close to my Mum and to my brother as well, and I think that should be, I think you should be close to your family.

When I asked what had happened to his father, he said he was not sure:

> I'm not sure where he is at the moment. He was a biker and a heroin addict. And, I don't really want to know him to be honest.

Jeff continued our discussion by saying that he believes it is important for him to support his mother emotionally, as she has 'been through a lot'. In a similar way, another teenager told me about his family structure using examples and words to convey feelings of closeness and warmth to all, apart from his biological father. Tom, 15, who had tried to escape from my school session through the fire escape, lives with his two biologically related siblings, and his mother and stepfather. Every weekend his stepfather's biological children come to stay. I asked Tom how he felt about that and he said he liked it. There was enough room for everyone, he explained; everyone got along well together and he was close to his stepfather's son, whom he referred to as his brother. In describing his Christmas day meal, Tom said:

> my sister's boyfriend comes around with my sister, she's got a little kid, so she comes around, all of us, we're just all of us sit down have a family meal together, a big Christmas meal. Lovely.

Here, he extends his idea of family to include his step-siblings and his sister's boyfriend, and his idea of Christmas to connote family, not religion.[4] A little later, when I was clarifying my understanding of his family structure, I repeated what he had told me, which was that he lived with his stepfather and mother.

TOM: Just put my Mum and my Dad. Or, does that matter?
ABBY: It sort of does, for me and for background.
TOM: If you prefer to put stepdad, for reasons for you, then put stepdad.

---

[4] Enjoying the 'big Christmas meal' in an otherwise non-religious family reminded me of a study from the United States: in her research of American cultural Jews, Davidman (2007, 58) reported that her informants told her that they strongly associated religious events with warm family memories and sought to recreate them even as they became less religious.

ABBY: Ok. And your other Dad, you don't see.

TOM: I don't want to see. I haven't seen him since I was about six.

I noted that although Tom had referred earlier in the interview to his 'stepdad', when it came to positioning him for my interview notes he initially wanted to be seen as living with his 'Dad'. One of the reasons why Tom may not have wanted to include his biological father in his 'family' became clear when I asked him one of my standard questions about what we was afraid of. He said he was afraid of his 'real Dad' returning and hurting his mother, because 'he was a drug addict and an alcoholic and I worry he's going to come back and hurt my Mum, things like that'. I asked if there was anything he did about that fear and he said, 'Not really, just care for my Mum, look after her, just do the usual things I can do for my Mum.' Both Jeff and Tom position themselves as a supporter of their mother against an absent, violent father whose authority or relationship with them they did not want to legitimize.

In a similar way Nadia, a 17-year-old student at the comprehensive school, said she believed in her religion (Islam), prayer, and her family. Her use of the term 'family' includes herself, mother (whom she described as her 'security'), and sibling, but no longer her father. Although she is glad her father, whom she described as a 'devil at home and angel outside' has left, there had been a difficult period of adjustment:

> I was really attached to my Dad. I really loved him, and he pretended that he loved me, and lied and everything. I do believe fathers should be there to an extent, but I think it's wrong to say – we're an example, as a family to everyone around us, that we can cope.

She explained that she felt that neighbours and other members of her extended family assumed that the family would not cope well without a father present when, for Nadia, the lying, insincere father was an illegitimate figure best living elsewhere. It was during that period of adjustment that she decided to wear the hijab and to pray regularly, she said, finding comfort in God and her religion.

Thus far, I have argued that young people 'believe in' family relationships insofar as those relationships are with those in whom they have faith, and with whom they have emotional, adherent relationships. The word 'adherent' in this sense was first proposed to me by Rick, 20, introduced in the previous chapter, as he was describing how he felt about the community where he lived and why he would not want to move away. He has lived in the same village all his life. His mother, siblings, aunts, uncles, cousins, grandparents, and friends live there; he plays for the local football team and when he walks into the local pub (where we held our interview) he knows everyone. He said there were things about a community like that which 'adhere to you'. It was perhaps a word he uses on a daily basis in his job as a painter-decorator and means to him, almost literally, 'to stick'. Adhere is also a term in common usage within the academic discipline of religion to describe people who have faith and some form of membership in a religion: they are 'adherents' to a faith. Adherent relationships are those, therefore, which 'stick to people', in which they believe and have faith. They are characterized by feelings of love, affection, trust, and protection gained from and given to certain people. Those are the people in whom they believe, and to whom they belong, often in a post-nuclear family, where the structures are flexible and the boundaries shift, defined and maintained by the members' conceptions of who legitimately belongs, or not. Although Rick now feels he belongs, only a few years earlier his sense of belonging had been severely shattered and his idea of 'kin' forcibly changed. As we talked further, he said that he had sometimes found it difficult to speak to his parents about their divorce, had sometimes been falsely accused of saying things he had not, and felt that people were saying things behind his back. His feelings of trust and of being protected were replaced by distrust and betrayal, which is why, he said, he now believes in 'freedom of speech'. He continued:

RICK: Apart from that I haven't really thought about what I believe in.
ABBY: Ok.
RICK: I believe everybody should have a goal in life.
ABBY: A goal in life?
RICK: Yeah. To achieve something.
ABBY: Have you always had one?
RICK: Well, yeah, silly as it might sound, to have a family, a semi detached house, a garage, kitchen, car, two kids, complete family, basically, like your general, English family so to speak. Always wanted to have that, really.

His mental picture of his family with the semi detached house, garage, and two children was an idealized version of how his life had looked before his parents separated.

And then all that disappeared, you see. That's probably why I want it, to make sure it stops[5] like that, you know.

---

[5] In Yorkshire dialect the word 'stop' is often used to mean 'stay' rather than finish or prevent.

His sense that 'all that disappeared' was raised again later in the interview when we discussed why he did not maintain contact with his paternal grandparents. It was not because he was too busy, he said, it was because 'it's just that whole family aspect of things. It's totally gone.' What had happened was that his father had gone and a series of misunderstandings which followed destroyed Rick's family as an entity being based on love, affection, trust, and protection. Here, he seems to be laying responsibility for the break with his father and by default the paternal grandparents. He did not review his family structure and conclude, as did Jeff and Tom, that he had a close, albeit differently-constructed family. Rick had a strong sense of the family to whom he wanted to belong.

A similar experience of betrayal during divorce was described to me by Briony, 19, in her final year at the comprehensive school. She lives with her mother and stepfather. She told me she had felt used and betrayed during her parents' divorce, so much so that she tried twice to kill herself. She believes in the importance of trust and honesty, she said. Gemma, 14, a classmate of Tom, Gavin, and Jordan, lives with her mother and stepfather and has been wholly rejected by her biological father. She said this was one area of her life which makes her sad, and she does not understand why her father will not see her, as he does not live far away.

I suggest that the emotional difficulties of being abandoned by a beloved father (as opposed to a dangerous, violent father) may lead some people to lose faith in 'family'. This particularly struck me when I attended a local village event in Rick's honour. One month following our interview it was Rick's twenty-first birthday and he was celebrating at the pub, together with the landlady's sixtieth birthday. Bill, my neighbour and the village football coach, had told me about it and encouraged me to go. When I arrived I was struck by the way the pub looked as if it was hosting a private party, although it was open as normal. There were 'happy birthday' banners and photos on the walls of Rick from various ages, and a large buffet supper. Everyone in the pub seemed to be talking with each other, which gave me the distinct impression that everyone was local. Throughout the evening, I observed Rick being constantly surrounded by friends and some members of his 'family'. My impression was of one large extended family. This was reinforced by a comment he had made in our interview that he had once thought about moving to London but had decided not to because: 'I'd miss my family, I think. I think if you're brought up in a community like this you adhere to it.' I will conclude here that Rick's use of family in this context referred to his large extended family; the small unit he had once thought of as 'family' had disappeared when his father left. Kinship for him was not defined by biology or structure: it depended for him on the success of the adherent relationships in which he has faith and feels he belongs.

Legitimate authority

It was striking in my interviews that the sense of affection and respect young people accorded to others they felt as legitimate authorities was not reciprocated in my interviews with older people. According to many of my older informants, young people today are immoral, disrespectful of authority, and even threatening. This contrasts with my findings, summarized in more detail in Chapter 7, where I found that the social code rights and wrongs young people discuss are the same as those described by older people. Young people believe in treating people well, not killing or stealing, doing well at school and getting a job afterwards or continuing to university. Gavin said his worst fear was doing badly at school and therefore becoming jobless and homeless. Other young people said they worried about their exams or whether they would be accepted at university. Even the most radical amongst them respect authority when they perceive it to be legitimate.

Charles, 15, attends the boys' grammar school, lives with his mother, and spends weekends with his father, a politically active man. Charles spoke at length about his interest in history and politics, describing himself as an 'anarcho-communist' (pointing out he was critical of some aspects of communism, particularly what he described as Stalin's abuse of power), and dismissed religion as inherently immoral. He often cited people whom he respected as authorities in the field and credited his school for his knowledge about history and his father as political inspiration. Like many young people, he would not respect authority for its own sake, particularly if perceived as authoritarian.

Older informants, however, think young people lead lazy lives showing no respect for others, and present a danger. George, 60, also felt threatened by young people. He said that one of the things which made him uncomfortable was going out at night because he perceived a threat from young people:

GEORGE: I don't go out at night. I don't go anywhere at night where I feel threatened.

ABBY: Where would that be?

GEORGE: Well, anywhere where there are groups of youngsters nowadays. I wouldn't, I wouldn't, but I'm not frightened going out, I just, it's like I said earlier, I've learned that if I don't want to feel uncomfortable then I don't do certain things.

He said he did not think there was a problem in his town with young people causing crime, but it was still a feeling he had. He is aware that the threat may be less real than imagined, but it alters his behaviour nonetheless.

I will return to how older people perceive young people in Chapter 7.

The examples reinforced for me the idea that young people offended their elders because they behaved in ways which did not demonstrate respect for the apparent authority of their elders. The older people, particularly the men, assume they deserve respect because of their age and, I suggest, their gender. Having reviewed belonging to kin, I will turn now to belief in other people, most particularly friendships.

Friendships

One month into my series of interviews with the students from the comprehensive school, Jim Smith told me that Tom and Gavin had decided they wanted to be interviewed. As they had not signed up at the time, partly because Jim and I had removed them from the classroom, I had not expected to see them again. At first I was hesitant and slightly worried because they wanted to be interviewed together, but Jim reassured me that they wouldn't be any trouble. Indeed, as they bounded up the stairs and cheerfully said hello it seemed they were different characters from the insolent, disrespectful boys I had last seen trying to escape from my class. I asked them to sit wherever they wanted. They moved to one side of the table and sat next to each other. I sat down across the table, facing them. I motioned to a small pile of individually wrapped chocolates that Jim Smith had left for them because, he had explained, in that day's lesson there was going to be a fun quiz with chocolates as prizes. The boys nodded impassively, but did not accept one. We began the interview in the usual way. When I asked what they believed in, Tom answered:

TOM: Like, by saying that you mean like I've got religion or something or what?

ABBY: That's a good question, and that's one of the things I want to know when I ask people that. Some people think it's about religion and other people think it's about other things. What does it mean to you?

TOM: I don't believe in really anything.

ABBY: Mmm.

TOM: I believe you've got to go to school, though.

ABBY: You believe you've got to go to school, yeah. Ok. What about you?

GAVIN: I believe in working hard.

ABBY: Mmmhmm. Any other things?

GAVIN: No.

ABBY: What about you, Tom? Anything else you believe in?

TOM: No.

We continued along those lines for another few minutes, me asking questions and them generally answering briefly, until we touched on what made them happiest. It was when he was fishing, Gavin said. Tom agreed: 'Same, when I'm fishing, when I'm just with my mates, having a laugh.' The subject of fishing animated them so much that they began to tell me stories of their different experiences. Later, when I was transcribing the interview, I was tempted to skip over what looked like fifteen minutes of boring, technical detail about rods and bait until it struck me: these were not fishing stories, they were friendship stories. I listened to the pronouns they were using and how pointedly they were plural. In telling me how they learned to fish, Tom said:

TOM: We just saw people. It was when we went to Whitby. You know when you've been to Whitby and you see those people off side?

GAVIN: Off pier, in the sea.

ABBY: Yes, I've seen them.

TOM: Well, we've seen them and all. We've seen them fishing and say, aw we'll have a bash. And you know when you go abroad, you can rent those things, it's just a line, and you put it in water and you just mess about... Well, what was it, we caught little fish, and we thought oh this is good we should catch more, and then when we got home we saved up and got a fishing rod, got more tackle, got more stuff.

While they fish, they talk. Tom explained that he likes to talk to Gavin and has confided in him about the problems with his 'real Dad' and 'he's told no one'. They are 'proper mates', Tom explained, because they will talk to each other and say nothing to anyone else.

Being able to trust friends was an important part of the relationship, as I found with other young people. Lizzie, 14, attends the same school as Tom and Gavin. She said she was happiest with her friends. She thought trust was an important moral value and described how hurt she has felt from being betrayed by other people:

LIZZIE: And I think trust is really important, especially with friends. I get annoyed with friends quite a lot about trust, because I think that's really important and some people don't.

ABBY: What sort of things do people do that you would get annoyed about in terms of trust?

LIZZIE: It's like, things if I told them something I didn't want anyone else to know, and then they said something, and so they'd say, oh, well, everyone else does that. And I'd say, ok but you know I don't and you knew I didn't want you to do that.

Lizzie added that it was important to her to be trusted as well as to be able to trust people. This added a dimension of reciprocity in adherent friendship relationships which I noticed amongst many interviews when people talked about their friends. Liam, 21, lives with his parents and is a trainer at a local gym. He talked often in the interview about going out to pubs with friends, but also about how he is able to share problems with one particular friend: 'so if I've got a problem I'll sort of go, you know, see him about it, or he'll come to me, ask my opinion about it'. Harry, 15, attends the boys' grammar school. He said his happiest times were 'When it's quiet and possibly you're with someone you like, sharing a moment with them, feeling peaceful and warm'.

Belief in adherent relationships does not obviate a belief in God or Jesus, but it may render those divine authorities subordinate to others with whom the young person more deeply belongs. Lindsay, 14, a student at the comprehensive school, told me she was a Christian who attends church, believes in Jesus and 'most' of the Bible. When we later discussed what influenced her in life, she said that Jesus influenced her 'in a sort of way', explaining that 'he can't be that much of an influence on my life now, if you know what I mean. It's just through what he preached in the Bible that's an influence.' I was curious about how she was experiencing his influence, and asked her to give me an example. She thought for a moment and then said that sometimes she prays to him about problems, and although she thought he was telling her what he thinks is best, she might choose to disagree: 'sometimes I think I'm right and he's wrong. It depends.'

That was a striking statement for a Christian to make. I asked her what it depended upon, and she gave me an example of when she might have problems with friends, and she would be inclined to talk to them to resolve matters, but Jesus would tell her just to leave the problem alone and see if it resolved itself. That, she explained to me, was the wrong advice: she understood her friends and how they behaved and it was definitely better to act quickly and seek to right situations as soon as possible. Jesus, she explained, did not have her first-hand knowledge of her friends and her relationship with them and therefore would not be in the best position to advise her. When I asked her if it ever bothered her that she was not accepting Jesus' advice, she said:

> No, not really. Sometimes it does when I know what he says is right and I don't do it, then that bothers me. But when I think I'm right, then, no, it doesn't bother me at all.

I note the self-confidence with which she is navigating territories of authority. She understands the difference between 'right' and 'wrong': her decision to trust her own judgement over that of Jesus was not a wilful act of disobedience, but a carefully considered, situated decision made in the context of her friendships.

Just as Lindsay presented her social relationships and her own judgement about them as sometimes more important than divine judgements, another classroom experience showed a similar dynamic at work. The discussion took place with students in a sociology class at the comprehensive school. After a considerable time discussing general beliefs, I asked how they might hypothesize the origins of the universe. All but one student answered in scientific terms. The only Muslim present said that she would answer 'Allah' to the question of how the universe came into existence. She then added, somewhat apologetically, that she '*would* say this' as it was part of her religious belief. Several people in the group immediately defended her, saying things like 'that's ok' and 'you don't have to apologize for that'. The students appeared to be eager to show respect for other people's beliefs.

When I held other class discussions, ideas like 'hate' or 'prejudice' were raised as examples of wrong moral behaviour. While I cannot claim that students are not racist, the ease and lack of embarrassment with which racist ideas were expressed by older informants suggests that older people found it publicly acceptable to demonstrate those opinions. In contrast, students did not, suggesting they do not want to be seen to support racist discourse. While that may be an example of 'morality' it is also, I suggest, a developing pattern that demonstrates the importance of relationality.

Locating belief

It seemed evident from my discussions with young people that few participated in conventional religious practices, most were indifferent to the idea of organized religion or deities, and they tended to find happiness and meaning in their relationships with friends and family. These findings reflected the trend seen elsewhere (Clydesdale 2007; Mason et al. 2007; Regnerus et al. 2004; Savage et al. 2006; Smith and Denton 2005). Those studies, from the USA, UK, and Australia, all found that young people derive meaning, happiness, and moral frameworks from social relationships. Quotes from their informants mirror mine and we often remark, during informal discussions as we meet at conferences, that our reports are uncannily similar. Some of our interpretations, conclusions, and suggested implications are, however, significantly different. The most important, for this chapter, concern the location and legitimacy of young people's beliefs in the social relationships to which they belong.

My findings that young people locate the source and maintenance of beliefs in their social relationships complicate some of Smith and Denton's (2005, 143) conclusions that describe youth as being 'nearly without exception profoundly individualistic, instinctively presuming autonomous, individual self-direction to be a universal human norm and life goal'. The difference in our findings may hinge on just what we suppose young people mean by 'individual'. For example: in her study of teenage witches in Britain, Cush (2010, 86) found that young people's concept of individuality was bound up in concepts of respect and choice, rather than selfishness or narcissism; Lynch (2002) concluded that the young clubbers he interviewed were seeking 'authenticity' and Harris (2010) wrote of young pilgrims to Lourdes rejecting institutionalized religion at home, but embracing collective belonging on their pilgrimage.

I found that young people's beliefs tend to be co-produced, through participating with family and friends in creating and maintaining beliefs. This problematized ideas about private, individualized beliefs, or a 'believing without belonging' thesis, as my work suggests that belief and belonging are interdependent, with beliefs being explicitly located, produced, and practised in the public and social realm.

Davie (2002) suggests that as people turn from larger, institutionalized forms of religion there occurs a dialectical process of transformation from public into private forms of belief: 'as the institutional disciplines decline, belief not only persists, but becomes increasingly personal, detached and heterogeneous' and shows a 'reverse' tendency (2002, 8). If by that she means 'personal' belief increases as faith in institutions decrease, I would suggest that the argument would not be supported by my work or those of other, larger studies in, particularly, Europe (Pollack 2008). Young people's beliefs do not seem to reflect more individualistic modes of being. That they did not believe in certain institutions such as religion or overly controlling classroom environments did not mean they did not believe in institutions per se. Their sense of communal identity was often strong. Singh (2010) reached a similar conclusion in his study of how young British male Sikhs were adopting the turban as a symbol of ethnic identity, often learning about the practice not from their parents, but from their friends, and wearing it as a symbol of belonging.

Legitimating belief

Legitimate families

The legitimacy of young people's beliefs is questioned by Smith and Denton, who suggest (2005, 156–8) that teenagers today live in a 'morally insignificant universe' where decisions are not guided by or grounded in larger, invisible, sources of religion, philosophy, or other supra-mundane moral forces. As will be discussed in more detail in Chapter 7, young people draw on the relationships that provide them with faith and love.

Through an open style of discussion, I was able to uncover how young people's beliefs are grounded differently, rather than insufficiently. Part of that was made possible through the methodological choice, relying more on open questions and discussion rather than questionnaires or closed interview questions, but much of it forced an ontological, personal challenge. Indeed, as a product of a certain historical era – and one raised in a church-attending family – it was initially difficult for me to explain Jordan and the many other 'anomalies' I was to meet in my research: atheists who believe in ghosts, agnostics who despise religion and yet say they are Christian, apparently 'rational' humanists who believe in life after death, and Christians who prefer talking to their dead relatives than to God or Jesus in prayer. Much of that did not correspond to what I had understood 'Christian' or 'religious' to be.

I was perhaps better able to overcome that challenge and refrain from delegitimizing their beliefs than could other, openly committed Christian scholars such as Smith, Mason, Savage, and others. This is not intended as a criticism of their scholarly approach, which I find exemplary, nor of their integrity as social scientists, but only awareness that their own commitments to Christ would at some point understandably force the question: can anyone be truly happy, safe, and secure without salvation in Jesus? I assume their answer would be 'no', as, indeed, Savage et al. expressed (2006, 170) when they suggested that young people's 'midi-narratives' are insufficient, because: 'true happiness requires a meta-narrative which can only be found in a Christ like way of life, for in him alone is true happiness to be found'.

A Christian commitment may therefore undermine the way scholars are able to privilege social and, particularly, family relationships. This recalls Cannell (2005), who argued that the Mormons she researched emphasized kinship, the body, and the material in ways which do not conform to majority forms of Christianity or beliefs in transcendence. She wrote that (ibid., 343)

> The undoubtedly powerful ascetic current in Christianity has generally been accompanied by an attitude to ordinary family life and kinship which regards it as, at most, a kind of second best to the spiritual life.

The young people I interviewed may indeed swim against a current of the ascetic, appearing grounded in their family and friendship relationships and networks. Belief was not absent but relocated to a social realm where it is polyvocal, interdependent, emotionally charged, and illustrative of experiences of belonging.

Young people, I found, may believe in their families, but are careful about how they define who count as legitimate family members.[6] My study illuminated many dimensions possible in the term 'family', and also how people change their meaning of family within their lifetimes, and also sometimes within the same interview. This is similar to a major finding in a long-running longitudinal study of families in the United States (Bengtson et al. 2002) where the authors described two strong theses within the field of family studies: the 'family decline' thesis and the 'family solidarity' thesis. They concluded that a belief in the importance of family was sustained over the three generations they studied, although the meaning of family changed, becoming progressively more informant-directed. They examined two of the main trends thought to contribute to the 'family decline' thesis: maternal employment and divorce. They concluded that maternal employment did not have negative impacts on children, measured in terms of children's self-esteem and attainment. They also found that the impact of divorce on self-esteem and attainment was only negative when there was evidence of the absent father's diminishing participation and emotional involvement in his children's lives. This mirrors many of my informants' feelings about their absent fathers as illegitimate sources of authority.

---

[6] For a discussion about how 'family' means an entity larger than a small, nuclear unit see, for example Jordan et al. 1994 and Bengtson 2001.

Tom, for example, would not include his biological father as a member of his family; indeed, he is an enemy of his family. That he has a biological link does not accord him a familial link for Tom in the same way that, for example, Tom's sister's boyfriend has.

Nevertheless, my discussions with young people reminded me that for all the changes that have occurred in and through family structure, this does not render 'family', howsoever conceived, as unimportant. In a review of how context shapes the social acceptability of cousin marriage, Kuper (2008) suggests that the study of kinship has fallen out of favour in the discipline of anthropology. And yet, he concludes (ibid., 733): 'It is only if we concentrate so much on symbols that we lose sight of social action that we can possibly doubt, even for an instant, that families crop up all over the place.'

This did not mean that family was unimportant; quite the opposite. This finding is important not only to illustrate the different types of relationships to which young people belong and in which they believe, but also to suggest that their acts of choosing may represent a shift from an externally imposed narrative to one that reflects their more immediate social norms. This shift may well provoke anxieties for older people in both secular and religious contexts. It is also a shift that may partly explain some of the changes we have seen in official religiosity. Indeed, when I identified the idea of 'family' and 'family values' as an important part of my doctoral investigation, my then supervisor Paul Heelas objected to that line of enquiry, saying that it had nothing to do with 'belief' or religion. On the contrary, as I argued then and here, the 'family', howsoever constructed, is one of the most important sources for meaning, morality, and even transcendence – all areas conventionally associated with religion.

Legitimate friends

Second only to family, friendship was most important to young people. The way friends supported and helped each other was often sustained through mundane activities, such as fishing, as illustrated by Tom and Gavin. The nature of men's friendships possibly requires more intensive research. Notably, a study of Basildon (Hayes and Hudson 2001) focusing on the decline of community participation pointed to aspects of friendships as evidence of that decline. In citing the most popular activity reported by respondents, having a drink after work with workmates, the authors describe this (ibid., 25–6) as the casual nature of work-based socialising in which people would meet for a few hours before going their separate ways. There was no sense of shared interests of activity above and beyond the immediate and transient moments of conviviality.

The authors appear to diminish the significance of these informal activities, privileging more structured, typically political, pursuits. They describe informal friendships as including 'even less sociable past times of cycling, walking, gardening and reading', defining those activities as 'individualized', and excluding other, presumably more legitimate, activities of 'communal and even joint interests' (ibid.). Once again, they appear to diminish the significance of the kinds of informal activities their respondents, and mine, participated in.

The influence of friends does not necessarily mean that young people are less religious. Vickie, 14, a student at the comprehensive school said she had begun to attend church again after a long gap because her friends attended. The effect of peers on such behaviour was noted in an American study that found the usual pattern of declining church attendance in teenagers 'disappears with the addition of friends' who attend church (Regnerus et al. 2004, 31).

The significance of belonging or not to certain peer groups was indicated by a longitudinal study of confirmation training in Finland (Niemelä 2008). Respondents were asked several questions about God-belief, one of which was designed to probe respondents' sense of both belief and belonging: 'I believe in God but I am not a "believer"' (ibid., 48). Forty-six per cent of those who had completed the confirmation training programme chose that answer, far outweighing those (9 per cent) who chose 'I am a believer' or those (7 per cent) who said 'I do not believe that there is a God.' I asked Kati Niemelä if that meant the respondents did not feel they belonged to a group of religious people, yet wanted to express their belief in God. In reply Niemelä (pers. comm.) said:

> When the youngsters in Finland talk about 'believers' they tend to refer to that small group of very religious and often also morally strict. So when one agrees to this item, she/he is most likely saying something like (and our open questions in the survey also reveal this): 'Yes, I do believe in God and have a faith in Him, but I do not belong to that small group of active ones nor do I totally live according to my faith.'

This chapter has thus far shed light on the location and nature of belief and suggested that young people are locating their beliefs and respect for authority in legitimate institutions and relationships. The question about why they are less religious than their parents will now be addressed.

Generational change

Generational decline in religion may reflect a decline in respect for authority in established institutions and meta-narratives. The perception that young people today have insufficient moral grounding was suggested by many of my informants as well as scholars, as discussed earlier, but it could be that such perceptions may rest on interpretations not so much of morality but what should be regarded as legitimate sources of authority. As George, cited above, suggested: the perceived threat from young people may be more imagined than real. The UK does not experience more youth crime than other western European countries, although it does have more 'anti-social' behaviour and more fears of young people than other western European countries (Margo 2008). Importantly, the same study notes that it appears that there are changes to youth culture and attitudes, with 'young people becoming less trusting of authority and more heterogeneous in their views of social issues' (ibid., 5). That final statement corresponds to my findings, particularly concerning young people's willingness to believe in some forms of legitimate authority and not others.

Further, evidence of decreasing racism amongst young people has been attributed to improved education, increased social diversity, and general societal discouragement of racist discourse (Ford 2008). Those changes may reflect a desire for more acceptance of pluralism and socially diverse modes of meaning and authority. Younger people are also less likely to express national pride than previous generations, argue Tilley and Heath (2007) because they have been growing up in more diverse areas and are more familiar with mixed, nuanced identities. Such studies corroborate my findings, I suggest, and the arguments that social relationships inform and are informed by who or what are seen as legitimate forms of both belief and belonging.

I asked Jim Smith, my teacher-gatekeeper, what he thought. He has been teaching successive waves of young people for more than twenty years. Has anything changed?

> If you want to use the word post modern, might be the word that fits... children realize that they live in a pluralistic world, that there are lots of options there and people are free to choose very minority options and be treated with respect.

Such an observation lends support to the idea of 'generation' as conceived by Mannheim (1952) as not a biologically constructed stratum but one defined by a social location seen in opposition to another generation. That view of generation may partly soften boundaries of class, geography, ethnicity, and distance to create what seems to be shown through this chapter's comparative examples.

Religion, and the accompanied faith in supra-human authority, is perhaps one of those institutions that young people no longer feel is a legitimate form of authority. If their highest regard is for people with whom they have loving, reciprocal relationships then it would likely only be those forms of expressive, social religions that they would find legitimate. Indeed, those are the only forms of religiosity that are growing in Euro American countries and the only forms that attract young people (Brierley 2000; 2006; Pollack 2008), but not in such numbers as to offset a general decline.

I conclude with a reflection on method and how it informed my theories of performativity that run throughout this book. My difficult classroom experience helped me consider the nature of 'performance' in ways that influenced my wider work. Being aware of teaching styles and being prepared with handouts was an internalized, subjective way of anticipating the social engagement yet to come, missing the reciprocal nature of the social performance being a specific, contextualized experience. All three boys who had been disruptive and non-cooperative in the classroom environment were respectful, polite, cheerful, and helpful in our private interviews. In the class they were performing much as Jim had predicted, but as I related to the boys in our quiet interview room, giving them my full attention and space to elaborate and expand on their ideas, they performed differently. They appeared intelligent, relaxed, and willing to talk and elaborate on points as I requested. The contrasting experiences of being in the classroom and the interview room would later influence my reading and interpretation of notions of 'authority' and performance. The classroom context had delegitimized my authority by making it dependent on institutional norms and power. In the interview room, where I positioned them as expert and me as learner, we met more equally.

Goffman (1959, 15) was correct in locating performance as: 'the activity of a given participant on a given occasion which serves to influence in any way any of the other participants'. I was, perhaps, reading 'performance' too narrowly, even if there was a 'performative' element as imagined by, for example, Austin (1962), who saw the linguistic power of the declarative statement as enacting a transformation. Following Austin, I had supposed that my act of declaring myself as, simultaneously, researcher/collaborator and researcher/teacher would bring that persona into being, quelling any contrary spirit in the classroom and creating a unique environment of cooperation and creativity. Austin did not discuss what I was to discover and Bourdieu

(1991) had anticipated by locating the performative within a specific social context: social realities are not created through linguistic utterances alone, but through the symbolic power already present, if unacknowledged, within specific social relations. What can and would be brought into being would depend on the context of the performers and how they legitimized their relationships. In future chapters I will return to the theme of performativity and power.

5

The Sensuous Social Supernatural

The previous chapter focused on how young people believe in their legitimate, adherent, affective relationships. Those relationships are often continued after the death of their loved ones, as young people transform bereavement from an experience of loss to an experience of continued belonging. This chapter explores that complex but common phenomenon of continuing relatedness with a deceased loved one. After providing descriptions of such phenomena, I will move to an analytical discussion of how they are experienced, communicated, transmitted, and embodied in a ritual of relationally located performative belief.

During my interviews, informants were not directly asked if they had 'experienced something outside themselves' or 'ever seen a ghost' or 'had a religious experience'. It was something I did not want to presume or impose, but wanted to observe as a potential dimension of our conversations. A third of my informants reported something of this sort, irrespective of age, religiosity, or social class, although significantly more women than men (39 per cent vs. 25 per cent). (I address that gender component in the next chapter.) Even those who described themselves as atheists reported such experiences.

While informants related experiences that may be described as 'supernatural', or 'metaphysical', or 'paranormal', they did not use those terms. Mostly, they told me about feeling the presence of a named, deceased relative. I did not hear any common word or language to indicate an other-worldly location, prefixed by such a marker as *trans-*, or *super-*, and nor did informants appear to be struggling to explain their experiences by using such cognate terms as paranormal or occult. While the experience was extraordinary, it was also deeply embodied: vocabulary most often described physical sensations such as smell, sound, and sight and affective, bodily responses such as calm or fear. The sensuous experience was usually, informants reported, shared with others who had either experienced the same direct experience with them or at least helped interpret the event as it was retold (or, as I will suggest, performed). These sensuous, social, extraordinary experiences require a different theoretical, conceptual framework from that usually offered through a religious, Tylorian, individualistic framework. I propose that broadening our concept of belief to include those embodied, emotive moments contributes to my theory of belief as performative and relational. Here, I review conversations with several informants who provided the stimulus for that theoretical renegotiation.

Atheists who believe in ghosts

Chris, whom I introduced in Chapter 3, positioned himself from the beginning of the interview as an atheist. As I described earlier, he answered my opening question, 'what do you believe in?' by saying: 'I think I'm a total atheist. I don't have any beliefs.' As it transpired, he believed in aliens, multiple universes, and ghosts, although not in God, the legitimacy of the church, or other religious ideas and institutions he had initially associated with 'belief'. He also reported, in detail, an experience that occurred one night in his partner's eighteenth-century cottage where he lives. He went downstairs at about 2 a.m. to get a drink of water and as he was standing at the sink with a glass in his hand a figure in a long, dark, hooded cloak walked by him and through the wall opposite where he was standing. His partner later told him that there used to be a door in the part of the wall through which he saw the figure pass. His partner teases him about his experience, he said, but he does not disbelieve what he saw: 'I'd take a lie detector test on it,' he said. He does not know how to explain it, other than by conceiving of a parallel world. It did not provoke him to believe in an afterlife, nor did he seem to find the question of what happened after death of much interest. When I asked him what he thought happened to people after they died, he looked momentarily startled. After a pause he said, 'I don't know. Unusual question. When you're dead, you're dead.'[1] The image he described reminded me of the black-hooded figure on a television ad for a financial product called 'Scottish Widows'. When

---

[1] I was curious about why this might be an 'unusual question' but am reminded of the conversations I had with students, reported in Chapter 2, when they suggested some questions might seem like a knowledge test.

I commented on this to Chris, he agreed enthusiastically that this was almost exactly the same image.

Another non-religious person with experience of seeing non-living humans (they tended not to use the term 'ghost') was Hannah, a single, 35-year-old mother of four children, who was heavily pregnant with her fifth child at the time of our interview. Hannah teaches mathematics part-time at a local college, and runs her own hairdressing business. She said that when her children have asked her if they will go to heaven after they die, her answer was 'I'd like to think so.' I asked if she had a strong belief about heaven and she said, 'not particularly, but I would like to think that's the case, but I'm pretty much of the mind that when you go to sleep, that's it'. She laughed when she said that, so I asked if it bothered her to think of death being final, and she, laughing again, answered, 'Yes it does!' She explained:

> Catholicism drums into you that you'll go to heaven, but you'll go to hell if you're bad, and for years as a child you firmly believe that, particularly the hell bit which is scary. You behave and you think about everything you do, you've this conscience the whole time. I think as you get older you need – I personally need – more proof of things for me to believe.

Seeing, for Hannah, was believing, and gave her sufficient proof that people from other time periods could appear here and now. She also describes heaven as a place to reward the godly and good – a description that is markedly different from how people I will turn to below describe it.

Hannah said that she had encountered beings from other eras on several occasions. Her parents had owned pubs and one pub in particular was well-known for its ghosts, she said, being featured on television programmes about haunted buildings. On one occasion she saw 'a man, a big man, and when I described his dress, it fitted to the 1600s'. She said her mother had, on a different occasion, seen the same man. Another time, at Christmas, she went to look for her daughter and found her sitting in the pool room saying she had been talking to a little girl, 'and I dismissed it'. Later, however, she also saw a little girl in her room. She said the girl just stood there, not speaking. Hannah explains this in a matter-of-fact tone:

> Never responded. They say they only respond in their own time warp, so she's from the seventeenth century she's not going to talk to you, and I believe that actually. You're seeing her but she's not seeing you. That's why they can go through walls. The door might have moved in that house, that's why they can go through doors, because that's what they're seeing in their era.

I said it must have been quite an experience seeing a ghost and I wondered if it had changed her life at all. No, she told me, it had not. Further, she volunteered that she was not frightened. She said she thinks one day an explanation for ghosts will be found. While she does not discount her experience, saying, 'I do believe it, I know what I saw', she also says that, 'I think there's an explanation for all those things.' Both Chris and Hannah told their stories in even, unemotional tones, as if the events were curiosities, related with a conviction that one day there would be an explanation.

That conviction, I suggest, is akin to a faith or a 'belief in' scientific rationalism. It is not, for example, irrational to believe in concurrent space and time dimensions. Further, they each noted in their narratives that they had discussed their experience with others, who helped enrich the accounts by, for example, describing the location of doors or modes of dressing from a different era. And yet, those sensuously experienced, socially mediated phenomena lacked the quality of emotion I witnessed with other people's accounts about deceased relatives. Several other informants who discussed extraordinary experiences spoke with emotional fervour strikingly different from the calm, detached accounts of Hannah and Chris. Such a difference can be explained, I will argue, through the nature of the relationship being described. Hannah and Chris were alone during their experiences and encountered strangers: most people I talked with who encountered spirits encountered the smells, shapes, and sounds of people they knew and loved and often shared the experience with others.

Patrick, for example, a male, middle-aged, educated professional, was proud to describe himself as an atheist. In answer to my opening question, 'what do you believe in?' Patrick swiftly answered:

I believe in the human spirit. I think that there are lots of things that have happened throughout history and happen now that we don't understand. And I think that almost exclusively must come from human beings. There are certain forces, certain, um, what feelings, all sorts of odd coincidences and, um, feelings that you have about other people sometimes having been present, and things like that . . .

Patrick is not explaining for my benefit an intellectualist, cognitive, propositional belief 'system', but 'feelings'. After describing the experience as an affective moment, he then went on to offer an explanation:

and I think that all has been generated from the human spirit, that human beings, extend beyond their body, and, I am pretty convinced that there is something that you could call a human spirit, but of course I don't know what it is. It's something that we can't, what it does and how it, it, moves about we can't possibly explain...

Further, he is keen to tell me that this is a reasonable, rational viewpoint:

> I think it's intrinsic to human beings. I think it comes from within human beings and is extended outwards. I think it's the only reasonable, plausible, explanation to things that happen, to the feelings that people get.

Patrick told me a long, detailed story about an experience that occurred on the day of his mother's funeral. They had been emotionally very close all his life and he was so stricken with grief when she died he did not think he would be able to attend her funeral.

> And, I woke up that morning feeling absolutely sick, physically sick, and I had a headache and felt absolutely dreadful, and I came into work for a little while and then went home, and when I went home I had a feeling of the most profound peace descend upon me, and at the time I thought, what is this and where is it coming from? It just feels so odd, and I was so utterly relaxed and calm, and I was that until I went to the funeral and saw it through. And I'd never had an experience like that and it was very strange, and afterwards I thought it must have been her, she must have come in some way to calm me down.

His account was permeated with references to his body and his emotions, bringing me, the observer, into the story as if I was watching him perform in a movie. It was not a neutral account told in cool, distant tones as I heard when Chris and Hannah described seeing strangers, and nor was it something for which he needed an explanation. He already had his explanation. I asked him if it was the experience of sensing his mother's presence that had led him to believe in the 'human spirit' or whether it was something he had already held as a belief. He responded by saying that it was something he had been thinking about for a number of years and had concluded it was the only explanation for otherwise inexplicable events:

> because I do not believe that there is any all-powerful force that is organizing human destiny. I think that is utterly ridiculous. And, I suppose, as I became an agnostic and then a convinced atheist I felt much more that this sort of humanist, spiritual idea was a much more, what, a much more sensible one.

For Patrick, seeing a 'spirit' could only be explained in relational terms, in contrast with Tylor, who supposed that such an experience could only be explained in religious terms. For Tylor, seeing a spirit was the invention of religion; for Patrick, it was the proof of his mother's continued love.

Patrick was one of several non-religious people who told me about their after-death relational experiences. Becca, 28, an education adviser, said she had been 'weaned off' her belief in God many years earlier. She said she could not remember what she had said on the census, but thought she may have said 'Christian' because she had been baptized. She was certain, however, that she did not believe in God, although she did believe in the spirits of her deceased relatives, who, she recounted, both she and her mother felt were looking after them.

Andrew, a martial arts instructor in his early 20s, said he was not religious and did not believe in God. And yet, he told me, 'I always jog past my grandfather's grave, and I always stop to talk to him.'

Although the above examples illustrate experiences relating to peaceful, positive relationships, it was not that specific feeling that marked the experience but rather whatever feeling was commonly associated with the specific relationship. Robert, the 73-year-old retired printer discussed in Chapter 3, spoke of sensing the spirit of his deceased father, an authoritarian man with whom he had had a difficult relationship. As I describe in more detail below, his experience with his father's spirit was accompanied by the sort of fear and anxiety he felt throughout their lived relationship: death does not change the nature of the relationship.

The unchanging continuity of both the character and relationship is a deeply culturally located idea. In his study of the Eveny in Siberia, Vitebsky (2006) describes how deceased relatives are often experienced as dangerous spirits who return to harm or even kill their relatives. It was also noticeable in his account that the experience of sensing the deceased relative was always collective. As one woman recounted: 'This man had been appearing in the dreams of all our relatives,' she said, 'they were all having the same dream.' In my study, the phenomena of communicating with deceased relatives were also experienced and reported in accordance with the structure of existing relationships.

The sensuous social supernatural

Many of my informants believed their deceased relatives retained a physical presence that continued in the world through direct communication. That sensuous, emotive experience is in marked contrast to the impersonal experiences reported by Hannah and Chris when the apparitions did not communicate with them or exude any material presence of sound or smell. Loved ones' presences, in contrast, were materially present, located and embodied for adherents through sight, smell, and sound and sometimes mediated through non-human physical phenomena.

Spirit location

Viv, 54, works as a technician in a hospital. After her mother died when Viv was 13:

> I used to go and, well, just sit on the bed where she died. Lay there, exactly where it was and everything. You know, I just wanted to be close to her, I suppose.

Her closeness was not a conceptual idea or a lingering memory: she felt it by physically pressing her body against the space where her mother had slept and where she had died. She also experienced being close to her mother in the intimate, domestic space of a bedroom – a common site for such encounters, according to many of my informants.

Vickie, 14, a student at the comprehensive school, continued her relationship with her deceased uncle. Although she attends church, she described how she does not pray to God or Jesus, but when she is alone in her bedroom at night she discusses personal problems and worries with her deceased uncle, who offers advice and solace. In a similar way, one of Vickie's classmates, Charlotte, 14, told me that when she has problems, she turns to her deceased grandfather. She talks with him in the privacy of her bedroom and tells him her deepest problems, particularly about the people who are bullying her at school.

Visual communication

Kevin, 32, a manual worker who lives with his parents in a small town in the region, sensed the presence and saw a shape he identified as his dead grandmother. Gary, 52, a lorry driver, told me about an experience he described as 'a near-death experience'. It occurred when he was about 12 years old and had fallen off his bike and suffered a concussion. He awoke in somebody's farmhouse and found himself lying on a sofa looking out of a window at his deceased grandparents, and their dogs that were 'looking through the window at me'.

Sightings of deceased relatives occurred only rarely amongst my informants. Most visual experiences were mediated through non-human phenomena. For example, Marge, 75, described an event at the funeral for her grandson who had died at the age of 23 seven years earlier. Marge is the mother of Liz, 55, a small-business owner cited in earlier chapters. At the funeral, Marge recounted: 'We stood outside and it was the most glorious sunset that I have ever seen. And never, never, seen that anymore.'

When I asked her what she thought it meant, she said her daughter had said it was her grandson communicating his presence. When I asked her what she had thought, she said she had not been sure, but she said she was sure that when she sees the north star, that it is her grandson: 'You see, and when it's dark and it's starlight and we're going down road, when you look up, I've got a star.' While she attributes the star, and to some extent the sunset, to her grandson, there is no particular message attached to it apart from a sign of his presence. Her daughter Liz, however, told me in a separate interview about the sunset at the funeral, and how she thought it was her son sending a sign.

Becca also talked at length about how non-personal phenomena bring her and her mother information about their deceased relatives. Thunderstorms, for example, sometimes portend bad news and have 'petrified' her since she was a young child. The night her brother was killed in a traffic accident there was a terrible storm, she recounted.

> ... there was quite a memorable electric storm which we could still remember years afterwards and my brother just ... because it was such a memorable storm. Sometimes in a thunderstorm ... and I can always sense them coming, and I suppose this confirms your sixth sense. Dogs can. We do have that sixth sense and we've written it off. And I'm still petrified thinking something horrible is going to happen.

Becca said there had been a thunderstorm the day after her Grandmother died as well. But then, she added, there have been storms when nothing happened, and sometimes there have been storms where good things have happened. Storms, for her, can be impersonal portents and they can also be a means of direct communication between her brother and her family:

> But then I know there was a storm, just a little one, for a few minutes the day my brother's best mate married, another good friend of his, and the day his girlfriend got married. So, it's, I look at this and they were very happily married, so it's not a case of him going oh no they shouldn't be doing it. We kind of thought he was saying, 'yeah, it's right'.

Thunderstorms, for Becca, can signify both good and bad events, but it is notable in her account how she uses the plural pronoun of *we*. The *we* is presumably her and her mother: together, they share and make sense of their grief.

Object manipulation

Liz told me about a communication from her son when she had felt he was communicating with her through manipulating materiality. She and her sister had gone one afternoon to tidy flowers on the grave, when suddenly she noticed that a candle which she had placed there some days earlier was alight. Both she and her sister were convinced that the candle had not been burning when they had arrived by the grave earlier. Its spontaneous ignition was, she said, a direct message from her son that all was well. It also, I add, reflects a generic religious symbol in Euro American cultures. This becomes particularly important when I reviewed Liz's explanations of why she believed in the Christian idea of heaven: having lost a child, she said, it was necessary to believe that they would one day be reunited.

Smell

Smells were also associated with spirit presence. Viv said she began to smell the cigarettes her father smoked, which she interpreted as a sign of his presence.

> While I was sat there, at times I was relaxing, I'd smell this Capstan Full Strength and I'd know that he was around, or I'd know he was in the car with me and things like that, and feel really, really relaxed and things like that.

Viv told me she also smelled hyacinths, her mother's favourite flower, just before her aunt died. This was her deceased mother trying to tell her of the impending event, she said.

Becca said that her grandmother had apparently told her mother that if there was 'something else' after she died she would communicate by sending a smell of violets, her favourite flower. A few months after her grandmother died, Becca was alone in her room when she became aware of a strong smell of violets. It reminded her of her deceased brother who had worn an aftershave with a similar scent, so she left her bedroom to go to the landing, where she used to sit and talk to him outside their adjoining rooms. The smell wasn't there and it was only recently, she said, that she realized that it had been her grandmother, not brother, who had come. The smell had disappeared once she had returned to her bedroom probably, she said, because her grandmother had been there and then had thought she 'hadn't got through' when Becca had left the room.

Sound

Earlier in this chapter I mentioned how Robert had experienced the presence of his deceased father in a manner that conformed to their living relationship. As he told me the story, his wife May joined in to echo and reinforce his comments. Both stressed the impact that sound made on them during the event. A few weeks after his father's funeral, Robert and May took his father's clothes to their house and sorted them into piles in their spare bedroom with the intention of taking them to a charity shop the next day. They told me they had both been asleep in bed that night when they were awoken at about 2 a.m. by the sound of heavy footsteps coming up the stairs towards their bedroom and the spare bedroom next to them. They said they were both terrified at the sound of the footsteps, but, nevertheless, Robert went to investigate, and found no one in the house but all the windows and doors locked. They were both convinced, they said, that it was the father who was returning because of his clothes. This act may be an example of 'unfinished business', a common trope in other accounts of relatives returning (see, again, Vitebsky 2006).

The above examples show the vivid, materially and socially located nature of after-death relational experience. The mix of private and public accounts reflects in many ways culturally embedded relational norms relating to blood ties. That people did not see ghosts of friends or other people known to them seems to correspond to a hierarchy of social structure. It notably does not correspond to notions of individualization.

Believing through bereaving: the performative social supernatural

I suggest that my informants were creating and sustaining beliefs in their continuing relationships by performing those beliefs through the telling. Their act of describing the experience with me and others was a repetitive performance (recalling Butler 1990; 1993), enriching, renewing, and rendering more plausible their beliefs. The experiences of sensing deceased relatives were not frequently repeated; for most people those experiences happened rarely, but their smooth narrative performances had the quality of practice through repetition.

People often wanted to express self-consciously how they were making sense of their extraordinary experiences, not through creating theories but through reinforcing their desire for a continuing relationship. It was, I suggest, the performance of reliving it and seeing the audience reaction that was important. Viv said she had experienced from an early age the impact of bereavement.

> I lost my Mum when I was 13. And my Dad when I was 22. My niece committed suicide. My brother committed suicide. My nephew, only a few months ago, committed suicide, and I think from a young age I've had to deal with – I lost my first child.

Her answer to that question began with her setting the stage with the bodies of her deceased family, as if she was introducing them to me one by one. She was answering the question not by offering a creedal or theoretical, rehearsed statement but by prefiguring her explanation with her social and emotional context and salience. Only then did she tell me how she came to make sense of it:

> You know, I think from being a young age I've had to deal with bereavement, and I think that it's, by taking this on board and really thinking it out, and reading bits as well, I really think that I – I want to believe that there's got to be something, somewhere.

Viv was pointedly trying to make sense of her loss through wanting to believe: it is a form of wishful thinking of which she is intensely aware. There had been cognitive effort in 'thinking it out' and reading, but her final point was more emotional: using whatever tools that might be available, she would believe because she wanted to believe.

Liz talked about losing her son and how it was important for her to believe in an afterlife to give her hope:

> Think especially when you've lost somebody, you need this belief, you need to believe that you're going to see them again, and I think most people feel, well, especially if you've lost a child, you need something to hang onto. You've got to believe that you're going to see them again. I think that's the thing that helps. It helps a lot to believe there's something else. You don't want to think you've got nothing there, and that you're never going to see them.

Liz used the word 'need' three times in her first sentence, followed by 'got to'. She is simultaneously telling me what she wants to believe, while also acknowledging it is hard work, almost a requirement, rather than a choice. The alternative – that she would not see her son again – would be intolerable. Such an explanation for belief in heaven ran through other interviews, notably with young people.

For example, Kathleen, a 15-year-old student, said she would like to believe in an afterlife while also suggesting such a belief was probably a result of not being able to cope.

> Again, I'm kind of agnostic. I'd like to think there's a heaven but again it seems to me that it's probably because people can't cope with eternal nothing, that they substitute something into that, because they can't comprehend it, rather than it actually existing.

Kathleen is presenting herself as an intelligent person who clearly recognizes the difference between something 'actually existing' and something people may wish existed. She then turns to the reason she might want to believe in something that may not actually exist: 'But, yeah, I guess, I'd like to believe in it because my granddad died when I was seven [. . .] and I'd like to see him again [. . .] or when my Mum died, I'd like to see her again.' Although she is struggling with the relative plausibility of belief in God and belief in human reunions in heaven, she is clearly drawn to the idea of continuing relationships.

Her classmate Sarah discussed heaven in both theological and secular terms. Sarah said she believed in heaven 'because I'm a Christian'. This reflected a non-performative acceptance of a propositional or creedal belief based on content rather than other dimensions. Nevertheless, she does have doubts and sometimes thinks it would make sense for there to be a final end after death, as if that were a more plausible stance. And yet, she continued, she would like to think that there is a heaven where she will see friends and family again.

The uncertainty but longing in the voices of Kathleen and Sarah were characteristic of many of my interviews with young people. Most young people I interviewed said they did not know what happens after people die, apart from those young people who had lost loved ones and said that they knew that their loved one had gone somewhere else and yet was still present in their lives. This connection between belief in an afterlife and experience of bereavement was reinforced when I asked people what they feared most, or asked them what they think happens after death. Informants, even young people, rarely spoke of being afraid of what happens to them: more often, they said they were afraid of losing people they love, and most often, they said that they wanted to believe in an afterlife so that they can continue their relationships, not their own lives. I suggest here that belief in an afterlife may increase as one ages, not because one fears one's own death, but because it is more likely that loved ones have died and the bereaved survivor seeks to maintain the relationship.

Performative belief rituals

The ritual of performative belief occurred during interviews in a processual manner I recognized, recalling three stages of a ritual identified by van Gennep (1960): leaving, liminality, returning.[2] First, the informant marked the beginning of the ritual by abruptly changing the subject. Typically, they, not I, introduced into our conversation the example of an uncanny experience. That conversational act separated us from the interview context I had created by forcing us to leave the semi-structured interview context for a different place of primarily their making. In that place, they performed their belief in after-death lives through telling me their story. My role changed from interviewer to audience, while theirs changed from interlocutor to performer.

I was not listening to coherent, cognitively-based belief statements, but stories with real characters, plots, and emotional content. These detailed stories, or belief narratives as I prefer to call them, did not fit with the idea of a belief system as envisaged by, for example, Borhek and Curtis (1975), whose analysis focused on mainly cognitive and empirical measures of a belief system's levels of commitment and validity. What I observed were not systems but narratives composed of emotionally charged components. The informant, as central participant in the ritual, was, as Bloch (1992) described, touched by the transcendent quality of the experience and 'returned' as a changed character. The presence, or spirit, of their beloved was not a character in the story, but seemed to be the purpose of the story. From Good (1994), I was to learn that examples, emplotment, characters, and multiple viewpoints are characteristic of such narratives. As he explains (ibid., 139), we can never directly access anyone's experiences, but might gain an insight through how they recount experiences and give them an apparently meaningful and coherent structure. In his study of belief, J. Day (1993) observed that it was through narrative that he began to understand his informants' beliefs and what those meant to them: 'Narrative as a feature of how things are framed is what establishes behavior in time, relationship, and identity, which are closely tied to situation in the world' (1993, 224). Bruner shows us that what is told is what is lived: autobiographical narrative is both a way of telling and a way of interpreting, such that it becomes a 'recipe for structuring experience' (1987, 11).

---

[2] Also see Bell 1997 and 2000 for discussion on the formal, visible nature of ritual.

A collection of stories gathered by Bennett (1999) is compelling through the detailed, emotive accounts of English widows' experiences of sensing their deceased loved ones. A folklorist, Bennett paid particular attention to the way the stories were told and commented on the dialectic between narrator and listener. The widow, she said, 'has a social need to have her definition of the experience confirmed in order that her view of reality may be sanctioned. The force of the story is therefore at once expository and heuristic' (ibid., 123).

When Collins (2008a, 152–3) studied how Quakers in a north of England meeting talked amongst themselves, he at first thought he was hearing unconnected and chance remarks 'until the penny dropped that these were not isolated phenomena... [but] a weave of narrative threads' that he analysed through three discursive dimensions: the vernacular, the individual, and the canonic.

Although theories of narrative were instructive to a point, my work here extends those theories by arguing that narrative can be performative, with informants' stories helping to bring into being both the presence and the belief in the presence of their deceased loved ones. Narrative is therefore a tool in the ritual of performative belief, deeply embedded in social relations and embodied through the performer. Patrick described himself nearly vomiting with grief and then overwhelmed with peace; Becca and Viv smelt the flowers, aftershave, and the cigarette smoke of their loved ones; Andrew ran to his grandfather's grave where he could talk to him. Belief, as they performed it then and through the telling later, was visceral, produced and performed through bile, olfactory senses, and sweat glands. As part of a ritual the narratives were, following Bell (2000, 383), how 'people can visibly, formally and explicitly attest to a whole cosmos of implicit assumptions about the nature of reality' and, as Tambiah (1985, 128) argued, reinforce certain values. It was more than solely a linguistic telling, it was an embodied, experiential, performance.[3]

And then they stopped. As unprepared as I was for the introduction of their story I was equally unprepared for how and when it would end. At some point they usually simply stopped, and looked to me to lead us back to the previous context, where the norms of the situation I had first imposed would be followed. This signalled the third phase in the ritual. There, after returning, my questions about how they explained their experiences and their associated beliefs met with polite but

---

[3] In their analysis of Mormonism, Mitchell and Mitchell (2008) call attention to the embodied, experiential nature of belief and argue that scholars should move beyond a linguistic analysis.

usually uninterested responses. Most had not bothered to develop a learned theory, perhaps because they did not need theory to validate their experiences. They did not appear to be wrestling with the problem Tylor supposed, or to be reconciling it through a religious explanation of gods. My informants did not need to explain the presence of their deceased loved one's spirit: that they continued to experience belonging to that relationship was enough.

Further, it is not something they would describe as religious. That finding challenges other studies of so-called religious experience and contradicts the tendency in wider social scientific literature to describe belief and experience in the continuation of life after death as 'religious'. That religion–belief–supernatural conflation reflects a Tylorian assumption, as discussed in Chapter 1, that belief in spirits is a religious, rather than social, experience. It echoes James' (1982 [1903], 31) idea that religious experience is what individuals experience alone 'in relation to whatever they may consider the divine'. In untying belief in spirits from religion, and situating it within sociality, I have showed in this chapter how beliefs are performed and performative – expressed, experienced, and embodied in non-institutional social places and contexts that rely both on pre-formed, already-held ideas and experiences and emotional improvizations.

Many of my informants, including those who said they were atheists, reported feeling the presence of their deceased relatives or seeing ghosts. They would not call those experiences religious or spiritual, in contrast with many scholars in the field who apply the label 'religious' to such experiences and describe them variously as common, folk, invisible, or implicit religion (Bailey 1990; Davie 1994; Hardy 1979; Hay 1982; Luckmann 1967; Sutcliffe 2004). Some scholars claim there is an enduring religiosity or 'common religion' on the basis of surveys where people say that they believe in fate, the paranormal, and so on, but what those surveys do not reveal is what such phenomena and concepts mean to people. Even those studies that claim people are seeking 'spiritualism' rather than religion (Roof 1993) may be missing the point that such terms are often a cover, or proxy, for sociality.

Hay (1982) and Hardy (1979) conducted research similar to mine, involving in-depth interviews. They were told similar stories about people's experience of something outside their 'everyday selves'. Hay (1982, 152) said that other than the named experience of God, experiences such as 'premonitions, encounters with the dead and encounters with an evil presence were often ruled out of the category religious'. He (1982, 162–3) concludes by saying:

On the basis of what people have said to us, then, I feel that 'religious experience' is not quite the right term for what we have been describing. It would be more correct to say that it is a type of experience which is commonly given a religious interpretation. For reasons of shorthand I intend to continue to use the word 'religious' while recognising that this is only one way of looking at it.

This 'shorthand', I argue, rather obscures the significance of the beliefs of people who reported such experiences and unfortunately has crept into the established canon within the field. It also removes as an appropriate object of inquiry the non-religious orientations of those who experience uncanny or transformative events.[4]

The extraordinary, supra-human experiences of many informants were akin to what Lévy-Bruhl described as a 'law of participation' (1926, 76), where distinctions between the material and the spiritual worlds are irrelevant and all interactions are experienced emotionally and perceived as relational. This is, he says, different from the 'laws of contradiction' that are taught and reinforced in our society. Even today, he concluded, people in contemporary society are also at times 'pre-logical' as they seek the ecstasy experienced through a sense of total participation. Although such terms as *pre-logical* forced much criticism of his work, Luhrmann (2007) points out that Lévy-Bruhl's idea of interconnection is the core of many contemporary spiritualist and witchcraft beliefs. For many of my informants there was no obvious distinction between the everyday and the ever-after. Transcendence is here shifted to an everyday, human, social scale, relocating a transcendent 'other' to an everyday experience of the ever-after. As Wood (2004) observed, the so-called spiritual experiences that sometimes may appear to be fluid and free-floating, such as certain forms of 'new age' spirituality, are in practice often deeply rooted in social and particularly kinship networks. The manner in which accounts were related in my study contributed to my theories about beliefs arising from and being performed through relational social engagement.

The socially embedded nature of supernatural belief was also discussed by J. Mitchell (1997), who, during fieldwork in Malta, experienced an uncanny sensation of a 'presence' while he was cleaning a statue of Jesus in a church. The experience provoked him to observe how he interpreted that experience in comparison to how many of his

---

[4] Other studies have worked on the belief/experience problem by situating the anthropologist in the centre of the experience as a participant as well as observer. See, for example, Luhrmann (1989) on witchcraft in the UK, Favret-Saada (1980) on witchcraft in France and Amiras (2008) on integral transformative practice.

informants, members of the congregation, might interpret the event. Of the many possibilities available some people might choose a sceptical, natural approach while others would choose a supernatural explanation, drawing on a 'corpus of religious knowledge' (ibid., 88). How they reach those conclusions is, he argued, based on their feelings supported by social memory. Of particular interest here is Mitchell's conclusion that an uncanny experience leads to feelings explained as a supernatural experience because:

> the logic by which it is felt in the first place depends on anticipation of supernatural intervention. Even before it is felt it is explained as religious experience. (ibid., 91)

The most important implication is that the religion–belief–supernatural connection can be broken through understanding that both religion and the supernatural are subsets of a wider set of belief understood as belonging.

6

Believing in Fate: Covering the Cracks in Belonging

How people explain what happens in their lives, and to what source or sources they attribute causality and control, were intertwined themes which arose, often spontaneously, in many of my interviews. There was a set question I had prepared to begin discussion about that topic: 'How much influence or control do you think you have over your own life?' but people often raised the subject as they discussed my first question about what they believed in. My analysis here begins with the observation that most people attribute causality to various agents, but their understanding of who those agents are, how important they are to the informant, and what they do varies enormously. I will discuss here my informants who believe in degrees of predestination: there is a plan or purpose for their lives over which they have little or no control. Those who do control it are described in terms of substantive agents that exist for the informant in an invisible realm with an independent reality. They name these agents variously as fate, God, destiny, 'something', a dead relative, the universe, or a guardian angel. Further, it is to sources with whom they feel they belong – typically, deceased relatives – that they turn for comfort, security, and consolation. Almost without exception, the force in control of people's lives is benign. Fate's function, it seems, is to propel the person through some tricky life moments with equanimity and reassurance. It is a kind, parental fate that is in control and, correspondingly, often takes a human guise in the form of a family connection.

Other informants believe they are mainly in control of what happens in their own lives, influenced by other visible, living agents who exist in their immediate milieu and described variously as family, friends, and other members of society. They may also believe in supernatural entities, such as spirits and ghosts, but do not accord them power over their lives. Their living social relations are the people who influence their lives. They also believe in something they call 'luck', by which they mean random events. These random events called 'luck' are happenstance: circumstances and events that occur as a part of the natural complexity of their wider environment. As will become evident, people use terms like destiny, luck, and fate to mean different things and only with probing during interviews does it become apparent what is meant.

What is common amongst most people I interviewed is the acceptance that it is not the individual who determines his or her fate, but an individual acting within a net of social relations.

Predestination

Many people I interviewed believed in what they called 'destiny', but not everyone meant the same thing by it. The difference, I will argue, lies in what areas of their lives and to what degree they feel they have power. Belief in such predestination is mainly retrospective and does not appear to manifest itself in any related actions or practices. Its main function, I will argue, is to comfort informants by explaining events that are otherwise hard for them to understand. Some selective events are explained by according power to a supra-human, supernatural agent. These agents tend to have four main functions: the grand planner, the life manager, the matchmaker, and the protector.

Grand planner

When people talk about the plan for their lives, most believe they have some control over their events but only within a larger plan. Antony, a 15-year-old boy attending a boys' grammar school, described himself as an atheist raised by parents who describe themselves as Christian. He said he believed everyone has a destiny that determines what happens to him or her: everything has been 'pre-decided'. Antony said no one individual controlled what was happening, describing the process as 'fate, or destiny, or something'. To illustrate his point he gave the example of Shakespeare, who, he said, always personified fate in his plays. In contrast, Antony said he did not believe it was possible to 'put a finger on what is controlling'. When I asked him how much control he felt he had as an individual, he said 'absolutely none'. I asked him if he liked the feeling, that everything was out of his control and he said yes, he did. He said it gave him a sense of security that what was going to happen was going to happen eventually. Further, he said he felt that whatever happened would be for the good. Although Antony does not know who or what is in control, he believes the controller is benign. As he does not believe in God, he could not name the source of the control but was in no doubt that his life was entirely mapped out for him: the constraints on his freedom were total. This reminded me of William, a young male in year 10 at a comprehensive school. He believes in a 'higher power' but does not accord it any power over his life now. He thinks most things in his life happen because other people decide they should, leaving him no control over what happens. He said he does have a sense that there is a higher power, which he described as 'a supreme intelligence' but this higher power does not act in any way to influence his life. Its purpose, he said, is to give him something to look forward to after he dies. His feelings of powerlessness were similar to those of Antony. I found it striking that only adolescent males amongst all informants in my study said that they had no power of agency in any part of their lives. Having been present in both their schools I was reminded of the regimented nature of their days and the constant reinforcement of subordination to older male authority. Whether this was repeated at home I have no way of knowing, but I will conclude by saying that believing in fate or a higher power is one way they rationalize the real lack of individual power they currently possess.

Life manager

The life manager is my term for the agent people describe which intervenes to prompt a person to return to specific parts of the pre-ordained grand plan. This life-managing agent is often called fate, the path, destiny, the universe, or 'something'. It appears to control only specific areas of people's lives and is experienced retrospectively as they are trying to explain something other people may describe as coincidence or bad luck. In the course of more detailed conversation, however, it became evident that the life manager is not an impersonal force but most often a deceased relative.

Paul, a 33-year-old year old restaurant manager, believes his vocation and his time of death are pre-ordained. He told me that 'If in my life I'm supposed to die at 66, I'll die at 66.' Some people, he said, die in car crashes, but are brought back to life because it was not 'their time'. Paul said he believed his entire life was mapped out for him. It was possible to diverge from a pre-ordained path, but something would always bring one back. I asked him to explain what that 'something' was, at which point he abruptly said, as if this would explain everything: 'I'm a twin. My twin died.' I said I was sorry, but he quickly continued with his story. His twin died at birth. Apparently there were complications and it was evident that one would die. He asked me suddenly: 'I didn't die. Why didn't I die?' He said this so forcefully it made me think that this question – why me? – had occupied his thoughts for some time. I was not sure how the effect of being a twin had any bearing on my question about the path being designed, but he continued to explain. Some people say that there is telepathy between twins, he said. 'They do say that', he repeated, as if he was not personally going to claim that assertion but the fact that other people said it made it more likely. I asked if he had ever had an experience that suggested his twin was sending telepathic messages. He said no, he had never had anything inexplicable happen, but after a slight pause, he told me a story about being in Tenerife and how he had nearly stayed but then got a sense that he should return back to the UK. When he returned he found a job in a hotel and settled into a career in the hospitality industry. That made him think that this was his true path, he said, but what, he asked rhetorically, gave him the sense that he should be doing it? He left the question open with the clear implication that it was likely his twin who had communicated with him. Why he had reached that conclusion is something I cannot explain, but it was clear from our conversation that he still struggles to understand the circumstance of his birth. It is possible that by according his twin power over his life he may be assuaging survivor-guilt. I do not think the experience should be read as evidence that he believes his twin has power over him but it does illustrate how some people struggle with an answer to the 'why me' question. As discussed in the previous chapter, interpretations are culturally embedded: for Paul, it was his twin; for the Azande in Evans-Pritchard's account, it was witchcraft. If a granary collapses as you sit underneath, 'Witchcraft explains the co-incidence of these two happenings' (1976 [1937], 23).

A 2007 study by Cancer Research UK[1] found that more than a quarter of those surveyed said that whether someone had cancer was determined entirely by fate. That percentage was higher amongst women, people over 65, people living in economically deprived areas, and amongst smokers.

In her research in Germany, Sammet (2011) analysed how unemployed people in Germany coped with their situation and, particularly, with feelings related to precariousness. Legislation had recently changed and reduced the level of benefits for unemployed people, in

---

[1] http://info.cancerresearchuk.org/news/archive/pressrelease/2007-01-03-more-than-a-quarter-of-britons-think-cancer-is-a-matter-of-fate.

an era when public discourse about people receiving benefits had become increasingly negative: 'This attributes responsibility to the unemployed and legitimizes social inequality. Unemployment is no longer discussed as a structural problem but turned into a moral issue' (ibid., 2). The effect was to increase the unemployed person's sense of isolation, worthlessness, and hopelessness and tendency to blame external factors beyond their control, sometimes to a degree that seems unwarranted. One couple, for example, admitted they smoked and drank excessively, but said (in phrases reminiscent of Mary Douglas) that everything in the world was so polluted that they could not improve their health no matter what they did.

Norris and Inglehart (2004) suggest that pockets of religiosity in different societies can be partly explained by conditions that promote and maintain 'existential insecurity' – even in such apparently modern countries as the United States. Religious beliefs in those contexts, they argue, provide some protection in this world and hope for the next. My findings suggest an even more complicated story: beliefs in predestination are usually informed by human relationships and performed by people who are seeking not only the 'alibi' of fate but, perhaps more strongly, the continued relationship with their loved ones.

Matchmaker

Many women describe finding a romantic partner as something that is controlled by an agent looking out for their best interests. What I will describe as a 'matchmaker' agency is a gendered type of agency that I only found being expressed by women. This agent usually either takes the form of a deceased relative, or, through some process of incarnation, imbues itself in a human on earth. Its main purpose in the women's lives seems to be to secure an ideal romantic partner and comfort them when their relationships fail. Women who believed this always talked about disappointing aspects of their emotional or sexual relationships and how they had concluded, following bitter experience, that they had to relinquish personal power over their relationships. The sense that they are themselves incapable of finding the right partner was intensely expressed by Becca. Although she lives with her child and with a partner, she described herself as 'single' and spoke frequently about her disappointment in love. Most significantly for my study, she spoke about how her disappointments were resolved by a power outside herself. She told me that once

I did have this wonderful life map of what I actually wanted, and it's the usual fairytale of getting married, settling down, and actually making a marriage that works. Nothing big. Just complete happiness for the rest of my life. And it didn't happen, and it doesn't matter how much I can picture it and see it, I don't think it will happen. It just didn't happen and so I've got quite cynical.

Her voice took on an edge of bitterness and anger as she described how the dream she had mapped out for herself did not come true. Attributing misfortune to a higher or at least distant power is a trait observed in other places and times. What is striking is the form those powers take. Becca, for example, does not blame a witch as might, in contrast, one of Evans-Pritchard's (1976 [1937]) informants. Nevertheless, in both cases, there appears to be a sense that whatever misfortune befell them, it was not their direct fault. The witch may have cursed them or, for Becca, 'it just didn't happen'. Fate becomes an alibi, as Fortes (1983 [1959]) described the situation in West Africa:

> the notion of Prenatal Destiny serves as a legitimate alibi. It relieves the sufferer's kin, and therefore society at large, of responsibility and guilt for his troubles and, indeed, exonerates him in his own eyes . . . he is not [even] aware that he is the victim of his Prenatal Destiny until this is revealed by a Diviner.

While a West African might turn to a diviner for help, Becca turned to her deceased grandmother. As discussed in the previous chapter, relations with supernatural forces reflect social relations. Becca believes that relationships are out of her control but are being managed by something else, probably her dead grandmother. Perhaps, she said, it is the spirit of her deceased grandmother who is helping her, describing this as 'something, like a guardian angel, that guides people to meet'. For example, she said, when she met her current partner it was such an unusual series of coincidences that it gave her the feeling that it had been pre-ordained and that they had met before in a previous life. She did not talk about a past life at other times in our interview and nor does she actively consult her grandmother on other decisions about her life. Her belief in predestination appears to apply only to romantic relationships. I conclude that Becca relinquished power in an area of life where she feels the most powerless to the benign, loving protection of her grandmother.

Rosemarie, a 49-year-old nurse separated from her husband and two children, expressed a similar belief that romantic relationships were pre-ordained. Recently separated from her husband after a lengthy period of unhappiness, she said she is hoping to meet her 'soul mate' eventually, but she did not think it would be as a result of her own effort. She said: 'I'm hoping it may find me. I'm hoping it may find me.'

This idea of waiting for the 'it' to find her was described specifically by Rosemarie as a feminine trait. It corresponded to what she said was her desire to 'go with the flow'. When I asked her to explain what that meant, she said that going with the flow meant 'stepping back'. Rosemarie concludes that being passive and submissive will improve her chances of finding her ideal mate. This mate will not be, she said, an ordinary man but some kind of god that she described as a 'higher being' in a man's form.

She described this 'it' as being exclusively male. It would be someone she could 'look up to', adore, and cherish, which was more important than he adoring and cherishing her was. I asked if she had ever found such a mate, and she said yes, 'fleetingly'. The feeling she had from that experience was 'that all-consuming love, that overwhelmingness' similar to how she used to feel about her father, and about God, she said. She did not feel that way about God anymore, she said, because now she was not sure that God was there as a higher being but was, perhaps, on earth or ultimately God was within her. Both she and Becca spoke about how they had to give up power over their romantic dreams and direction in order to allow something more powerful than they to act for them. Both women had first been disappointed and emotionally upset in relationships. This has led, I conclude, to a sense of powerlessness that is only ameliorated by believing in and subordinating themselves to a more powerful agent that acts for them.

In a similar way, Briony spoke of chance meetings as significant events that helped her recover from emotional suffering. She identified her willingness to link her significant relationships to fate as being 'a bit of a romantic'. She, like Becca and Rosemarie, thinks that sometimes she is destined to meet certain people. She quoted an author saying that people meet some people for a specific period of time in their lives because it is important for them to learn something from that other person, or to impart some specific piece of knowledge to them, or to find the ideal mate: 'I like that idea.'

I note how she slightly distances herself from the belief by saying she likes the idea, as if acknowledging an element of wishful thinking. Briony relates some of her experiences to her idea, saying there have been times when she met someone purely by chance who became important to her, causing her to believe that 'it's almost as if we're supposed to'. Belief in the matchmaking agent exists here, I conclude, to comfort women that the lack of power they feel over their romantic lives is being managed by a wiser, more powerful agent – a grandmother or male protector/lover.

Protector

Linked to the matchmaking agency above, this type of agency watches over and loves people, performing a protective and comforting role. This type of agency is personified, being most often referred to as a guardian angel or a guide embodying the spirit of a deceased loved one who performed a protective role in life. In the previous chapter, I discussed at length many examples of people who believe their deceased relatives are watching over them; I will not repeat those points here. I raise the theme in this section to include their protective role as linked to predestination. People do not accord their dead relative the power of a manager agency who creates and enforces a plan, but rather a different form of agency who protects them through warning them or comforting them. The deceased relative does not impart knowledge of which the informant would not become immediately aware through the normal course of events: a death in the family, for example. The informant, I conclude, draws comfort from the idea that their deceased relative is protecting them and present with them during times of crisis.

Deities

I will turn now to examine specifically the role of deities in people's lives. Sometimes, the deity may perform some or all of the functions described above, but seems to have a more robust role than simply one of justifying how things are meant to be. About a fifth of the people I interviewed experienced the sense of something they variously described as God, Allah, Jesus, goddess, or, in one case, 'garden deities' such as fairies and gnomes. They described their experience as giving them a sense of peace and calm in their daily lives as it reassured them that their lives fit into a larger pattern. As I described in Chapter 2, those who believed in God or wanted to profess a faith in a religion almost always introduced that belief immediately, answering my first question by stating their belief precisely. What I will discuss here in more depth is how they experienced sensing the presence of a deity.

Informants who describe experiences with God or Jesus say they have a sense that God or Jesus is communicating a feeling. They sometimes say this as 'words in my head' and most often relate feelings of calmness and peace. Jane said that her faith in God has helped her through many difficult situations. When she prays to God it is a form of emotional release, she said, of letting go or, as she described it, 'handing over'. During those times, she never hears anything back from God in the form of actual words, but feels a sense of peace that leads her not to worry about her problems. Nadia told me she felt peaceful when praying to God, saying she feels God's presence when she prays and believes he answers her by bringing her peace and happiness.

A different kind of experience with a deity was described to me by Veronica, 48. She raised the topic of her unusual experience at the end of our interview, as we discussed how she had filled in the 2001 census. We were talking about Buddhism, and the concept of past lives, when suddenly, she leaned forward and said with an urgent tone in her voice: 'Have you ever, you know, seen something?' I said, 'Like what?' Having now marked the moment when we would advance into a new territory, she began to tell her story. The experience had occurred at Christmas, two years earlier, when she had been very stressed with the pressure of work. One evening, she went to bed crying, when suddenly in the corner of the room she saw something she described to me as a kaleidoscope. Each piece of the kaleidoscope contained a picture, of 'all the most horriblest things that have happened in the past horrible things. Starving children.' It was silent, and circling slowly, and in the middle was a man's face. As she looked at the face she felt calm, and felt she was receiving a message that while terrible things have happened, nothing she is going through now is that bad, so she should not worry. After some time, how long she was not sure, the image faded. She left her room, went next door to her son's room, and said: 'I've just seen Jesus.' Her son replied, 'What you been on, Mum?' He did not believe her and neither did her husband. The urgency with which she introduced the topic during our interview was a feature of the performative belief ritual she was conducting, and her desire to tell the story and to be believed. Veronica said she never discussed this experience with a religious person, nor did she start attending church, or do anything to build the event into a larger religious framework. But she has no doubt that she saw Jesus, and that the feeling of peace that accompanied the image and message has remained with her.

Veronica also thinks much of her life is her choice, apart from areas where she feels particularly vulnerable. She spent most of the time in our interview stressing how it was up to every individual to make his or her own choices in life. She said she had grown up on a council estate in a large family with abusive, alcoholic parents. Nevertheless, she stressed, she had broken away from that life and had not followed the pattern of her parents. She said that sociologists categorize people and say if you were an abused child you will abuse your children; that it is the way you were treated before you were 10 years old that determines what you will be, adding: 'That's a crock of shit.' She did, however, speak about the role of God as being important in determining one event in her life. She said: 'I believe in fate. Well, I believe in God, actually.' By way of example, she told me about how she had come to buy the local shop. She had lived in the village for several years, working as a cleaner. And then, she said, one day she popped into the local shop to buy a strawberry tart, and the thought suddenly struck her that she should buy the shop. It was, she said, a preposterous idea as she had no relevant experience or money. She went home and announced the idea to her husband, who thought she was mad, but she continued in her quest and eventually succeeded. She found each step surprisingly easy, she said, as if it was 'meant to be'. I suggest that the shift from being a domestic cleaner to owning and managing a business was an area outside Veronica's experience and one in which she felt inexperienced and vulnerable. Here, she could not rely on her own sense of self but rather had to attribute her progress to a power well beyond herself. She explains her success as something beyond her control and added that she thinks life is sometimes like that. She said:

> I think some things are meant to be. Sometimes, you don't know why, you start to go down one road and then go a different way. Or maybe you get to the airport and you've forgotten your passport and then the plane crashes.

I identify in Veronica's account two themes. One is her sometimes fierce sense of responsibility and accountability for her own life; the other is how 'some things' are meant to be. In her case, the agent called God intervened to provoke her into following the path in an area she would normally feel was outside her control or power of agency. Another, much younger informant described God's intervention in her life in much the same way. Laura, a 23-year-old single receptionist who lives with her parents, answered my first question – 'What do you believe in?' – by saying that 'life is what you make it'. She said she thought she was in control of her life, asserting with a self-confident air: 'Life is what you make it. Meeting people, going to places.'

Here, she sounded much like Veronica had sounded in the first part of her interview. Nevertheless, like Veronica, she switched her tone and her position when she discussed an area that she felt lay outside her control. Within certain defined areas of her life, she qualified, she has control, but not over everything. She said she thought that God had most things planned, although it was possible for a person to change certain things. She identified those mutable areas of life as certain aspects about a job, relationships, how one looks, friends, and holidays. That, I commented to her, was quite a long list and seemed to cover most aspects of her life. I asked her what areas of her life she could not change. She said that God has 'more major concerns about your life in general, your health, and stuff'. She went on to say that she believes God is 'against me for some reason' as she has had two major operations in the last two years for tonsillitis and appendicitis. These are the kinds of health crises that are, indeed, outside one's control. The operations had forced her to take time off work, she said, with a tone of anger and resentment. Consequently, she had less money and was not able to socialize as much with her friends.

A slightly different feeling expressed by some informants discussing deities was the sense of one's place in a bigger plan. Melanie, 42, a nurse and reflexologist, is single and lives with her young son in a small town. Melanie said she believes in and has felt the presence of 'garden deities'. Although they are invisible, she said, she has felt their presence in her garden and near certain plants. She said she believes in fairies, gnomes, angels, gods, goddesses, 'the big white spirit', and a benign source of everything. This gives her a sense of being alive and being part of the 'planet', she said.

Being part of something bigger was a feeling also described by John. He said that when he felt close to God it was 'a sense of relationship, this sense of knowing a God who knows and loves me and is drawing me to know and love him'. He said he not only felt this when he was praying but he felt it all the time. Jane said God gave her a reason for being: 'I couldn't contemplate life without him, and I couldn't contemplate life without there being something at the end of it.' Jane also said that she could not imagine a better community to belong to than her church. This reminded me of Ozorak's (1996) study of American Christian women, where she found that their acceptance of the church hierarchy and male domination was partly explained by their sense of having their own space where they felt empowered (see also Day 2005; Eccles 2008).

The informants above described sensing the presence of a deity in ways strikingly similar to those who reported feeling the presence of their deceased relatives. The difference was to whom or what they attributed the source of that feeling. People I interviewed who affirmed their beliefs in God and their religion did not usually talk about feeling other supernatural presences apart from his, but the sense of a relative, or God, watching over people is the same. I did not find a similar quality of protective emotion in interviews with people who had lost children. The sense of being protected appears to relate to a deceased older relative in a parental role, or to God performing the same role. I will examine that proposition in more detail below.

On one occasion, an informant told me about receiving a sensuous sign from God, later mediated through social experience. David, 48, recounted how he and his wife had been confirmed recently, renewing their vows to Christianity. Within the context of that conversation he said there had been a lapse in his church attendance while he was in his 20s, but then all that changed 'after an experience when I was fishing, in the river'. He paused for a moment, invoking a short silence, a pause in what I now recognize as the beginning of his performative belief ritual. He continued to talk about the church he attended as if there was no need to expand on his reference to the 'experience'. I let him continue on that topic for a few minutes before I asked him directly to tell me about the experience. There was, I now recognize, a moment for audience participation in his ritual where my role was to provoke him to embark on his narrative.

It was an experience that still sends shivers down him thinking about it, he said, although it was 20 years ago. He was standing, fishing, in the centre of the river when it suddenly began to rain. The strange thing was, he noticed, it was not raining on him. As he told me the story he rubbed his arms as if he were cold. The excerpt below conveys his emotion:

DAVID: It was peculiar, I was actually in the river, I was fishing in the middle of the river, um, sort of, nearly waist deep in the river, and it started to rain, but I was stood, almost in, it's making the hair stand up on my head, on my arms, just thinking about it, um, stood in like a shaft of sunlight and it was raining all around me, and it was like a shaft of sunlight all around me in the middle of the river. It was most peculiar.

ABBY: How long did that last for?

DAVID: Couple of minutes, it wasn't just an instant.

ABBY: So, what did you think it was?

DAVID: I don't know, I still don't know to this day. It was just peculiar, and everything, I could see all the rain splashing on the water, and it just like, really quiet.

David and I paused at that point. I shrugged and shook my head in a way that indicated the experience sounded inexplicable. He laughed, nodded, and shook his head. After I had non-verbally communicated to David that I accepted his story at face value, I asked him directly: 'Well?' He just shook his head. I continued to press the point: 'Well, you must have thought about something.' Again, he said nothing, so I continued: 'You said that prompted you to go back to that church group, so what was it that made that connection for you?' He replied: 'I don't know.' Given that he had made that connection, that he had introduced the experience in the context of his return to church, I decided to continue to press him. I said, 'You didn't say this is an interesting scientific odd thing. It was something more than that for you.' He nodded and then said:

> Well, I suppose it seemed like a sign, I don't know. 'Cuz I went down to speak to, to sort of tell somebody about it really.

He then told me that he went to speak to people at the church on the army base where he was living, and although he could not recount exactly what they had said, it was enough to convince him to return to church, which he has done more or less regularly ever since. I asked him what he felt at the time and he said 'sort of calming, really'.

The belief in fate as the grand plan, sometimes known as God, can therefore be selective and situational. Neither Laura nor Veronica spoke about God at any other time in our interview. He seemed to have no other function but to explain events over which they felt they had no personal power, providing, as Fortes might put it, an 'alibi'. Further, their invocation of God, *aka* Fate, performed a specific purpose in a specific instance, what Stringer (1996) referred to as 'situational beliefs'.

Conclusion

In this chapter I have explored how people believe their lives are influenced or controlled: they vary not so much in whether they believe in any supernatural personal or impersonal entity guiding them but the salience and function of those entities. It is not belief or disbelief in God or other supernatural entities that influences people's sense of their own destiny but the reverse: I have argued that it is people's need for something to control their destinies that leads to their belief in such entities. Having said 'people', the distribution of those beliefs was not equal in my study, and nor does it point to a simple correlation between such beliefs in modernity.

A recent cross-cultural example from a study of Christianity in China (Xiaowen et al. 2008, 59) found that those most likely to convert to Christianity were women, migrants, people from ethnic minorities, and farmers/peasants: 'believers are disproportionately drawn from some of the socially dislocated and disadvantaged categories in society'.

Although I observed a gender difference in how men and women claimed spiritual power, it may be instructive to examine an age difference. Berger and Ezzy (2007) found in their study of teenage witches in Australia, the UK, and the USA that the females were attracted to the idea of the witch representing the powerful woman. Young female witches, they found, shared 'a belief in the supernatural, a connection with nature and an appreciation of the importance of the feminine' (ibid., 50).[2]

Apart from some variations, I found no evidence of the systemic, ontological, pervasive insecurity some theorists argue is an inevitable consequence of modernity (see, for example, Bauman 2001; Beck 1992; Beck and Beck-Gernsheim 2002; and Giddens 1990). Nor did it appear that belief in fate was linked to degrees of rationality or to higher or lower levels of reasoning. For example, Caldwell et al. (1992, 1179) argued that an under-reaction to Aids in Africa could be explained by deeply-held beliefs about fate because 'Africa is still in a theological and philosophical transitional state'. That implication of an evolutionary process of modernization is not supported by my study. Africans who accord power to fate may be doing so for the same reasons people in my study did: they are covering the cracks in belonging. Also, as Dawson (2008) discovered in the rapidly modernizing state of Brazil, some forms of religion are increasing. He studied the Brazilian new religion of Santo Daime, largely composed of urban middle-class people who were attracted to traditional themes of millenarianism, and noted that while the urban middle classes did not experience the same conditions of systemic marginalization as rural people, 'their status as urban professionals in contemporary Brazil nevertheless engenders a kind of systemic insecurity' (ibid., 188), fear of a decline in standard of living and status.

In summary, in the above chapter on predestination I have described several kinds of agents to which people accord power. I have argued that the power they accord is over areas where the informant feels least power. Whatever the extent or limitation of the powerful agent, the common strand linking the above informants is their belief in a benign plan or purpose to their lives that they will, to at least some degree, be guided to follow. Whatever created this plan is supra-human and supernatural and yet the agent who communicates the plan, who nudges the informant in the right direction, is almost invariably human.

---

[2] In her research into witchcraft amongst young people in Britain, Cush (2010) observed a gender difference with young men being more explicitly oppositional to Christianity than young women.

7

Boundaries of Belonging:
Doing Unto Ourselves

Terms such as 'moral' or 'ethical' abound in both popular and professional discourse, the former tending to imply overarching truth-based or
'deontic' principles and the latter more situational, practical, 'con-
sequentialist' rules, with each, in practice, overlapping and often used
synonymously. Thus, as Castañeda (2006) points out, the American
Anthropological Association has a 'Code of Ethics', reflecting an apparently non-moral approach to professional conduct. In practice, the
code is embedded in both deontic principles (it is good and worthy to
study people) and consequential rules (ensure one does not harm or
place informants in danger). Heintz (2009, 4) suggests that in academe
morality is evoked to refer to what is 'right' with a deterministic over-
tone, whereas 'ethics' refers to what is chosen by individuals to be
practical and lived. Heintz introduces (ibid.) her edited collection by
saying that such distinctions were not accepted at the outset by contributors, who wanted instead to show how moralities and ethics might
be understood and enacted in different cultures (see also Barker 2007).
Different people might, for example, have different views about what
was individual or societal and what might be constructed as freedom or
choice. For example, in the analysis of my own case study below it will
be evident that perceptions of what is right or wrong vary situationally
amongst my informants and are discussed in terms of abstract, perhaps
deontic, morals as well as practical, everyday acts.

Debates within the sociology of religion centre on whether religion is
necessary for a 'moral' society and whether changing moralities would
illuminate other debates about changing religiosity or secularization.
Implicit in those debates are deeply embedded questions and, I will
suggest, anxieties about meaning, order, and coherence. Those are
themes interwoven throughout this book, beginning in Chapter 1

when links were made between coherence, order, and meaning – apparently inherent needs, summarized by Berger (1967, 22) as 'a human craving for meaning'. Without a sacred canopy of order and meaning, chaos would reign. For example, Wilson (1966) wrote about non-regulated, laissez-faire collections of changing beliefs leading to an inevitable relaxing of moral standards, creating a level of moral freedom that is 'enjoyed by man individually, but is costly to society as a whole' (ibid., 63). The same sentiment was expressed by Ward (1992, 21) who wrote:

> Our whole understanding of morality really does depend upon the existence of God, upon seeing human conduct in the context of a wider spiritual realm, if it is to make sense.

Gill (2001, 291) supports the idea that Christian beliefs are linked to morality, but more specifically suggests that those beliefs are strengthened by regular church attendance: 'attitude data suggest strongly that those who attend monthly have less distinctively Christian beliefs and values than those who attend weekly'. Other studies also link church attendance to morality and even to 'niceness': see, for example, Ellison (1992) and Morgan (1983). Contrary studies are difficult to find, although Allport (1966) argued that some forms of religiosity are strongly associated with prejudice. The role of religion in racism is a complex area replete with contradictory evidence.

Schnapper (1994) argued that prejudice was higher amongst more religious people. Edgell and Tranby (2007) examined a range of attributes including age, gender, ethnicity, and religious affiliation. They found that while the more religiously involved respondents held less progressive views about racial equalities than those who were less religious, they concluded that too little is known about religious sub-cultures and about how wider societal structures shape how people use religious tools.

Given the low levels of regular church attendance in the UK, I expected that most of my informants would not be regular attendees and was interested in how they would describe their morals. As the fieldwork unfolded it became increasingly interesting to me that it was not so much a matter of how people behaved morally, but with whom.

When probing my informants about morality I heard less about belief and more about belonging. For example, people I interviewed said that they have strong moral beliefs about treating people fairly, but it soon became evident that 'people' and 'fair' were not neutral or universal terms. The focus of analysis here is consequently not so much on what morality 'is' but rather on where and with whom people perform it.

Most of my informants clearly distinguish between the people to whom they belong and the people with whom they do not. Their sense of morality was expressed in terms of relationality, particularly amongst family and friends. I suggest this goes beyond a material concern only, an 'amoral familism' as (Banfield 1958) proposed, or an ethos of 'limited goods' (see, for a wider discussion du Boulay and Williams 1987).

Here, I will explore how clues to understanding morality as a key marker of belonging lay in the methods people employed in their narrative performances, using resources of time, space, memory, and shared tropes to help bring into being, however fleetingly, the sense of a shared social identity.

Social code morality

Although I had prepared a question about morality, intending to probe people's ideas about what they believed was right and wrong, the question was sometimes answered immediately in response to my opening question, 'What do you believe in?', demonstrating, I will argue, an explicit link between belief and morality but not religion and morality. For example, Barry, 48, said:

> What do I believe in? Um, I believe in right and wrong, I believe in having good morals, I believe in honour.

The links were also made specifically to how morality was performed through certain social relations, most often with kin, friends, and neighbours. Rarely was there something larger or more concrete, such as 'justice' or 'country', or, as Stewart, 71, a retired accountant, said 'what the laws of the land demand'. The exception was something people often described as 'fairness'; I will turn to an analysis of that in more detail below. First, I will briefly summarize how people described the place and relations of morality, succinctly described by May, 68, a married housewife, who said the right thing was 'to do the right thing to your family, your neighbours, your friends'.

Kin morality

Charlotte, 14, said that 'stealing and stuff' was wrong, but that 'doing stuff for your parents and being good, is good'. Jordan said it was a good thing for him to help his father with the washing up, particularly because he worked the night shift. It was, he said, also good if someone asked to play football, but 'if someone asks "go smash that window" you know that's wrong'. Andrew, a martial arts instructor in his early 20s, related the idea of 'good' to being a good father and partner. James, a 32-year-old policeman, said he believed in the law, and family values. Frances, a 26-year-old advertising executive, engaged to James, said that 'wrong is stealing, murder, affairs, breaking laws. Right is to have an honest life, to work hard, be loyal.'

Friends and neighbour morality

Many people, particularly young people, expressed clear ideas about how to treat others they associate with on a daily basis. Violence was, many young people suggested, always wrong. Gavin, 15, attends a large comprehensive school and lives with his father, a manual worker. He said, 'It's right not to fight with your fists' but better to 'sort it out man to man, not fighting'. He said he had been in trouble on a few occasions for fighting and now believed it was wrong to do so. The rights and wrongs of the school environment were frequently mentioned amongst young people. Gavin's classmate William, 14, said it was right to listen to what other people said and wrong to be 'messing about' in class. Kathleen, 15, said it was wrong to lie, although she admitted she often did when she had not completed her homework on time. Tom said it was wrong to play truant because it would just lead to trouble at school and at home. Kevin, 32, a manual worker, said it was wrong to kill and steal or hurt people and right to be positive, generous, and pleasant. In his work, involving customer deliveries, many people are unpleasant, which makes his job more difficult. Chris, 43, a manufacturing supervisor, said the 'right way' is 'the expected way, shall we say. To blend in with the rest of what's going on.'

   In a similar way, another informant passionately spoke about how he and the people he knows should be treated fairly, irrespective of how much money they make. Bill, 54, a self-employed salesman, said it was important to treat people 'properly' and 'equally'. He said, for example, he always calls people by their first names and expects the same in return. He would never call anyone Mr or Mrs, choosing instead to use the name they were 'christened with'. (I note here his used of the term 'christened': Bill had described himself as an atheist who never went to church.) In his job, he said, he does business with people like managing directors but also meets labourers 'who can barely read or write'. He treats the labourer the same way as he treats the managing director, he said. He would never pass someone he knows without stopping to say hello and he expects the same in return, he said. As he spoke about treating people fairly 'whether they're up there or down there', I asked him what he meant by 'up there' and 'down there'. It seemed to resonate, for me, with an explicit Christian 'golden rule' to do as one would be done by. Bill said he meant someone with money or someone without. This had a startling echo of Burridge's finding (2004, 82) in his fieldwork amongst the 'cargo cults' of Melanesia that the regulating moral force in Tangu life was 'equivalence': 'The ideal was equivalence, neither more nor less, neither "one up" nor "one down".'

Nevertheless, if equivalence in Tangu society is enacted through food, in Yorkshire the resources at stake vary from practical, material goods, such as housing or pensions, to the way people behave with each other in public. Further, as I shall argue, it was not so much equivalence or equality that was being sought as a redress of what is sometimes perceived as unfair distribution of resources to 'others'.

For example, the idea of equality was a strong theme in my interview with Veronica, who is 48 and owns a village shop. She talked at length about her difficult childhood growing up on a council estate in a family of thirteen children with unemployed, alcoholic, abusive parents. She told me several stories about how some people treat her as if she is beneath them, just because they have more money and bigger cars than she does. The contrast, she said, was a certain wealthy female member of the aristocracy, whose family has owned a nearby estate and stately home for generations. Veronica says Lady X is very nice and talks to her 'just the same as anyone else' because she has 'proper money', unlike other people 'with flashy expensive cars' who may have made money recently but 'do not have the right to it'.

For the most part, people's stories were situated in the everyday reality of their social lives. There appeared to be a notable lack of anxiety about any contradictions, instabilities, and changing nature of their moralities. Indeed, many informants emphasized their disinclination to make absolute moral judgements and follow them through absolutely.

Being Christian

Whether people were religious or not, they still tended to share what may be described as 'social morality', whether that was expressed as being nice, law-abiding, or non-violent. Some religious people specifically mentioned the importance of religion as a source of morality, just as some non-religious people criticized religion for being immoral. Charles, 16, who discussed in depth his interest in history, said that people look back to earlier times with a false view of that period's morality. Charles said that in earlier periods when people were more religious, society was less moral than it is today:

> Now in this country I think it's less than one per cent of people go to church every week, but we've got less crime, we don't have 12-year-old prostitutes like we did a couple of hundred years ago, we don't have the same sort of immorality as then and yet religion has declined.

David, 48, recently reaffirmed his faith through being confirmed in the Church of England. When I asked him to describe his view of morality, he said:

> It's being Christian, you know. Like the other day there was an ambulance crew struggling with a patient, when I drove past in my car, so I pulled up and gave him a hand because I think that would be a Christian thing to do, rather than just driving past and thinking, well, I'm not on duty.

He gave other examples of 'being Christian' as helping in the village with local events, such as the annual bonfire and pantomime. Being Christian, he said, is 'doing things for other people. I do the cycling proficiency at the school every year.'

It sometimes made me wonder during these kinds of conversations if people who said their morality derived from Christianity would think non-Christians were immoral. I put that question to John, 51, a teacher.

> One thing, which I almost weep for society, is that society seemingly becomes lost, that even just on the issue of its moral framework, where does it go? Where does it get its moral framework from, so then, this elevates mankind because now we can work out our own moral code, now is a great challenge to humanity to rise to the moment and look into genetics, look into gender issues, look into relationship issues, and we can work the answers out ourselves.

John's reference to 'society' may reflect a deeper theme about other-world/this-world tension reflected in Christian theology, echoed within the sociology of religion discourse about 'pick and mix' or 'do-it-yourself' religion and within a pervasive political discourse beginning with Margaret Thatcher's famous comment that there was no such 'thing' as society, only individuals and families. John spoke further in our interview about how it was wrong for people to try to make their own decisions about, for example, sexuality or reproduction rather than follow what is God-given:

I think there have been huge, huge consequences with the opening of the abortion gate. You look at, and again I think this is a personal take on it, I think there's big issues in the homosexual debate and gender issues there.

The perceived superiority of Christian morality nearly prompted Chris, cited above, to describe himself as a Christian in answer to my census question, despite already having identified himself as an atheist. When, at the end of the interview, I asked him how he had answered the 2001 census question about his religion, he struggled with his answer. After I had read the choices, he said he had ticked 'none', but he added: 'I may be very close to being a Christian. I'd help anybody out, things like that.'

Sarah described herself as Christian. She regularly attends church with her family but talked about some of the difficulties she is experiencing in remaining Christian:

I used to be very judgemental, but now that I'm a teenager, I've learned not to be, so my morals have slightly changed, cuz I am a Christian but the morals that go with being a Christian I don't necessarily agree with now.

One way to understand the difference between religious and non-religious moralities was proposed by Middleton and Putney (1962, 142), who distinguished between social and ascetic moralities. They described 'social standards' as those that proscribe actions seen to be harmful to the social group, such as shoplifting, stealing towels or cutlery from hotels or restaurants, cheating, lying, hitting another person, or unjustly blaming someone else. Ascetic standards, they suggested, are those seen to be 'spiritually harmful to the perpetrator', such as gambling, drinking, looking at pornography, and engaging in extramarital sexual activity. They found that social standards were shared amongst religious and non-religious people 'as part of a general social ideology: The fact that religious ideology may also proscribe these actions is incidental' (ibid., 143).

Absent from the above study, and most of my interviews, was a description of morality as 'doing unto others' when the 'others' were conceived in more abstract terms, such as 'justice' or 'alleviating world poverty'. The exceptions in my study were young females who included environmental issues as morally important and two politically-involved men who described their morality in terms of social justice. Patrick, for example, expressed his view that rights and wrongs were related to wider social issues outside his personal milieu. Those examples illustrate broader, less parochial ways of thinking about morality, but they were not typical. For the most part, people

135

I interviewed were intent upon bringing out the meaning that the people they know and care about are the people with whom they perform their moralities. Yet, whom they define as 'people' requires more examination: it is not a universal term, but is specifically applied to family, friends, and members of what informants variously describe as their community, culture, or society.

Doing unto people like us

I will return now to Barry who said he thought morality was about right, wrong, and honour. When I asked him to expand on what he meant, he did what most people did when I asked such an abstract question: he told me a story. He said that if someone broke into his car and stole something, then he would think that person had done something wrong and should be punished. On the other hand, he continued, if a bank inadvertently credited his account with a large sum of money, he would be tempted to say 'tough luck'. The bank, he explained, has millions of pounds; why should he bring the error to their attention? Yet, he added, 'there's an argument that says there's no difference between those two things'. He offered a further example by saying that it would be wrong for him to rob somebody, but he would probably inflate an insurance claim although he knew it would be wrong to do so. The difference, he explained, lay partly with the nature of the so-called crime, but also with the nature of who was being offended. One was a person, much like himself, while the other was a corporate entity, an international banking organization, which is 'making billions of pounds out of people like you and me'. He said he did not approve of 'unfair' bank charges to which he has been subjected in the past, and therefore did not think it was a particularly bad thing to 'get my own back'. He added that it was probably also possible to do that because the entity was 'an unseen, it's just an image, it's not anybody in particular'. Two arguments are at work to justify his choices. One is about moral entitlement, a defensible evening-out of the score. The corporate entity has, in effect, robbed from him so it is not wrong for him to get some of that money back. It is not the sense of moral entitlement, however, that enables him to act on his feelings. That action was only made possible, he explained, because the entity 'wasn't anyone in particular'. It was, to substitute his words with social science vocabulary, the impersonal, abstract 'other'.

Barry's example reminded me of a similar example I heard about from Becca, 28. Becca spoke strongly about the need to be 'fair', saying,

'It's about how you treat people.' Becca talked about morality by saying some things were right and wrong, and some things were 'grey'. She said, for example, that when she was younger her family would go on holidays and stay in large hotels with buffet breakfasts. Her father would always tell the children to take from the breakfast buffet some bread and cheese for lunch. Other people, she said, would describe that as stealing and would only take what they needed for breakfast, and not more for the rest of the day. Becca said she would not take extra from the buffet in a small hotel because it would affect 'that one person' but she would do it in a big hotel because she knew customers were 'paying over the odds anyway, because they were charging one pound for a bread roll when it doesn't cost that much'. Like Barry, she is distinguishing between a small entity on a more human scale and a larger, more distant, less human organization. This distinction was made more visible when Becca said that while she thought it was justifiable to take bread and cheese from a hotel buffet, she would never steal from a school. I will note here that Becca works in the education sector and therefore I can assume that schools for her are a familiar environment populated by people she knows.

This reminded me of Jenkins' observation (1997, 193) that people 'act in common sense ways to gloss morality and identity in ways that are not trivial'. If at one level of analysis it is apparent that moral actions might apply differently to people like 'us' or impersonal 'others', further analysis revealed the situated particularities of who might be the 'others'.

Ethnic, racialized others

In Chapter 3 I described how May and Robert described themselves as having a 'Christian outlook' on life, although they do not go to church. May said:

> Yeah, we try to respect other people's beliefs, um, if we go to another country we accept their religious beliefs, whatever, we do accept that, but if you're asked to do something because it's their religion, we will do that, because we're in their country.

There was something in her voice as she spoke the above passage that signalled to me an emotion behind the words. I suspected that there was a silent corollary to her logic, that she was also meaning that people who come into 'our' country should act as she says she would in 'their' country. The hidden meaning was something I extracted later in the interview and will discuss in a later section of this chapter. For now, I am reminded of our discussion, detailed in Chapter 3, about how May and Robert thought Muslims treated women badly. The view that 'others' had inferior morals ran through many of my interviews, recalling Anderson's (1983) argument that morality was linked to Englishness in the rise of nationalism. Like Colley (1992), Anderson argued that imagined moral superiority over 'others' was part of 'English' identity, but he linked that rise to nationalism, classism, and colonialism rather than to Protestantism.

A link between morality and nationalism sometimes appeared when informants described 'ethnic others' as either acting in dangerous, immoral ways or receiving what appeared to be better treatment than English people. George, 60, had strong views about morality and entitlement. In answer to my first question, 'What do you believe in?' George said:

> I do believe that I expect people to treat me as I treat them, so if I want to be treated properly by people I will treat them as I expect to be treated.

I inferred from his answer that if people treat George as he expects to be treated, he will treat them likewise. Later in the interview he expanded on 'who' he was talking about by saying: 'I'm not a great believer in this positive discrimination that goes on nowadays, but neither am I a sort of a racist in a sense.' George then related to me an event that occurred when he was working in a senior position in Burnley and an Asian man applied to him for a job for which he was not qualified. George said that the man had just graduated from university with a degree in American Studies, had no accountancy background, and had applied for a job as a senior accountant. That possibility was so far-fetched and unlikely to be true that I nearly challenged George, but, as with so many other belief narratives I heard, I decided to listen for the meaning his exaggeration was illustrating. The story continued. George told me he did not shortlist the man for an interview, with the result that the applicant accused him of being racist. In relating the story, George's voice began to rise, his face tensed, and he clenched his fists. If he had passed the man in the street, he exclaimed, 'I would have cut him straight, if I had seen him in the street I would have cut him, that's how I would have been.' As he repeated the phrase and spat the words out, I had to remind myself that he was using the word 'cut' to mean 'ignore', not physically to do any harm. He added, his voice beginning to calm, that this was not because he was racist; he would have felt the same if the applicant had been a white man. He continued by saying he felt everyone should be treated the same.

Later in the interview George expanded on his theme that all people should be treated equally by referring to a project of economic regeneration in Burnley:

> Then you got political correctness coming in, that's what I mean, political correctness, a lot of money was spent on deprived communities mainly in Burnley, of course Asian communities. The poor white communities weren't keen on that.

He explained that the 'poor white' response to Asians receiving money was to vote for the National Front. I asked if the backlash in favour of the National Front could have been avoided and he said yes, 'If you treat people as a person not for what they are. Just as people and that's it.' He told the story in such an unbroken way that it led me to assume that George has probably told the story many times, and exaggerated certain aspects. In an unsympathetic, firm, sometimes punitive tone he is expressing his anger that the 'others', in this case poor 'Asians', apparently receive more public resources than people like himself. Similar to the belief in 'fairness' discussed above, George's belief in equality demarcates boundaries, acts to rebalance power, and calls for reciprocity.

George, and others I interviewed, usually say they are not racist before raising points about 'political correctness' or immigration. I sensed this keenly partly through my own experience as a white, middle-class immigrant. In many interviews the topic of immigration was raised, yet no one appeared uncomfortable to be talking about immigration negatively in the presence of an immigrant like me. An example is my interview with Rick, 20, to whom I referred in Chapter 3. Like George, he ignored the fact that I was an immigrant and talked at length about the problems of 'Asians' who 'claim off me'. His reference to elderly people who do not have adequate pensions while 'we pay a lot of taxes to keep these immigrants and that in our country' echoed almost verbatim the sentiments of Veronica, discussed in Chapter 3. She objected to 'asylum seekers' who come into 'this country' and have everything they want 'made easy for them', while there are 'old people living just down the road who will be cold this winter'. People described as 'asylum seekers' were often mentioned by informants as undesirable 'others' unfairly receiving resources. The trope of elderly people being neglected in favour of asylum seekers who are not 'genuine' is one that runs through protests about asylum seekers elsewhere.

Grillo (2005, 236) reported on a seaside town's protests against a proposed asylum centre in south-east England. One of the placards at a demonstration read: 'Homes for our elderly not for phoney asylum seekers.' An elderly person said (ibid.): 'We're scared to death. Everybody in these flats is over 80 and some are in their 90s. Some say they'll be afraid to go to the post office and get their pension.' Grillo observed in his study that negative discourse about asylum seekers has been increasing over recent years and tends to include claims that the objection is not racist, but reflects concern for the ability of the locale to absorb increased newcomers.

He concluded that the protests contained coded signifiers, or hidden narratives, about disease, crime, and degradation that reflect historical racialized prejudices. A similar study by Hubbard (2005) reached the same conclusions after analysing a protest movement opposing the construction of an asylum centre in Newton in Nottinghamshire, UK. Hubbard conducted a content analysis of the letters of protest and concluded that the main themes were related to issues about the asylum seekers themselves, not to the economic or environmental impact. Protestors referred to being afraid for the safety of women and children walking the streets, with asylum seekers who might 'wander round our villages looking for trouble' (ibid., 59) 'with no thought for our customs or culture' (ibid., 60). Like Grillo, Hubbard found that the 'discourses of opposition' were racist in nature, despite the frequent claims of the protestors that they were not racist.

The language of uncivilized, alien peoples threatening civilized people is a key component of racist discourse, argued Gilroy (1987). In what he describes as the 'new racism' Gilroy (ibid., 43) said that a populist view of 'race' was illustrated by Enoch Powell's 'river of blood speech' of April 1968, with which 75 per cent of the population, in at least one survey, registered their support. Gilroy argues that the careful coding of Powell's rhetoric helped push 'race' from a discussion about colour and immigration to a more complex discourse linking multiple themes of 'patriotism, nationalism, xenophobia, Englishness, Britishness, militarism and gender difference' (ibid.).

This complexity characterized my interviews when people discussed 'race'[1] in typically coded terms of wild, dangerous interlopers. Marge, a 75-year-old widow who has lived all her life in the same area, does not feel her own streets are safe anymore. She says she used to be able to leave her door open when she talked with neighbours across the road or went to the shop, but now she locks her front door when she goes

---

[1] In common with current anthropological and sociological practice I use 'race' with inverted commas to signify that I do not recognize its validity as a means to classify people but rather as a term to describe the act of so doing. The tendency to avoid using 'race' in anthropology may have led to a discussion instead about 'ethnicity', but both are unstable, contested categories. See Harrison (1995) for a comprehensive review.

outside to her dustbin at the back of the house. While Marge said she cannot venture outside her door for fear of the others, Barry felt that his small village was safe but the next town, Keighley, about three miles away, was more populated with 'Asians': 'we're talking about no-go areas'. Many of my informants talked about the perceived boundaries between their homes and nearby places like Keighley, Bradford, and Burnley, home to large immigrant populations. Andrew had told me he was not religious and did not believe in God (although he did, as I discussed in Chapter 5, communicate with his deceased grandfather), but he invoked God when describing what he found to be a troubling inter-ethnic, non-Christian relationship:

> You never know what might happen – look at my uncle. He died young, in his 30s, left two daughters and his wife. A really lovely family. Then his daughter started going out with this Asian guy from Bradford and now they're together and have twins. Her mother's gone off the rails. If there was a God, how would he let that happen?

Penny, 60, a retired social services manager, said that she would not walk on her own out of the small town where she lives about three miles from Keighley:

> I once walked up there, on my own, a few years since, about seven years since, and when [her *husband, George*] came home at night he said to me 'I'd prefer it if you wouldn't go up there because I think it's quite dangerous for a young woman up there'. And I don't walk on my own up there now because it is, sort of, if someone came, I wouldn't be scared of walking up there, I'd be scared of, if, putting myself in a position when someone might come along in a car and drag me into the car.

The idea that Penny would be attacked by someone in a car reinforces the common theme from my interviews that criminals come from elsewhere. Most of my informants refer to crimes committed in their local communities by people who do not live there but come from, typically, nearby towns with large immigrant populations. Barry, for example, said that people in nearby poor areas come to small towns and villages like the one he lived in from Leeds because:

> they don't steal off each other, they go to different areas to steal. It's where all, well not all, but a lot of the villains and thieves and vagabonds live. They don't steal on their own doorsteps. They go to other areas.

Marge believes the same: 'Fellas from out of town what's done it.' She referred at one point to the criminals as 'rogues' and said if someone broke into her flat it would be so contaminated (polluted, as Douglas (1966) might observe) that she would be forced to leave forever. The emotion conveyed in the language Barry and Marge use, the antiquated terms of 'vagabonds' and 'rogues', and the deeply felt horror Marge expressed about her space being invaded by such people suggest this is an emotional connection which runs far deeper than simply an opinion about who or what is good or bad. The language is of an earlier time, a lawless, uncivilized era where 'rogues' and 'vagabonds' roamed the streets. Here, my informants position their locale at the edge of a frontier that is slowly being invaded by uncivilized hordes. The invaders, it is evident from their coded language, are the 'Asians' who live in Leeds, Burnley, Bradford, and Keighley.

Absent from the above discussion were the views of the student cohort I interviewed. As I discussed in Chapter 4, notions of 'race' and ethnicity did not arise other than in the context of racism and 'hate' being wrong. While this does not prove that young people are not racist, it may indicate that at least the expression of racist beliefs is more socially acceptable amongst older people than younger.

I will now turn to another stigmatized group, young people, who were also identified as having different and threatening beliefs to older informants. These were not, however, the young people in the families of my informants but 'other' young people with whom they do not belong.

Young others

George, just cited, told me a story echoing, almost verbatim, the story of another man more than ten years his junior. Both George, 60, and Barry, 48, talked about the days in small villages when life was better: there was always a local policeman then who knew all the children and would report to the children's father if any were misbehaving. Also, neighbours would see what children were doing and would also report on their behaviour. Nowadays, both said, the policemen are gone from the villages and people who live there do not know each other anymore and are often not home during the day. The difference to which they are referring here is that women are no longer home during the day because they are working. Specifically, I suggest, it is the absence of male dominance that Barry and George are noting. Barry described it thus:

> I well remember a village I used to live in where the village bobby used to put the fear of God into all the kids, and if they misbehaved, he used to give them a clip around the ear. And you went home and said PC so-and-so gave me a slap because I was pinching apples out a tree, and so on, and my father

would say quite right, and I'll give you another slap. Whereas now, you wouldn't be able to do that.

His story was tinged with his nostalgia for an earlier time of male corporeal authority.

Both George and Barry employed the same tropes as the Nottingham protestors cited above: children played in the streets, old ladies could safely walk home at any time of day or night, and the world was a safer, friendlier place.

Vera, an 83-year-old widow and former housewife, living in sheltered housing, said in answer to the first question that she believed in the church and her faith which she described as being 'the church, the Church of England'. She continued that she believed in 'fair play' and honesty. She added that young people today behave differently from the young people of her generation. This makes it difficult for her to get along with them, she said, although she tries to be 'fair-minded' and non-judgemental. It became apparent in our interview, as I will discuss later, that she was often judgemental and critical about young people.

According to many of my older informants, young people today are both immoral and disrespectful of authority. This contrasts with my findings, summarized above, where I found that the social code rights and wrongs young people discuss are the same as those described by older people. Young people believe in treating people well and not killing or stealing. They believe in doing well at school and getting a job afterwards or continuing to university. Even the most radical amongst them respect authority when they perceive it to be legitimate, as I discussed earlier in relation to Charles, the young 'anarcho-communist' who respected authorities in the field and credited his school for his knowledge about history. Older informants, however, have views about young people that suggest that young people lead lazy lives showing no respect for others. What they mean by 'others' tends to imply older people like themselves. Vera said that young people today lack self-discipline and expect to earn money for doing little. This is mainly because they do not have enough discipline at home and in the schools, she said. Given that women are the ones usually charged with raising children, I suggest here that Vera's criticism of young people is also a criticism of their mothers. I will discuss this further in the section below. Here, I will note how Vera also mentioned that young people swear loudly on the streets, which offends her. I heard a similar comment from Margaret, 74, a housewife who moved to the area seven years ago to nurse her dying daughter. She said the changing role of women, and the behaviour of young women, is something she finds 'frightening'. She called young women 'creatures' and spoke vehemently about how offensive she finds their swearing: 'that to me, in a young girl is still totally unacceptable'. More than simply disagreeing with the changing role of women, Margaret is emotionally distressed by it. She said, 'The female frightens me now, because I think she's changing.' Other older people described young people as disrespectful. May and Robert told me about how young people today do not give up their seats to older people on buses or trains. Robert said:

> When I was a teen, when the train halts, I think every child from the age of 10 would have stood up on a bus when an older person came in. They don't today.

The above examples reinforced for me the idea that young people were behaving in ways that offended their elders because they behaved in ways that did not demonstrate respect for the apparent authority of their elders. The older people, particularly the men, assume they deserve respect because of their age and, I suggest, their gender.

Apart from young people and ethnic others, the third category of people that arose frequently in discussion of good and bad morals was women. This was particularly striking in light of the way that women, particularly mothers, are often revered in discussion. I will analyse this apparent contradiction in more depth below.

Bad mothers

Women frequently are blamed for the downfall of society, in my study as in others. Dilger (2008, 216) showed how women in rural Tanzania are blamed for the spread of AIDS. The people Dilger studied maintain regulations to protect the stability of society. Of particular concern, Dilger noted with reference to Douglas (1966), is how to define with whom, where, and when one might have sexual relations, because transgressing those boundaries will lead to contagion and the breakdown of society. As men die in increasing numbers, young women begin to fill roles in business and commerce, leading to a blurring of gender boundaries. In response, Dilger says (ibid.), 'A morally conservative discourse on sexuality and gender relations has evolved' with women being accused of having excessive sexual desires leading to promiscuity, the breakdown of family units, and the spread of Aids.

In Larner's (1984) review of Scottish witchcraft trials in the eighteenth, seventeenth, and sixteenth centuries she shows that witchhunts were not random but coincided with other specific movements in popular beliefs and anxieties, such as the rise of the ideology of the Christian nation-state. The identity of those accused of witchcraft was also not random, but primarily reserved for older women. Other studies (in particular, Macfarlane 1970) stress the link between witchcraft and social tensions.

I mention those studies to foreground the findings in my own case study: women were frequently blamed in interviews for acting in ways that differ from the roles they held in society in a previous generation. This, many people argue, resulted in a general breakdown in the family unit, leading to an increase in bad behaviour amongst young people. I will suggest that Yorkshire women are seen as the carriers of moral purity in ways similar to contemporary women in Tanzania and Scottish and English women in the middle ages. This theme will be revisited in the next chapter when I examine what people identify, and protect, as the sources of their beliefs.

The idea that women's roles have changed arose in many interviews when people referred to the values they were raised with being different from those today. It is a change that unsettles some people, like Margaret. She said that her generation accepted that 'you did the washing, you looked after the kids', and women had taken on that role, which, she said, she thinks is the most responsible job possible. She had stayed at home raising her children, even when they had little money. This might be, she said, 'a bit old fashioned' but she believes that a wife is 'first and foremost a mother, and if we all did that job you wouldn't get these creatures that I no longer recognize'. She makes a causal link between young women using bad language and their not being raised properly because their mothers do not stay at home.

Mary, 54, is a technical assistant at the local hospital. She is married to Gary, a lorry driver, whom I also interviewed. They have an adult son. Mary said she thought women today had a different idea of commitment to husbands and families than they had twenty or thirty years ago. She said her father had left home a few times and her mother had taken him back when he returned because women did not think they had a choice in those days. They did not think they could earn a living on their own, she said, but had to be looked after by a man: 'I think that's altered a lot. I think it's practically turned itself around, really,' she said. Mary continued her discussion about women's roles by saying that more women work nowadays and can be 'career-minded' and 'self-sufficient'. She added that she is uncertain whether that is a good or a bad thing. She said she had chosen to remain home with her child until he went to school, and then had worked part-time from home to be with him. Her mother made the same choice. Today, she said, children are not being brought up to have good manners or respect for other people, and with both parents working no one seems to know that their children might be misbehaving. This not only affects those children, but the children of people who are trying to raise them properly, she said. Her own son 'altered' when he went to secondary school, she said, becoming friends with other children who were not raised properly.

Other informants also blamed women for influencing a change of values and behaviour. Barry, cited above, blamed women for how society has changed 'beyond all recognition, really'. Barry described himself, echoing Margaret, as 'an old-fashioned person' who knew he should behave with honour and loyalty. Those are values that 'seem to be disappearing from our world', he said. He said he had been brought up to:

> hold doors open for women. And all of that kind of thing seems to be disappearing a bit. And no one has time for anyone else anymore. It's a very selfish world that we live in.

I infer from him that it is women who do not have time for people and who are selfish. The word 'self' either as selfish or self-sufficient recurred in interviews when people talked about women. It is seen to be wrong for women to be concerned with focusing on their own 'selves' instead of others. The virtues of the selfless woman were widely discussed, whether the informant was male or female. The selflessness both genders thought was appropriate for women appears to be exclusively for women. The same concept did not arise about men, even when men talked about their families being important. They never talked about situations when they sacrificed themselves for their families in the same way that women do. Neither men nor women raised a changing role of men as contributing to problems in society. This is clearly not a 'gender' issue but an exclusively 'female' issue. It is also one that appears to cross socio-economic lines and reaches down through the generations. Katherine, for example, is a 26-year-old single department secretary who has lived at home with her parents, both professionals, until recently when she moved in with her boyfriend. When we were discussing morality, she said she thought her morals resulted from her parents' influence. The influence of parents in raising children properly is very important, she explained, and she feels concerned that this is changing now. She explained that: 'Yeah, I think perhaps, there seems to be a lot more people getting pregnant nowadays, at a younger age, who perhaps can't look after the children.'

She continued in the same vein, explaining that 'people' go out more, socializing to the detriment of their children:

> People seem to go out more, be more sociable, have their friends around, get drunk, more than perhaps when I was younger. So, it seems to me that perhaps children are put into positions sometimes that they shouldn't be in, like, people take them to pubs and things, and the swearing that goes on.

Both Vera and Margaret express their distaste for young women swearing. The portrait of the 'good woman' is one who does not swear, drink too much, or socialize to the point she neglects her children. Nicola positions herself as such a woman. I had quoted her earlier as saying that if she had a spare day and no one to look after she would not know what to do. Marge, also discussed earlier, had said she spends most of her time helping her children, now in their forties and fifties, with their own children or households. Laura, a 23-year-old single receptionist who lives with her parents, said that 'right is trying to abide by the law and trying to keep everybody happy, not just yourself'. Lindsay, a 14-year-old student at a comprehensive school whose parents own their own small business, said she prays and she believes God answers her prayers unless it was a 'selfish' prayer. When I asked her what she meant by a selfish prayer she said that it would be about something just to do with oneself and not anyone else. While I am drawing links here between gender and selflessness, I note similar findings from another study (Collins-Mayo 2008) amongst 11-to-23-year-old young people in the UK that found young people generally prayed for other people, particularly family.

Viv, 54, described being 'good' as 'being loving and caring towards other people, definitely. Thinking of others before you think of yourself'. Fran said she thought being morally good was 'not behaving selfishly or greedily'. Evil was 'something you do for yourself that upsets other people'. Nicola, 37, said being moral was remembering others. For example, she said, she might be at the pub enjoying herself one evening and might like to have another drink, but realizes she can't because she needs to get back to see her children:

> My morals say I've got to go because my children need me there, they need me back. If I didn't have the kids it would be a different moral altogether, wouldn't it? I'd only have myself to think about and I'd probably stay there till I dropped down – and that's only one aspect.

Having another drink in the pub would be either good or bad depending on how other people would be affected, she explained. Making those judgements is not something she seems to take lightly, adding,

'My morals are treat people as you treat yourself. I know it doesn't happen all the time, but I try to think it a lot of the time.' Nicola is not only talking about morality being context-dependent, but being specifically dependent on the people affected by her moral choices, a version of 'doing as you would be done by'.

Barbara, 69, a retired cook, nursed her terminally ill husband for several years and also cared for her elderly parents. Margaret, discussed above, described herself as nursing her daughter when she was dying of cancer. She did not mention her own husband or her daughter's husband contributing to that task. The labour of caring for others seems to be exclusively female both in perception and in practice. What people criticize is what they see as a change away from that, where women will no longer be carrying out that labour. In the absence of women carrying it out, the proposition that men might do it instead is not raised. This work is evidently perceived as woman's labour, and when she chooses to withdraw it, everyone suffers. If women are not performing roles of carers and men are not picking up that task, then it will not be done and children, sick people, and other vulnerable members of society will be cared for less.

In a small-scale qualitative study of thirty-six middle-class couples (Jordan et al. 1994) the same finding regarding gender responsibilities arose: men and women alike do not question women's roles as primary carers of the young, the husbands, the infirm, and the elderly. This may help explain the apparent contradiction between statements about wonderful mothers, spoken with tenderness and regard, and bad mothers, as discussed above. Women are described in terms related to domestic labour and in that context are revered when they perform it. When women withdraw that labour or at least behave in ways that show they have turned attention away from their families and to themselves, they are reviled.

Further, I found no criticism of the structural inequalities and lack of societal support for lone mothers pervading Euro American countries (with the notable exception of Scandinavia: see, for example, Christopher et al. 2002; Zuckerman 2008). Lone mothers are aware of their precarious position in society. Hannah, introduced in Chapter 5, is a 35-year-old mother of four children, heavily pregnant with her fifth child, who teaches maths part-time and runs her own hairdressing business. The pressure of work and family commitments sometimes makes life difficult, she explained, but she would not choose to live differently. When I asked her my first question, 'What do you believe in?', she said the question made her immediately think about values and morals, particularly family values. For her, belief triggered thoughts about ultimate value or meaning, rather than doctrine or creeds. She said that by 'family' she meant herself and her children. She said that although she had very strong ideas about morality, this might appear as 'a contradiction in terms'. She continued, saying, 'Being a divorcee, I do have quite big family values.' I asked her why she thought that might be a contradiction and she replied, 'Well, you kind of think, how can I have big family values when I'm a single parent?' I note not only that she understands belief in terms of social and personal values, but also that she is conscious of how she is using the term and is able to comment reflexively on it.

The juxtaposition Hannah was posing between family values and divorce reminded me of several theorists who argue that a change in family structure caused by divorce or by mothers working outside the home leads to moral decline in society. For example, Wilson (2001, 44–5) referred to the modern family being 'split apart' with parents insufficiently present to take a role in the moral inculcation of their children. This, he says, is not only because family structures have changed but also because individuals are being encouraged today to 'discover their own identities', to 'be themselves', to 'do their own thing'. The, I suggest, hidden code here is that women are 'doing their own things'. Davie (1994, 3) also relates changes in the family to changes of morality, saying that: 'the nature of family life, including the traditional codes of morality, are altering rapidly'. Not sure how to reconcile the apparent contrast between what I had read and what Hannah was saying, I decided to put the problem to her. I said that, yes, some people do link changing family structures to changing moral codes, and what did she think about that? She said that she thought that when people get married and have children, they bring them up in a family unit and they say, 'This is the correct way to go.' When, however, that unit breaks down, 'you've got to sort of re-examine the way . . . the way you make it all right to them'. She explained: 'I don't think it's that your morals change, so much, but your way of life has to change slightly, and you're far more answerable to children if you're on your own with them.'

Here, the changed family structure increased her feelings of account-ability towards her children. I found a similar strength of feeling about responsibility towards children in another interview with a divorced woman. Nicola, cited above, is a 37-year-old mother of two young children. Although she lives with a partner, she never discussed him in our interview in terms of her role as a parent. She said her purpose in life was 'to bring my family up', to look after her children until they leave home, at which point she will spend more time on herself. Until then, she said, if she had a spare day and no one to look after, she would not know what to do. She explained why:

And that's because I don't spend a lot of time on myself. I might have a bath, I might do my toe nails, I might take the dog out, but that's about it. I don't really – I can't remember what I like to do.

Throughout our interview she returned to her narratives about being caregiver, not attending to her own needs, but looking after her family. The family appears here to consist of herself and her children, with her role being to spend time on them rather than herself. Her comments, together with Hannah's, bear little resemblance to the picture of mothers abandoning children in favour of 'doing their own thing'.

Social tension and moral panic

The above section demonstrated how my informants often raised the spectre of an 'other', often ethnically/racially constituted, young, or female, as responsible for immoral behaviour. By marking clearly the boundaries of 'them' and 'us', and by attributing social problems to 'them', my informants are essentializing and demonizing the 'others'. This not only legitimizes their distaste for the 'others' through providing a scapegoat, it also excuses the informant for not accepting responsibility for social problems. It is the act of essentializing which is the core of discourse about others and deviance, argues Young (1999, 104): 'Essentialism is a paramount strategy of exclusionism: it separates out human groups on the basis of their culture or nature.' Criminal or other behaviour viewed as anti-social is a ready marker to reinforce essentialism and demonization. Following Bauman (1992) I conclude that the act of allowing difference without actively engaging with that difference is partly a device to maintain distance, where people can fail to 'acknowledge not just the *otherness* of the other, but the legitimacy of the other's interests and the other's right to have such interests respected and, if possible, gratified' (ibid., xxi–xxii). This makes such apparent beliefs in equality and fairness reduced to beliefs in equality and fairness amongst people like themselves, in particular, amongst the dominant group of white men. I will argue below that how people attribute the sources of their beliefs provides insights into how they legitimate authority and power.

The act of attributing negative attributes to the 'other' can be explained in several ways. Not only did my informants allude to their friends and families for confirming moral categorization, they presented such behaviour as rooted in seemingly fixed categories of, for example, gender and ethnicity. That claim to common-sense, inherent, unchosen, natural, or pure identity also recalls Anderson's comment (1983, 131) about people having a 'halo of disinterestedness' when they make such claims, particularly when their views about 'others' could otherwise be seen as reprehensible.

The conformity of my informants' vocabulary, and the common tropes upon which they drew, may reflect what they read and listen to in the popular press. Anderson (1983) argued that it was the novel and the newspaper that permitted the rise of nationalism and the promotion of certain values deemed to be English. Cohen (1972) stressed the important role of the mass media in communicating 'moral panics'. In his study of English 'mods and rockers', he identified scapegoating, or the formation of folk devils who bear the cultural anxieties of a certain time. Mason (1995, 112) also refers to the 'moral panics' incited by media-supported stereotypes which relate crime to immigration and certain peoples. The region I studied borders two sites, Bradford and Burnley, of riots in 2001 related to racial tensions. One study (Ray and Smith 2004) argued that such tensions and the related violence were exacerbated by discourse in the locale, particularly in the media, that accentuated and reinforced ethnic differences.

Hunt (1997) summarized three theories about how moral panics occur and spread: cultural anxiety theory (where moral panics mask deeper cultural anxieties), the elite-hegemony theory (where powerful interests fuel panics to divert attention), and the grass-roots theory (where people are responding to real, not imaginary, incidences of crime or injustice). Those three theories seem to play through most of my interviews, although the cultural anxiety and grass-roots theories have predominated in this chapter. What I observed was not a 'panic' but a tendency to allocate blame to, in their minds, well-defined others. Nevertheless, any of the above theories will need to stretch to accommodate what I observed as the agent-directed, socially located, performative nature of morality. As I discussed in Chapter 1, Firth (1948) explored how individuals created and manipulated beliefs by using their beliefs as modes of action to manage the sometimes contradictory demands and positions between an individual's social and physical context, and her own 'set of impulses, desires and emotions' (ibid., 26). Further, it was not so much the content of moral beliefs that distinguished some informants from others, but rather where they located the source of those beliefs: it is the identification of that source that provides the most important boundary and means of social reproduction.[2]

That most of my informants are confident about locating that source in their everyday, changing environments is clear. Robbins (2009) studied how the Urapmin, a people of the Sanduan region of Papua New Guinea, adapted forms of Christianity during a period of rapid social change. He points out (ibid., 74–6) that Urapmin moral consciousness pervaded all aspects of daily life; and suggests that such heightened awareness of morality results from the experience of cultural change and tension between two competing logics: Protestant individualism and Urapmin relationalism. Robbins concludes that people who find themselves trying to reconcile competing cultural logics will seek to apply morality to even the minutiae of daily life. Nobody in my study has told me that morality does not matter, only that it is a matter in many cases of deciding on each issue in a particular context. Sometimes, people chose to focus on 'others' as those people thought to be held responsible for social problems. In doing so they engaged in a process of categorization between the 'in' and 'out' groups (see, for example, Tajfel and Turner 1986). That process seemed to happen collectively: their polyvocal narratives of morality explicitly referred to other people close to them who apparently shared the same ideas about morality and common tropes about who was responsible for moral and immoral behaviour.

---

[2] See Bialecki (2008) for a detailed example of how Vineyard Christians in southern California reconcile their relationship with money through shifting applications of the related concepts of stewardship and sacrifice.

Section 3
Relocating Belief and Belonging

In this final section, the data from the fieldwork and cross-cultural comparisons are used to develop more general vocabulary and more useful analytical categories. Chapter 8 discusses how an orientation to believing in belonging to either the human or divine captures the mood of the mainstream more clearly than apparent divisions between 'religious' and 'secular'. Further, it is argued that belief is best understood not as a single statement reflecting its content, but through at least seven dimensions in an holistic, organic, framework. Chapter 9 returns to an opening question in this book relative to why otherwise non-religious people may choose a religious affiliation. That understanding helps inform an under-explored phenomenon described as Christian nominalism, arguably the largest form and fastest-growing style of Christian belief and belonging in the world. The final chapter summarises key findings and seeks to bring the book's empirical and theoretical arguments together in a substantial rethinking about belief and identity.

8

Theorizing Belief: A Holistic, Organic, Seven-Dimensional Model

The preceding five chapters introduced portions of informants' cos-mologies through the core empirical data gathered initially in northern England and then compared with some cross-cultural examples. What has become clear is that belief means different things to different people and varies according to the social context. That insight presents a problem first raised in Chapter 1: if belief is different according to places, people, and times, how do we identify it, define it, measure it, or compare it cross-culturally? We could ignore it, of course, heeding Needham's advice (1972, 188):

> The notion of belief is not appropriate to an empirical philosophy of mind or to an exact account of human motives and conduct. Belief is not a discriminable experience, it does not constitute a natural resemblance among men, and it does not belong to 'the common behaviour of mankind'.

On the other hand, as social scientists we are not engaged primarily in 'an empirical philosophy of mind', nor would we try to create an 'exact account' of anything so messy as human motives or behaviour. Further, we would not assume that belief is 'a natural resemblance' or a 'common behaviour' or employ it 'as a term of universal application' (ibid., 206). We need to do something more socio-scientific, and simply dropping it in favour of another blanket term, such as 'faith', only takes us to the same problematic place. Further, while belief is not universal or ahistorical, it is, howsoever defined, important to the people at the heart of this book – Euro Americans – for all the historic, Christian-centric reasons Asad (1993) identified. To them – to *us* as the case must be for me and my colleagues researching religion – belief is a term, rightly or wrongly, used frequently in our disciplines by informants and researchers to describe and even measure religiosity – yet it is also, particularly within sociology, remarkably unexplored. As Lindquist and Coleman (2008) discussed, such a term, while problematic, is too important to be dismissed and therefore must be 'written against', by which they meant, properly historicized and contextualized. Nevertheless, the question remains, how should we do that? We needed an interpretive method to allow us to analyse cross-culturally and compare what belief means to different people in different places at different times. The seven-part heuristic I developed explored not just the content but also sources, practice, salience, function, place, and time. Analysing belief holistically and organically helped me to resolve what I introduced at the outset of this work as the 'census question' puzzle: why would so many non-religious people choose to claim a Christian identity on the census? Applying that analytical framework helped me identify two prominent belief orientations: anthropocentric and theocentric. I will summarize briefly here what I mean by those 'orientations'.

Belief orientations: anthropocentric and theocentric

As I first summarized in Chapter 2, what became quickly obvious after the first few interviews, and maintained consistency throughout, is that most people believe in their relationships with other people. Those I interviewed did not generalize about 'people' but were specific about the sorts of people who were important to them: these people are those with whom they have adherent, affective reciprocal relationships, most commonly partners, family, and friends. With those people, as I discussed in Chapter 7, they believe it is important to act morally, which for the most part meant treating people as they would like to be treated. From those people, they trace their moral heritage and consider the roots and the formation of their beliefs to be a result of those personal relationships and the experiences they have had with those relationships.

The majority of people I interviewed rarely talked about God or other divine beings. They generally think the universe was created by a 'big bang' to be explained one day by 'science', believe that when they die they do not go to another place such as heaven, and if they are asked a forced question about religion and answer 'Christian' they do so, as I discuss more fully in the next chapter, because of family or 'ethnic' reasons. While I was tempted to describe those people as 'humanists' to reflect the primacy of their beliefs in human beings, and to add to an existing body of knowledge that such people are 'secular' in their scientific and rational beliefs, they have slightly confounded those bounded categories by their enduring beliefs in spirits. I have explored, particularly in Chapters 5 and 6, how many of these same people believe that their dead relatives watch over them, talk to them, guide them, and sometimes protect them. Some believe that such influence covers them with a protective canopy under which all is well, preordained, and meant to be. For the most part, they are reluctant to call that influence 'God': some who believe in the eternal influence of their relatives are affirmed atheists. Their orientation was to people, not to gods, and thus *anthropocentric* seems to convey best the idea that human beings are 'centric' to their lives and it is with them they locate power and authority.

A minority of people were markedly different when they discussed the content of their beliefs. As I discussed in Chapter 2, this minority responded either immediately or very soon into the interview that they believed in God. They also tended to say at different times in the interview that their most important relationship was with God, indicating that their God-belief was highly salient. The way they described their moral beliefs was often spoken in reference to what God would want. This theocentric type of discourse never occurred with the anthropocentrics. This minority also described their relationship with God as the overarching canopy, protecting them and giving them meaning in their lives; one day they would be united with him in heaven. They tend not to have contact with the spirits of their dead relatives. They, like the anthropocentrics, had strong human relationships but they did not describe those relationships as the centre of their beliefs and therefore I have described them as 'theocentric'. It is their orientation rather than their practice here that I am identifying. That theocentrics practice relationality even while their discourse subordinates it is a theme dealt with extensively elsewhere – see, for example, Day (2005) and Bielo (2008) – and often requires subtle and strenuous work to reconcile theological and experiential positions.[1]

In summary, anthropocentrics articulate their beliefs primarily in reference to their human relationships. Unless coaxed into seeing belief in non-religious terms, they may say that they believe in 'nothing', as if they do not regard their human-centred beliefs in the same category as religious beliefs. Theocentrics cite God and their relationship to him as central to their lives.

Below, I will relate in more detail how I reached those conclusions through deconstructing people's belief narratives and analysing them

---

[1] Elisha (2008) discusses, for example, ethical dilemmas facing Christians involved in activism.

through the holistic, organic, seven-dimensional model. The way people described beliefs was not typically through coherent, cognitively-based belief statements, but stories with real characters, plots, and emotional content: holistic belief narratives. Like Good (1994) in his exploration of narratives of illness, I was to learn that rich examples, emplotment, characters, and multiple viewpoints are characteristic of such narratives. People did not typically articulate their beliefs in grammatically grand language or in flat, rehearsed creedal monotones; their belief narratives were polyvocal, enlivened with the stories and voices of other people, alive or dead, who meant something to them – in whom they 'believe'. In deconstructing the narratives, I learned that their stories were about themselves and other people, not about beliefs in terms of creedal statements. This may reflect a shift from a propositional, content-oriented form of belief to a form that is multidimensional and expresses faith and trust as discussed in Chapter 1 (see also, for example, Robbins 2003, 2007; Ruel 1982).

The practice of using multidimensional models for religiosity is widely accepted, beginning with Malinowski's analysis of the Kula's beliefs and behaviours (1961 [1922]) and his later reflections (2002 [1935]) on the ritual properties of language. Glock and Stark (1965) proposed that the religiosity of a congregation could be analysed by considering five dimensions: belief, practice, experience, knowledge, and consequences. In considering how their model would apply to an analysis of belief, rather than religiosity, and to a person, rather than a congregation, I encountered problems in analytically separating belief from knowledge, experience, or consequences. Further, my informants' narratives did not correspond to such distinctions or cognitive 'belief systems' as described by, for example, Borhek and Curtis (1975) and nor did they seem to reflect a coherent, shared system of symbols that would reflect how Geertz (1973, 112) defined religion, as a cultural system whose sacred symbols inspire people's 'moods and motivations'. It was more plausible to consider belief more in terms of 'worldview', as Smart (1998) so described in his multidimensional approach to analysing religion.

Seven dimensions of belief

I will now turn from the generalized to the particular/empirical through revisiting several key encounters mentioned in preceding chapters to illustrate how I interpreted those data through a holistic, organic belief framework and concluded that there were, broadly, two separate belief orientations of anthropocentric and theocentric.

Content

This is the 'what' of people's beliefs. As discussed in Chapter 2, while some people needed initially to contextualize their beliefs before describing them, most people I interviewed were willing to state what their beliefs were and then elaborate at length. Anthropocentrics and theocentrics may sometimes share the same 'content'.

Gemma, 14, said that she thought God had created the universe. At a cursory glance, we might therefore say that the content of her belief reflects a belief in God. Yet, she continued the conversation by saying 'don't, like, worship him or anything'. Gemma might likely qualify as a 'God-believer' on a survey, but in our interview I heard the tone of her voice, as she said 'don't, like, worship him or anything'. She almost spat the words out, as if the idea of worshipping God was distasteful. The *content* of her God-belief related only to an explanatory function about which she thought or cared little, and had no other salience or function for her. Her desire to disassociate herself from the act of worship seems to be both a rejection of a relationship with a god, and also with those who maintain that relationship. 'Worship' is a word linked with public, communal expressions of belief: churches, synagogues, and mosques are often called 'places of worship' where people gather for what is called a 'service of worship'. While Gemma may believe 'that' God exists, she does not 'believe in' him and did not want to be seen as someone who does – in contrast to, for example, Jane, a 61-year-old married teacher, who said:

> I believe in God, one God, which I define as a spiritual being or a spiritual presence, no gender, all loving, all powerful, all mighty, creator.

That statement indicated the *content* of her beliefs, but to understand more fully what Jane believed we need to appreciate both the salience and function of her beliefs. Jane said God gave her a reason for being: 'I couldn't contemplate life without him, and I couldn't contemplate life without there being something at the end of it.' Just those two examples of Gemma and Jane illustrate the importance of not only looking at 'what' people say they believe but, as I will analyse below, how, when, why, and with whom.

Far from the green spaces of North Yorkshire I suggest an example from urban Singapore to make a similar point. In his study of Filipino migrants who belonged to a large church, Cornelio (2008) argued that their commitment to the church was deepened through intense socio-emotional relationships and participation in collective tasks. This is not to say that the content of their beliefs did not, of course, include God or Jesus, but rather that it also included other salient content, such as belief in each other.

Sources

People I interviewed expressed what they considered to be the origins of their beliefs. Once again, the examples they gave were of people with whom they have had or have a strong emotional relationship. The other occasions when I observed a strong emotional response to questions about the origins of belief were when people were criticizing other people's beliefs, or lack of them, as I discussed in Chapter 7. It was sometimes through what I observed as a tension between their beliefs as somehow indigenous to what they described as their 'culture' and others being foreign that the importance of 'cultural' influence emerged, reinforcing, as I discussed in Chapter 3, the importance of 'culture' as a performative trope to define and reinforce difference.

Anthropocentrics traced the source of their beliefs to family roots, followed by life experience, by which they usually meant the consequences of events. People described their familial influences partly as 'being told what to do' and partly by observing what people do, most markedly observing the ideal behaviour of, usually, a mother or grandmother. The effect of social sources on beliefs was sometimes described as a continuous process, where people were being, as one young student described it, 'socialized continually'.[2] Harriet, 14, a student at a grammar school, sourced her understanding of morality in a form of social code Christianity derived from the social, but not from the church. When I asked her what she believed in, she said she was open-minded, but she would believe in 'Christian morality', which she described as recognizing that there is good and bad in people, and that people can be forgiven. She said she used to attend church when she was younger. When I asked her if that was where she had received her ideas about Christian morality, she said: 'Not really. We just did colouring in.'

---

[2] A similar observation was made by Hoge et al. (1982) in a large quantitative study of values transmission in the United States. While they identified important dynamics between parent and child (parental agreement about religion, age of parents, and good relationship), their conclusion that membership in a denomination influenced children more than parental values emphasizes here the importance of sociality.

Occasionally, people said that feeling the presence of their deceased loved one was what convinced them that there was an afterlife, a phenomenon I explored in Chapter 5 and described as 'believing through bereaving'.

Many people who specifically disassociated themselves from a religion cited the 'Ten Commandments' as a source of moral authority. While this may suggest a religious orientation, if we examined only the *content* of that belief, it became evident through discussion about the *source* that what they were referring to were not Ten Commandments but the six excluding God, a faith, or the practice of a religion. I discussed sources of morality with a sixth form sociology class where, as I noted in Chapter 2, the students had agreed to pilot my questions. In our discussion, they initially offered a variety of sources for their moral beliefs, ranging from family to friends to experience. One male, Matt, 15, commented as we shared their lists that it seemed the ideas fit into the 'the big tens'. I asked how he knew about these and he said he did not really know about them, although he thought they were about the things we had just been discussing, such as not killing or stealing. He may be illustrating how even non-religious young people reflect the wider tropes in society. Schofield-Clark (2007), in her discussion of young people and their religious understandings, found that American teens expressed disapproval of atheists, and discussed their moral beliefs within a wider discourse of Protestant Christianity: even 'teens who claim no interest in organized religion itself, may use religious language and images as means of identifying themselves as good moral people' (ibid., 79). Other young people I interviewed had similar explanations for their moral beliefs. Leah, 14, said she was a 'Roman Catholic' because she believed in the 'Ten Commandments', although 'they don't really apply to me yet'. Her religious identity is tightly bound to the Ten Commandments even if she is uncertain about their content. Terry, 49, cited earlier, said he did not believe in God or attend church yet answered my questions about morality by saying there were certain 'obvious things' like 'the Ten Commandments, thou shall not kill, thou shall not steal and all that carry on'. In a similar vein, Barbara, 69, cited the Ten Commandments despite her earlier comments about being anti-church:

> Well, going back to religion, the Ten Commandments are probably the best moral guide I can think of, and while I don't use the religion I have certainly tried to practise, probably because of my upbringing, the commandments, you know. Don't kill, don't steal, you know.

I note that she distances herself from 'the religion' but emphasizes commandments prohibiting killing and stealing. Like my other informants who discussed the Ten Commandments, Barbara made no mention of the first four commandments relating to one's relationship with God, but only to those governing relationships with other people. This was an omission I raised more specifically with Antony, a 14-year-old who said he was an atheist although baptized as a Christian. When we discussed morality, he said that medical ethics were important, as were the Ten Commandments. He said he tried to 'stick by' the Ten Commandments in that he does not steal, has not killed anyone, and tries to love his parents. I suggested that sounded as if he believed in living by some commandments but not the first four. He agreed: 'I believe in them after four to ten.' The understanding that there are more commandments beyond those prohibiting killing and stealing was expressed by Georgia, an 18-year-old student. She adamantly positioned herself away from the Ten Commandments, saying:

> I wouldn't class myself as a Christian. I'm not devoted. I don't live by the Ten Commandments. I don't attend, so I wouldn't define myself as Christian at all.

I do not infer from this that by not living by the Ten Commandments Georgia steals and murders, but rather I infer she is referring to the first four commandments, with the comment 'I don't attend' being an elision of 'attend church' and indirect reference to the fourth commandment. Wide current knowledge about the Ten Commandments and Christian doctrine amongst young people may in part be explained by the UK's Religious Education curriculum and its material about the Ten Commandments.

In contrast to anthropocentrics, theocentrics attributed the source of their beliefs to 'God'. They believe that God reveals his presence to them through feelings of love, peace, or awe, and that he laid down moral guidelines through the Bible and Jesus or, in the case of one Muslim I interviewed, through the Koran and Mohammed. Discussion about source and content was frequently intertwined with theocentrics, such that I conclude that for them content and source is indivisible. Theocentrics trace what they see to be a decline in good morality in society to a decline in the effect of the church and religious teaching, a consequence of which is, to them, an unacceptably high divorce rate, acceptance of homosexuality, abortion, and premarital sex. Anthropocentrics also see a moral decline in society, but trace this to inadequate teaching in the home, particularly by mothers, leading to poor behaviour amongst young people. Although I cannot rule out how people were actually influenced by such institutions as the church and schools, how people say they have resourced their beliefs relative to those institutions is part of what separates the anthropocentrics from the theocentrics. They unite, however, in their common derision of some women and young people, a point to which I will return under 'salience' and 'function'.

In Chapter 7 I concluded that the social code morals of both groups are broadly the same, but in conversation it was striking that they would not admit to that. I am reminded here of Cohen's observations (1985, 16) about symbolic communities: the 'quintessential referent' of community is that its members think they make sense about significant matters in ways unique to them.

Anthropocentrics frequently expressed sentiments about religious people being hypocrites and about God being either negligent or absent. Theocentrics often identified a lack of moral adherence in society as a problem caused by those who did not have a religious upbringing or practice and rely instead on their (selfish) self. In their study of values, beliefs, and morals, Geyer and Baumeister (2005, 419) reflect that concern: 'Historically, a central and explicit goal of religion and morality in general has been to restrain the self and to override people's tendency to act out of self-interested motives.'

Yet, on the broad 'social code' morality I discussed in Chapter 7, both groups believe much the same things. It does not appear, therefore, that the content of people's beliefs is what sets some apart from others as much as what they see are the sources of those beliefs.[3] Claiming the source of morality as religious is an important characteristic of religion and is part of what sets religion apart from non-religion, argued Johnstone (1975, 20):

Religion is unique in claiming a 'higher' source or basis for its morality: You should do such and so or refrain from such and so because God willed it, or because it's in tune with cosmic forces – not simply because one group says so or only because it's the only natural, logical, sensible or humane thing to do. In other words, religion ultimately invokes the sacred or the supernatural in order to influence the behaviour of individuals.

---

[3] The tendency to dismiss other people's beliefs and practice as different from our own may also be symptomatic of a tendency to distinguish between 'their' beliefs and 'our' knowledge, as Good (1994) discussed.

Practice

Not everyone believed there was a direct or necessary link between belief and practice. Highly self-conscious and reflexive in interviews, people often noted disparities and contradictions between their beliefs and practices, indicating that belief must have another purpose than simply to guide behaviour. How people interpret their practices and relate it to their beliefs requires multidimensional analysis. As Cohen noted (1985, 16), 'behaviour itself is not meaningful but only becomes meaningful through the actor's subjective interpretation'.

Once I had identified with people what they believed in, including their moral beliefs, I would ask them how they put those beliefs into practice. This frequently stalled the interview, as I described in Chapter 7. There did not seem to be to most of my informants a seamless transition from what they believed in to what they did in practice. The people whom I am describing here as anthropocentric tended to be taken aback by the question. Only a few said anything more specific than 'treating people right' or in some cases, 'recycling'. For the most part, they had already covered the answer in responding to my first question, 'what do you believe in?' or in discussing their morals and values. As I described in earlier chapters and summarized above under 'content', people who are anthropocentric described their beliefs and morals in tangible, human-related terms giving specific, human-oriented examples. I suggest here that they do not separate the idea of belief from the idea of practice: belief, for them, is practice and emotion. Having already answered my question about what they believed in, they often appeared confused that I was, in effect, repeating it.

Those who seemed to separate effortlessly the idea of belief from practice were those I refer to as theocentric. These people tended to answer my 'what do you believe in' question in theological terms, as in: they believed in God. When I asked how they put those beliefs into practice they said that they practised in their everyday lives, through their work, which they sometimes saw as a vocation, and through behaving in ways they described as kind, helpful, and loving. Their separation of belief and practice may go some way in explaining why it is that theocentrics think people who do not believe in their religion would not carry out similar practices, such as being kind and loving. It does not seem to me that anthropocentrics do not believe in being loving and kind, but that they would not engage with the discussion in the same way. This is a good example of discursive hegemony: as anthropocentrics do not attest to beliefs that conform to the belief orientation of theocentrics, it may be assumed by the theocentrics that they do not practise in equally loving and kind ways. While the term 'belief' signifies to the theocentric person both the source and content of their beliefs, to the anthropocentric it signifies its practice. For the anthropocentric, the term 'belief' is largely irrelevant. For the theocentric, it is central to their identity as religious people. As I have noted before, they often describe themselves as 'believers' and refer to people who do not believe in gods as 'non-believers'. The elision that often followed 'belief' indicates how natural it seems to them that the word would be essentially theistic. I could discern little difference in the way that anthropocentrics and theocentrics said they lived or should live their lives. Both kinds of 'believers' were convinced it was best to treat people as one would like to be treated, and both deplored the behaviours of women, young people, and people from other ethnic groups whom they saw as disrespectful and damaging to society.

How people practise their beliefs will be affected by the nature of the religious group and wider cultural expectations. Turning to a cross-cultural example, Çarkoğlu (2008) reports that in his study amongst Turkish Muslims, it was noticeable that the more someone practised their religion (through making the Hajj, sacrificing a lamb, and attending mosque) the more likely they would be involved in philanthropic giving: 'Higher levels of, not belief or faith, but rather of practice, or worship seem to be more effective in shaping people's likelihood of making donations for different causes' (ibid., 120). He also found it was important to distinguish between types of giving – whether to known people such as family or friends, or unknown strangers or associations.

Salience

The degree to which certain beliefs mattered to people differed amongst my informants. Some beliefs seemed to be of only passing importance, like a half-remembered taught or residual belief that they had not reviewed recently but to which they still adhered. Other beliefs were spoken about with conviction and sometimes passion to indicate to me the high degree of salience they held for people. Belief in the importance of adherent relationships had a high degree of salience for those whom I am identifying as anthropocentric. The significance of relationships appeared in most answers to most of my questions with those informants. The degree of salience was also reinforced by their tendency to tell me detailed stories about real-life experiences that illustrated for them the importance of relationships. Several young people, as I have described particularly in Chapter 4, told me about their important friends and what they did with their friends, as well as about ex-parents and how they felt threatened or rejected by them. These were not sanitized, neutral, narratives, but emotional and per-formative. In a similar way, older people told me about losing or gain-ing a partner and how that made them feel, and about their unresolved relationships with children and parents. If I was informed by their stories of adherent relationships, I was also informed by their accounts about people with whom they did not want to be associated. Once again, in striking and vivid detail they recounted their experiences or their friends' experiences with bad, or at least different, people with whom they do not want to belong.

I contrast those emotionally loaded stories with the tone of indiffer-ence with which most people greeted the questions I assumed would give them enormous pause for thought, on the themes of our origins, destinies, and purpose in life. Most people answered those questions briefly and with little apparent interest. This was probably most striking, as I explored in Chapter 5, when talking about people's the-ories about an afterlife. Anthropocentrics tend to believe that death is final, that there is no heaven, and that there is no coming back. That view changes, as I discussed in Chapter 6, relative to the power and authority they feel they have over their own lives. The exceptions most often occur with people who have lost their loved ones: here, there was often a description of experiencing the presence of their dead loved ones, or even having detailed conversations with them. My evidence and analysis points to belief in an afterlife increasing with age not simply because people may ponder their mortality as they age but also because people tend to lose loved ones as they age. Many young people I interviewed who had lost a loved one believed in their continued relationship with their deceased beloved. Further, when I discussed with people their worst fears, it was rarely their own death they mentioned but most commonly the death of someone they loved.

To refer to a point I made above about the content of people's beliefs, the salience dimension allowed me to understand that people formed a belief about their relationship to 'x' when 'x' was something important to them. People I spoke with discussed God, Jesus, marital problems, abuse, seeing visions of their dead ancestors, talking to their dead ancestors, their feelings of joy and despair, and other deeply personal and sometimes disturbing issues. Indeed, a problem I originally had as a fieldworker and discussed frequently with my supervisors was my personal level of embarrassment and discomfort when listening to some of their accounts. It became increasingly unlikely to me that people were withholding important aspects of their beliefs. What, therefore, is an important corollary of what I have just said must also be examined: if I know what is important to people in their beliefs, do I also know what is not important to them? I cannot answer that question exhaustively, but I can answer it within the context of my study: what appears not to be important to the majority of people I interviewed, irrespective of age, class, and gender, are the so-called religious or metaphysical questions to which I referred in Chapter 1: the meaning of life; why we are here; how we got here; and where are we going. Most people, I conclude, are far more preoccupied with the mundane matters of their lives to give such ontological questions much thought. When they do so, primarily because I provoked them to, they answer in ways that convinced me they did not really care about such issues. The people who do discuss these 'religious questions' are those whom I have identified as theocentrics. The imponderability of some of those questions can only, they say, be answered through the mystery of God. Indeed, asking those questions is an important characteristic to theocentrics. I will therefore explore under *function* how holding certain beliefs as *salient* allows them to function not only to support one's personal insecurities or worries, but to differentiate amongst those who have such beliefs and those who do not. People, for example, who sometimes say they are Christian to reinforce their membership of an ethnic group may do so only when it becomes important to them as a form of symbolic ethnic/religious identity.

Function

Fourteen-year-old Jordan had answered my question 'what do you believe in?' by saying 'nowt', although, he added, he was a Christian 'but I don't believe in owt'. His grandparents, whom he described as 'really strong Christians', believed in God, Jesus, the Bible, and 'stuff' but he did not. He believed in doing well at school, helping at home, and being responsible and kind with his friends. He had no difficulty in discussing rights from wrongs or what made him happy, sad, or worried. Jordan rejected the doctrinal *content* of Christianity but embraced the *function* it gave him of familial identity. Other people believe in the afterlife because, I suggested in Chapter 5, it functions to help them continue their adherent relationships. The bereaved have an experience of sensing the presence of their dead loved ones in a way that conforms to their experience of the loved one while living. The feelings they had with their loved ones before death are retained after death. From what my informants have told me, it seems that the nature of the experience functions to prolong the sense of the dead loved one's presence, to continue the adherent relationship. The belief allows the bereaved to continue a relationship with their deceased loved one that would otherwise be denied to them if they did not have that belief. This was most poignantly expressed to me when people said that they 'had to believe' in an afterlife because they could not tolerate the idea that they would never see their loved one again.

Belief in the importance of adherent relationships also had a performative function in terms of identity. As I argued in Chapter 7, when people talked about treating 'others' right, they were in fact referring only to people they knew and with whom they belonged. This could be more properly expressed not as 'doing unto others' but as 'doing unto people we know'. Although this belief may function to maintain boundaries, the nature of demarcating between 'them' and 'us' functions to strengthen 'our' sense of belonging to 'us' through both a process of affiliation and disaffiliation. How this is operationalized will be further discussed in Chapter 9 with my analysis of Christian nominalism and conclusions that the majority of people who said they would have ticked 'Christian' did so mainly for three reasons: because they were affiliating to a family group; they were affiliating to and disaffiliating from perceived ethnic groups; they were aspiring to belong to a group perceived as respectable.

I therefore concluded that the most important function of anthropocentric beliefs was to nurture a sense of belonging. In desiring to belong with people they love, they must not only prolong relationships in this life and the hereafter, they must also separate from those whom they do not love by demarcating the boundary between them and us. Theocentrics may do the same in their adherent relationships, but rather than refer to this belonging in terms of people they love here and now, they refer to people who share similar beliefs as part of their community, or church, united in their love of God. Although they say that the source of their morals and their sense of being loved comes from God, they also emphasize the importance of their church community.

As I have previously observed, anthropocentrics and theocentrics denigrate each other's forms of believing and belonging. Theocentrics often decried what they saw as a breakdown in society stemming from a lack of church participation. While noting that the church provided a strong sense of community they sourced the 'true' source of love and comfort as coming from God, not from the community or its members. I recall one Christian who criticized churches that focused too much on the congregation singing, dancing, and striving for happiness. Those Christians not only disapproved of adherent relationships existing outside what they considered to be God-given parameters, they actively criticized them.

In a similar fashion, it was a common theme amongst anthropocentrics that religious people were weak and needed to believe in God to give them a sense that they were important and belonged to someone, and yet the anthropocentrics did not see their own self-confessed dependency on their adherent relationships as a weakness or a character failing. I will conclude here that the way people regard each other's beliefs often serves to function as a means of strengthening their own identity as part of a certain group or community, marking and sustaining boundaries. In this sense, belief functions as an ideology, a way of promoting a certain view of ourselves, the world around us and most specifically how we want it to be.

Above all, informants impressed upon me their desire to have their beliefs understood and respected as their beliefs, not the beliefs of others imposed on them. This did not, I argue, arise from an ethical position wherein they respect the rights of all people to hold divergent beliefs. Informants are often critical and dismissive of other people's beliefs, while retaining the conviction that their own beliefs are to be respected. This is not, I suggest, a contradiction or hypocrisy. Belief, to many people, is a statement of self; a way of saying who they are: 'I believe, therefore I am.' Defending their own beliefs is an important way to enhance their identities: opposing other people's beliefs functions in the same way to the same end.

Place

When Malinowski (1961 [1922], 4) began his ethnography with the invitation to imaginatively join him 'suddenly set down surrounded by all your gear, alone on a tropical beach close to a native village, while the launch or dinghy which has brought you sails out of sight' there was no doubt that 'place' was both geographically and ontologically configured. The point was not simply that he was in a physical location but in an unfamiliar and potentially lonely space. Collins (2008b) described how he and colleagues explored how hospital chaplains negotiated a space for themselves within a social space that was, at least superficially, constructed to be rational, efficient, and based on scientific and technological principles. During his period of ethnographic research carried out among hospital chaplaincies in the north of England, he found that research participants foregrounded practice and rarely used the term 'belief'. Those spaces were also populated by representatives from different religions and therefore open to religious contestation. This multi-faith context resulted, the researchers discovered, in more collaboration than conflict. Collins indexes here the multidimensional relationship between content, practice, and place.

When my informants talked about important places, they also interwove senses of belonging or alienation. An adherence to place therefore acts performatively, helping to develop and animate a sense of belonging through temporal and physical experience. Their explanations of their beliefs were securely rooted in a non-religious discourse of family, friends, and places. As I discussed in Chapter 7, 'place' sometimes refers to areas of habitation, or what people describe as their 'communities', being, typically, perceived safe places segregated from 'others' and where my informants felt they belonged.

Places were always relational, deterritorialized, or embodied. Significant relational places for my young informants were their bedrooms, where they sometimes prayed but more often communicated with their deceased loved ones. That particular experience of 'place' represents a relocation of the common theological representation shared by theocentrics that transcendence is supra-human and located in a place within another, non-human, realm populated by deities. For my anthropocentric informants, transcendence is a place located in their most intimate and everyday social spaces. The most important relationship people talk about is family or partners, followed by 'friends'. I would then put 'place' next because the 'communities' about which people talk as their own, typically, safe places tend to be segregated from the ethnic communities of the 'others'. These are important distinctions to make because the discourse of 'treating others right' is so prevalent. When people talk about their relationships, they are usually being quite specific about what kind of relationship and what kind of others they mean. There is a sense here of tension between them and us. There are people with whom we belong, and others to whom we do not belong. The 'others' have emerged from my study to have distinct characteristics: they are young, female, or non-white.

Place also refers here to the location of the set of beliefs to which many people claim they adhere. As I discussed in Chapter 3, the act of locating a cultural identity is relational on both small and large scales. Recalling Barthes' (1988 [1973], 288) evocative reference to the *déjà lu* or 'already read', place is also a discursive space already prepared by a wider society and into which informants often desire to insert themselves. An empirical example of the place of belief was offered by Elliot (2008) who examined whether or not the experience of snowboarding, or more specifically 'soulriding', was spiritual for his informants. While he concluded that the majority of the snowboarders interviewed felt that in some way snowboarding was indeed spiritual for them, he found that it was not the experience itself that made it so, but their pre-existing expectations. He contrasted his findings with Durkheim (1915), discussed in Chapter 1, who argued that religion is an a posteriori result of certain experiences. Elliot further suggested that 'when we encounter the "spiritual" it is because at some level we expect to do so, it fits with our primary framework'. Wuthnow (1998) reached similar conclusions in his study of contemporary spirituality, where he found that such experiences did not change a person's orientation towards religion and propel them into joining a church, for example, if they did not already belong.

Time

A common theme from my interviews, irrespective of age, is how people usually placed belief formation as an activity in the past and now complete. How people relate to 'time' is often relative to specific discourses of power, legitimacy, and authority. While they may identify multiple sources and life experience as belief-builders, the building is now, for them, a finished project. That, however, may not be so for others, they will say. Those 'others' are often responsible for infecting the beliefs of 'people we know'. Indeed, in the field of religious studies the impact of other people of different faith backgrounds is often described as pluralism and cited as one of the reasons for the decline[4] in Christian practice, although how less than 6 per cent[5] of the population in, notably, positions of little influence would actually achieve that is not clear. This may be part of a tendency I observed that while people claim their beliefs are intact, they often suggest other people's are not and are easily influenced by, typically, the 'wrong' sort of person.

Rudiak-Gould (2010) explored how people's beliefs are not always consistent as they respond to different temporal contexts. He tried to make sense of two different versions of the 'past', described to him by his Marshallese informants. Depending on whether they were talking

---

[4] Although, see Warner (1993) and the rational choice theorists discussed in Chapter 1 and 2 about how pluralism may stimulate religious demand. See Voas et al. (2002) for contrary evidence and analysis.

[5] UK census 2001 figures: 6 per cent identified themselves as members of other religions, the largest single group being Muslims at 3 per cent and all others accounting for less than 1 per cent each, together accounting for 3 per cent. Figures for the 2011 census are predicted to reflect a slightly higher number of non-white English responders, but the greater proportion will still be overwhelmingly white English.

about the 'past' being a pre-Christian past or pre-Western past, accounts stressed either present-day decline or present-day progress.[6]

My own fieldwork took place in Yorkshire between 2002 and 2005, when tensions between whites and Asians were high, occasionally spilling over into street violence. It was also a time that coincided with the rise of the BNP (British National Party) and its offshoot, the more hard-line EDL (English Defence League). In 2005 BNP leader Nick Griffin unsuccessfully contested a seat in Keighley, part of the region in my study.

Further, mindful of Asad's analysis summarized in Chapter 1, focusing on only one aspect, such as the doctrinal content of belief, and ignoring the significance of a particular *time* would perhaps hint at another agenda behind our scholarship. Asad (1993, 40–1) argued that in a more scientific, modern period the church worked to assert its authority by delegitimizing the advances of science and history. It thus began to privilege 'belief' over 'knowledge' and private conscience and sentiment over discipline and monastic authority, 'shifting, as they did so, the weight of religion more and more onto the moods and motivations of the individual believer'. What had been previously regarded as true religious practice – intellectual and social discipline – would recede from the religious space, 'letting "belief", "conscience", and "sensibility" take its place'. As an example, Asad cites the theologian anthropologist Robertson Smith (1912, 110), who, as quoted in Chapter 1 here, claimed that in a more modern age, belief takes precedence over theological or historical interpretations: 'it will no longer be the results of theology that we are required to defend, but something prior to theology. What we shall have to defend is not our Christian knowledge but our Christian belief.'

Using seven dimensions of content, sources, practice, salience, function, place, and time helped complexify and nuance people's beliefs and demonstrate their social nature in what I theorize as holistic, performative belief. Through applying that model to these data I concluded that it revealed two predominant belief orientations of anthropocentrism and theocentrism. In using this analysis I have concluded that most of the people I studied are 'anthropocentric', situating power and authority with people, not gods. Further, I have suggested that in practice there is little difference between the two orientations as they both share similar functions of creating a sense of belonging. This is a Durkheimian (1915) interpretation that moves away from a

---

[6] See also Gellner (1970, 45), who speaks of a 'socially essential discrepancy between concept and reality'.

supernaturally oriented view of religion. For Durkheim, religion is not rooted in a belief in the supernatural but in those activities that bind people.

What I have argued throughout this work is that most people believe in their relationships with other people. They believe in how they treat other people and how they feel about other people, although they were specific about who those people were: they were people with whom they have an adherent relationship, people similar to themselves with whom they want to identify as belonging, in life and sometimes after death. I described that predominant moral framework as 'treating people right' and treating people in a manner in which they themselves want to be treated. This finding bears some similarities to Ammerman's (1997) 'Golden Rule' Christians who also share beliefs in a general ethic of treating others in the way one wanted to be treated, but tended to centre their caring on their families, friends, and neighbours, They were markedly different from people she described as 'activists', who believed in working to remove injustice from society. I argued that the form of 'fairness' and 'doing unto us' morality I found is a perverse twist of the Golden Rule edict to do unto others as we would have them do unto us. Most people I interviewed will treat people well only if they are people like themselves.

Those who are not like themselves are 'others', most frequently identified as young, non-white, or female, and mostly responsible for the ills of society. This leads me to conclude that most people I interviewed shared a belief in the supremacy of white male dominance, a belief located in and reinforcing a social place of 'white patriarchy'. I will return to this theme in Chapter 10. In the next chapter I will turn to a specific instrument that I have thus far referred to as the UK 2001 census but which, as I will discuss, can also be read as a performative tool, with many parts of the population participating as both a legal, civil duty and also as a collective rite of intensification.

9

Understanding Christian Nominalism: Rethinking Christian Identity

Introduction

In this chapter I return to the opening question posed in this book: why would 72 per cent of those who answered the religion question in the 2001 census opt to identify themselves as Christian? In addressing that question here I will link questions of self-identity with belief.

Many people without faith in God, Jesus, or Christian doctrine self-identify as 'Christian' in certain social contexts (Day 2009a; Day 2010b; Voas 2009; Voas and Day 2007; Voas and Day 2010). That phenomenon, often referred to as 'nominalism', is arguably the largest form of Christianity today (Brierley 1999) and the least understood. The term 'nominalism' derives from the Latin word *nominalis* – 'of or pertaining to names' – and in philosophy refers to a doctrine that abstractions, or universals, have no essential or substantive reality. This chapter explores how nominalism is far from an insignificant, empty category but a social, performative act, bringing into being a specific kind of Christian identity. Further, if the analysis presented here is correct, it suggests that many people who self-identified as 'Christian' on the UK 2001 census – and will likely again in 2011 – may have been Christian Nominalists. This has important sociological and political implications relating to religious and national debates about identity and about how census data inform political decisions affecting a range of issues, such as health, welfare, and education.

Central to the discussion here about Christian identity was the overwhelmingly 'Christian' response to the first-time inclusion in 2001 of a religious question in the UK decennial census.[1] As explained in Chapter 3, how and why a question about religion was placed on the census was a significant political act. Of interest here is why 72 per cent of respondents self-identified as Christian in a country where most forms of Christian participation have been declining (Brierley 2006; Gill et al. 1998). Applying Converse's (1964; 1970) theory (that most people answer open-ended questions without really thinking about the issue and their answers, therefore, do not reflect an ideology or belief system) to the census is tricky, partly because the census was based on closed, tick-box questions and also because it did not measure attitudes or beliefs (although many people, as I will discuss presently, interpreted the results in those terms). Nevertheless, the possibility that people might have just ticked the boxes at random must be borne in mind and it is probable that many did. I will argue, however, that many who chose the Christian response did so for more complex, and less random, reasons than Converse might suppose. One answer may relate to the wording and location of the question, asked differently in the three regions of the UK, as discussed in Chapter 3. Such wording is incompatible with other surveys about religion that probe issues of belonging and find considerably lower affirmative responses.

Another partial explanation for the overwhelmingly Christian response will be introduced in this chapter and described through what I see as performative, nominalist Christianity. 'Performative' has been used in this work thus far to describe how language sometimes has the effect of doing something other than merely conveying something (Austin 1962). Butler (1990; 1993) extends the idea of performativity beyond single language acts to incorporate a function or purpose: a lived, embodied performance brings into being an identity through repetition, regulation, and normative adherence. As Butler pointed out, it is not just the repetition of the act that is important but its nature, context, and significance. A performative act precedes itself, as it were, as its efficacy requires an already-present discourse. Interpretations of a speech act must also account for the cultural framework in which it is being used, the relative power relationships within that context, and the function, or 'meaning-in-use'. In this chapter I develop those ideas and relate them to the act of responding to a census.

---

[1] Somewhat confusingly, in 1851, on the same day as the population census was taken, a separate exercise called the *Accommodation and Attendance at Worship* census was carried out. That census, popularly called 'the religious census', asked questions about church attendance, not affiliation.

What is nominalism?

Bill Bright, founder and President of Campus Crusade for Christ, describes nominalism both using the Latin-derived definition given above and a more Christian-centric version, writing:

> 'Christian' nominalists make up one of the largest mission fields in the world and quite possibly the largest in the United States...a Christian nominalist is one who claims the name Christian, but who has no authentic, personal, sin-forgiving and life-changing relationship with Jesus Christ. His allegiance to Jesus is in name, not heart. (http://www.greatcom.org/resources/tell_it_often_tell_it_well/chap10/default.htm)

Those nominalist Christians are the focus for many evangelizing Christians worldwide. In a report on its world mission, Operation World 2000 described nominalism as a challenge, estimating that 60 per cent of Christians worldwide are 'non-practicing' or 'nominalist'.[2] All Nations Christian College, based in the UK, explains its decision to send missionaries to North America: 'Christian nominalism and liberalism are the two challenges to mission in the United States and Canada' (http://www.allnations.ac.uk).

The anti-nominalist rhetoric reflects a particular kind of Christianity, one that stresses the lived experience of being with Jesus Christ. Another American Christian website put it even more starkly by stressing that Christianity was not a 'belief system' 'reiterating the propositional tenets of its founder's teaching' but 'Christianity is the function of the Spirit of Christ as He continues to live in Christians.'[3]

Rick Warren is probably the best-known American evangelical minister, whose Saddleback church in California ranks as the eighth largest church in the United States. A best-selling author, Warren is a credible figure to many Americans: he hosted a debate between the two Presidential candidates, Barack Obama and John McCain and gave the invocation at Barack Obama's inauguration. Warren is concerned about what he describes as the 'notional Christians' identified by Christian research company, the Barna Research Group:

> Recent data from the Barna Research Group reveal that 50% of Protestant churchgoers in the United States are not born again. In addition, Barna has discovered that 44% of Americans are 'notional Christians.' These 90 million people describe themselves as Christians but do not believe that their eternal hope is based on a personal relationship with Jesus and a belief

---

[2] http://www.methodistmessage.com/nov2006/nominal.html.
[3] http://www.christinyou.net/pages/Xnotbs.html.

in His death and resurrection. (http://www.pastors.com/blogs/ministrytool-
box/archive/2002/09/13/Church-initiative-launches-strategy-to-reach-
lost_2C00_-notional-Christians.aspx)

It is evident that there therefore arises a tension amongst Christians
about what sort of Christian is the true sort, but it is not my intention
to enter that debate. Rather, I want to focus on a type that figured in
my study prominently, the anthropocentrics who sometimes identify
as Christian, who may be described by others variously as notional or
nominal and occupy a central place in contemporary society. Davie, for
example (1994, 8), described the UK religious landscape as exhibiting 'a
prevalence of Christian nominalism alongside the hardening of religious boundaries'. Nominalism is presented as something different
from those other, harder boundaries, something perhaps softer, or
even, as Voas (2009) suggests, 'fuzzy'. Further, the category by implication suggests an opposition to another, perhaps truer or more authentic
form of Christianity, measured by church attendance and/or subjective
questions about the importance of religion. Winter and Smart (1993),
in their study of a locale in 'rural England', concluded (1993, 641) that
nominalism provided 'merely a sense of cultural belonging to Western
Christendom'. The use of the word 'merely' provides a tone of insignif-
icance, creating an implicit contrast with something more substantial
(as if whatever is meant by 'Western Christendom' is not significant
enough). They elaborate (1993, 642) by suggesting that 'belonging'
represents 'vague notions of belonging', which is, they suggest, 'of a
nominalist or minimalist kind'.

Such taken-for-granted notions as 'Western Christendom' may,
indeed, lurk within a nominalist sense of belonging, but such associations are deeply cultural, located, and loaded. By closely examining
people's sense of Christian 'belonging' we may discover other, more
subtle, interwoven 'belongings' related to, for example, history, nation,
morality, gender, and 'culture'. I will argue later in this chapter that
nominalism is not always soft, fuzzy, vague, minimalist, or, even,
benign.

If nominalism minimally describes the practice of self-identifying as
Christian while not attending church (although, as I will discuss, it
is more than that) then levels of nominalism are indeed high in
Euro American countries. Surveys of religious identification in the
United States provide data[4] that show that 76 per cent of the

---

[4] American Religious Identification Survey (http://www.americanreligionsurvey-aris.
org/).

population self-identify as Christian and that around 40 per cent say they attend church regularly, if not weekly.[5] Actual, versus reported, US church attendance may be much lower (Hadaway et al. 1993; Hadaway and Marler 2005). Fewer than 2 per cent of the British population attend a Church of England service weekly, and less than 7 per cent attend even monthly (Brierley 2006; Heelas and Woodhead 2005). This is slightly lower than a European average of about 10 per cent who attend church monthly (Davie 2002), notwithstanding considerable geographic and denominational variation. For example, church attendance is lower in European Protestant countries than in Catholic countries (Lüchau 2007) and in the UK lower amongst Anglicans than amongst Pentecostals. There has also been a dramatic and steady decline not only in regular church attendance but also in participation in all other church-based Christian rituals, such as weddings, funerals, confirmations, and christenings in the UK and other Euro American countries (Brierley 2006; Gill et al. 1998).

In Canada, the percentage of those claiming a Christian identity – 72 per cent in 2001 – has been decreasing. The Canadian census offers denomination subcategories and the percentage of those who affiliate with the general category 'Christian' rather than a specific denomination has more than doubled between censuses, representing the largest percentage increases among all major religious groups. This tends to support the tendency, as I discuss later, to associate with Christianity as a cultural symbol rather than as a practised religion. Reported weekly church attendance in Canada is around 20 per cent.

If, therefore, we seek to compare European and North American affiliation and practice, it would be fair to say that three-quarters or more of North American Christians do not attend church weekly; in the UK and most of continental Europe the figure approaches 90 per cent, but 'nominalism' is high in both regions. Measuring nominalism in relation to church attendance, however, prioritizes a social practice over potentially significant private practices and does not provide sufficient understanding of what is meant by 'church'.

Demerath (1965) analysed Lutherans according to whether they were 'church-like' or 'sect-like'. Those who were church-like not only attended church but also participated in a variety of church-related organizations in the church and parish, unlike the 'sect-like' people, who attended less and participated less, but were more (following Glock and Stark's 1965 typology) experientially, ideologically, and

<hr>

[5] Table #79: 'Self-described religious identification of adult population: 1990 and 2001', Section 1 Population, U.S. Census Bureau (http://www.census.gov/).

consequentially involved. Demerath related those types to social class to demonstrate that people in different social classes may be seeking different things from their participation and affiliation.

As discussed in Chapter 1, several authors (see, for example, Davie 1990, 1994; Stark et al. 2005) suggest that while the 'unchurched' may not be participating in public, social practices they may be privately and individually religious or spiritual. They may also, I suggest, be privately non-religious or non-spiritual, rejecting traditional religious beliefs and yet also choosing to identify as religious for other reasons.[6]

Davie (1994, 2), for example, draws on European Values surveys to conclude that the majority of British people believe in God but 'see no need to participate with even minimal regularity in their religious institutions', arguing (1994, 12–13) that it is more accurate to describe such people as 'unchurched' rather than secular. The familiar short-hand in the sociology of religion field for this thesis is 'believing without belonging' (Davie 1990, 1994; Gallup and Jones 1989). That claim, however, has been challenged by studies looking at decline in both beliefs and practice over generations (Gill et al. 1998; Pollack 2008; Voas and Crockett 2005).

The problem remains, however: why self-identify with Christianity at all? There are many, and growing, numbers of atheists who were baptized as Christian, yet do not call themselves Christian. Part of the answer to that question, explored below, can be found in specific social contexts. As Inglis observed (2007, 218) in his study of the decline of traditional Catholic beliefs and identity in Northern Ireland, identity 'operates within specific contexts, such as encountering people from other religions, going to Mass, going abroad or watching the national team in sports'. To understand more about 'why' people self-identify with Christianity we should start with the social context: 'when', 'where', and 'how' they do that. The two main contexts explored below are the act of self-identifying as Christian when filling out the 2001 census form, and the explanation of being Christian during research interviews.

Anthropocentric nominalism

In this section I will apply two of the most important theoretical con-cepts I have developed in this work: performative belief and a belief

[6] For a non-Christian example see Davidman's (2007) research into 'unsynagogued' cul-tural Jews.

orientation I termed 'anthropocentric' arising from a holistic, organic belief analysis. Of the sixty-eight people I interviewed, slightly more than half (37) answered 'Christian', a response in line with other non-census surveys mentioned above. What interested me was that of those Christians, half were anthropocentric, as defined in the previous chapter. They often overtly disaffiliated themselves from religion in our interview, were agnostic, non-church attending, and described their beliefs in a non-religious discourse of family, friends, and places. The word 'Christian' usually only arose when I introduced it as part of the census question.

When I asked them why they had ticked the 'Christian' box, a common explanation was because they had been baptized, or had attended Church of England services when they were younger, or had otherwise been 'brought up' Christian. To be a Christian, for them, did not include participating in liturgy or ritual, or engaging with Christian principles such as faith in God, the resurrection, or the life of Jesus. It was an ascribed identity from which they could not apparently disassociate themselves. The criteria of ascription and, therefore, criteria for membership, varied during the interviews: sometimes, it only required being 'named' through baptism; sometimes it was conferred by attending church when children; sometimes it was only by being born into what was described as a Christian country and therefore becoming a member of the Christian 'culture'.[7] These are likely the people referred to as 'nominalists', but the matter is more complicated than mere residual, habitual identification. For some, I suggest, 'performing Christian' for the census cemented a sense of belonging and exclusion in a national, collective practice similar to what has been described in anthropology as a 'rite of intensification' (Chapple and Coon 1947), where the performance of selecting shared categories of identity relating to ethnicity and religion was consciously understood as a collective, political act.[8]

In selecting 'Christian', respondents were choosing the institutional form of Christianity as the site of their Christian identity – after all, as one informant explained, what is more institutional yet non-religious

---

[7] For a further discussion of how anthropologists consider how religion is learned and, as the editors describe it, does not just arrive 'out of the blue' (Berliner and Sarró 2007, 5) see Berliner and Sarró 2007.

[8] In a completely different cultural context, it is interesting to see that in Davidman's (2007, 59) research into unsynagogued Jews, she found that many people adapted traditional events, such as the *seder* (sometimes served with neither *matzo* nor traditional prayers): 'The unsynagogued Jews freely chose how to practice, but many of the elements they chose were intentionally Jewish. And, like other Jews, identity was measured by practice and not belief.'

than the Church of England? Terry, 49, repeatedly said during the interview that he did not believe in any supra-human force, nor attended church. Yet, when he heard me reading the census question aloud, he said he would have selected Church of England (although that was not an option given on the census or when I read it in the interview). When asked why, he replied:

> Well, only because they asked us to, not because, we wouldn't have any qualms, but that's the British way, isn't it? If people are not religious, they're C of E. Church of England. Weddings, funerals, and christenings.

His repetitive, self-mocking, tone – 'weddings, funerals, and christenings' – marks moments of the performative process. As Butler (1990) described it, performativity brings into being an identity through repetition, regulation, and normative adherence. Terry performs Christianity through attending the public, institutional events, through self-identifying as Christian on the census, and by talking about it in the social context of the interview when, and only when, I invited him to choose it as an identification amongst others. That he and others did so not only reflected 'identity' but also 'belief' as understood now as 'belief in belonging'.

That assertion complicates a 'believing without belonging' thesis that Davie (1990; 1994) conceived as a private belief in God or other Christian-associated ideals, without church attendance or participation. Those people I describe here as performative, anthropocentric Christian Nominalists appear to eschew regular church attendance and even Christian doctrinal beliefs as they align themselves to institutional Christianity and what, for them, it represents. Adding now to the emerging picture of 'nominalism', a performative, anthropocentric Christian Nominalist may be someone who neither attends church, has faith in God or Jesus, accepts the creedal beliefs of Christianity, nor thinks religion is important in everyday life, but does find the institution of Christianity important when asked, usually in relation to 'others'. The next section will explore in detail why that may be so.

Hardening boundaries of belonging: performing Christian Nominalist identities

Following Barth (1969), I will now return to the earlier discussion in Chapter 3 and pay particular attention to how boundary-marking constructed a nominalist identity. When I asked the non-religious people why they had self-identified as Christian, while distancing themselves from religion throughout our interview, a common reply was because they were baptized or born to Christian parents. When analysing their interviews for further clues about their self-described identities, three separate but sometimes overlapping identities emerged.

Natal nominalist identities

Many people who say they are Christian because they were baptized, or because members of their family are Christian, usually also say they rarely, if ever, think about their religious identity: it seems to them to be inherent and inalterable, like their 'ethnicity', 'race', or 'class'.

Barbara, 69, a retired pub cook, distanced herself from Christianity and organized religion of any kind from the first question in the interview: 'What do you believe in?' She said, laughing: 'Not a lot. I'm not religious at all. Haven't been for a number of years, so I believe in today and now and not the hereafter and all of that.' She said she had been christened and went to church as a child, but became 'disenchanted' through what she saw as hypocrisy in the church. When I asked the census question, she replied 'I would put Christian because I was christened, so, yes, I'm a Christian.' Gary, 52, a lorry driver, said he would have ticked Christian on the census because: 'How I was brought up. I don't believe, but I don't disbelieve either.' Barry, 48, a bookkeeper, explained, 'I suppose it was instilled into me from an early age that I was a Christian.' Penny, 60, a retired care-team manager, explained, 'Because I was christened Church of England.'

In summary, the above examples illustrate an internal logic. Informants' Christian identities were expressed as an ascribed identity they believe was conferred upon them at birth, one that has not engaged them often in later life, until asked. By assuming someone is Christian because – and sometimes only because – one is born into it, the corollary must hold: one is not Christian if one is not born into it. By extension, once we collapse Christian into British, or more specifically, English Protestant, it follows that anyone not born in Britain to a Christian family could be properly neither Christian nor English.

Ethnic nominalist identities

Use of the term 'ethnic' here does not presume an inherent identity, but rather one constructed and reinforced in different social contexts and at different times. Following Weber (1978, 389): 'ethnic membership does not constitute a group, it only facilitates group formation of any kind'. Certain forms of Christian Nominalist behaviour, I argue, facilitate group formation of a white, English Protestant kind. What is described here as 'ethnic' nominalist behaviour was mostly found amongst people over 30 and most markedly over 50, corresponding to the age group which tended to answer 'Christian' on the census.

A desire to claim a Christian label as a marker of ethnic identity was sometimes immediately obvious as people interrupted the reading of the census list during the final interview question. This was particularly marked during the interview with Robert and May, a couple in their 70s. He was a retired printer and she described herself as a housewife. Although they had both said they were not sure if they believed in God and never attended church, they had no difficulty answering the census question. As the choices were being read aloud May interrupted:

ABBY: They offered you some choices, Christian and -
MAY: Yeah, yeah, we would be Christian. Definitely. Yeah.

Robert asked:

Was it on that census where you were British, you could be British but not English or something. Is that what they're talking about bringing in?

When I said I could not quite remember the exact wording, he interrupted me, saying:

You could be a Scot, you could be a Welshman, you could be Irish, but you couldn't be English.

Robert's linking of religion to ethnicity recalls a suggestion that a heightened sense of ethno-religious identity may have been triggered through the census itself both because of the affirmative form of the question and its location on the census document.

Veronica, 48, said she thought she had selected Christian, explaining, 'Well, I'm not Catholic so I must be Christian.' Catholic had not been one of the options I read out; neither was 'Church of England', which many informants claimed they had selected. I suggest this is not a case of misunderstanding the question, but of reinterpreting the question to conform to pre-determined social understandings, particularly the value of institutionalized Christianity.

Voas and Bruce speculated that the high 'Christian' identification in the England and Wales census response may 'represent increasing anxiety about national identity rather than increasing commitment to Christian faith' (2004, 28). They also suggest that ethnic-religious identity was further triggered by the atmosphere at the time of the so-called 'race riots' in northern England and the general media presentation of ethnic relations. As I discussed in Chapter 7, Ray and Smith (2004) argued that local tensions and violence were partly stirred by racist media discourse.

My evidence supports Voas and Bruce here that the proximity of the ethnicity and religious questions on the England and Wales census may have triggered some people's anxieties about ethnicity. Further, I suggest that the wording of the ethnicity question, particularly its omission of 'English', may have antagonized some people and prompted them to be more careful when answering the following question on religion. I suggest here we can see how 'nominalism' may work to harden boundaries.

Terry, cited earlier, explained that religion did not play a part in his life, or the lives of others he knows: 'I don't know anybody who would say grace before a meal or anything like that.' He went on to say that there was no trouble in the village about 'whether somebody was a Catholic or anything else'. While to him 'Catholic' may indicate a more serious form of religion than the low level of religiosity in his own social group, his comment is also reminiscent of distinctions between Christian and Catholic reflecting a cultural history in the UK and, specifically, to the role of Protestantism. Until 1829 Catholics were not allowed to vote in the UK and they still cannot become (or marry) the monarch. Colley (1992, 31) said that in the eighteenth century church attendance in Britain was in decline but:

the Protestant world-view was so ingrained in this culture that it influenced people's thinking irrespective of whether they went to church or not.

She argued throughout her work that a sense of superior Protestant identity was created by and maintained through often military dominance over Catholic cultures thought to be inferior to the British and often specifically to the English. She discussed, for example, the way Britons in the eighteenth and seventeenth centuries argued that Catholics were lazy and their cultures politically, morally, intellectually, and commercially inferior to the British. As I discussed in Chapter 3, Terry had elaborated his point by referring to 'a bit of anti-Muslim feeling as anywhere else', mainly because newspapers like *The Sun* 'stir it up'. The 'fears of others people' may help explain why some people want to accentuate ethnic difference by relating it to Christianity. That is not to say such inscriptions are reflexive. The Catholic–Protestant divide may be similar to the Muslim–Protestant divide, not a new phenomenon, but one taking on new identities. The current discourse heard in the interviews is one where terms like 'Muslim', 'asylum seeker', or often just 'immigrant' have, to adopt a contemporary turn-of-phrase, become 'the new Catholics'.

Further, Terry's reference to 'our culture' has a specific sense of ownership, belonging, and exclusivity. That culture is learned and acquired may be taken for granted amongst sociologists and anthropologists, yet strikingly conceived differently by most of my informants. While academics might wrestle with culture as a contested term, exploring the balance between homogeneous and heterogeneous depictions, whether culture is a flow, a field, or a repository (or, indeed, all and more), my informants' views were untroubled by those varieties. They belonged to 'their' culture because they and their ancestors were born here, and they were proud of it. As Terry said: 'I'm proud to belong to this culture. To put it in a flamboyant sort of way.' I asked him what he meant by 'culture' and he replied:

> Well, it's the country culture, farming culture. It is a culture. Craven culture [*Craven is the region in which Skipton and nearby villages are situated*], Skipton culture, whichever. I can relate to anybody between Keighley and Bentham and Ingleton. And anybody from the countryside, better than I can to, let's say, townified people.

When I asked him what he meant by 'belong', he again situated it within immediate and bounded, physically related concepts.

> How do I know? Well, I walk out of here, drive down that road, call into every fifth house and know that I'd be able to talk to whoever lives there, for about thirty miles that way and well, maybe only about fifteen miles that way. Anyway, in a square, a patch, a fairly big patch. And I could, I could go with you and point to all the farms round and about and tell you he lives there, he lives there, and that's my sense of belonging, really. Know your way round, for a start. And I am a countryman, I mean I'm not really at ease in a city, and I'm useless at driving in a city to start off. Have to go around a round-about about four times. But I can find any back lanes and byways and footpaths.

As Cohen (1982) observed in his study of Scottish Shetland Islanders, culture is performed through everyday acts, not through grand rituals. People may emphasize the history of a practice not to 'demonstrate its consequent sacredness but to exhibit its appropriateness to those particular social circumstances and to portray the ingenuity and skills of those who originated them – and, by implication, of themselves' (1982, 5–6). Terry was demonstrating his personal and inherited ingenuity of local landscape knowledge, particularly when I asked him if he could find his way around so well because he was good at map-reading: 'No, it's because I'm familiar with the area. Anyone can find them if they have a map.'

The sense of being better had a moral authority for some other informants. This was clear in the interview with Robert and May, who, as described in Chapter 3, explained that they were not sure if they believed in God, although they had a 'Christian outlook', unlike Muslims who treat women badly. Robert's comments resonate with Colley's observation (1992) that Britons compare their laws, their treatment of women, and other parts of their societies with societies that they do not understand yet consider inferior. Like Robert, another informant positioned himself as better than others who were not Christian or, I suggest, English. Graham, 34, a technical analyst I first introduced in Chapter 3, discussed in the interview how his beliefs were derived from his family and life experience and that they had not changed in the 'small community' where he had grown up. Graham described Britain today as 'massively multicultural', saying 'with them come their beliefs and I don't know whether their beliefs filter out to the rest of us, I don't know'.

When asked what he said on the census, Graham said:

> I think I probably would have put Christian, actually, because that's how, what I was raised as. Not that I'm a practising one, but, I was born and raised that, so if I were to mark a religion that would be it.
> ABBY: Would you prefer to say Christian rather than none?
> GRAHAM: I've been baptized and confirmed as a Christian so in effect I was, I am a Christian but I'm not a practising Christian believer.

Graham admits he is not a practising Christian believer, but seems also to think that even without practising or believing, through merely being named as a Christian at birth he is inherently a Christian and not one of the multicultural others. This brings a non-trivial, powerful meaning to those who say they are Christian 'in name only'. It is therefore not the practice that is being labelled as different but the people who are practising it. The word 'community', as Graham invoked it, also stresses who is better and who is different. Thus, as discussed in Chapter 3, 'community' serves as a reference group, a real or imagined entity used to distinguish between one group and others, and provide apparent external validation for one group's beliefs.

Some of those symbols and meanings may converge to give an impression of a cultural religion. Demerath noted (1992, 46) that in the UK:

> The Anglican Confession has become a symbol of much more than religion itself, given its ties to the throne, the past, and to civilization at its zenith.

This tendency to merge symbols of power and history with religion was noted by Winter and Smart (1993, 648), who found that people who did not attend the Church of England regularly were twice as likely as regular attendees to oppose any change in traditional elements of church services. Non-attendees also said they were Christians because they were brought up as Anglicans 'or implied in some way that their belonging was by virtue of their "Englishness"' (ibid.).

Demerath (2000, 127) also looked at cultural belonging in Europe in a study of Northern Ireland, Poland, and Sweden.[9] The people he studied

> join in illustrating a common syndrome of 'cultural religion' by which religion affords a sense of personal identity and continuity with the past even after participation in ritual and belief have lapsed. Arguably one of the world's most common forms of religious involvement, it is also one of the most neglected by scholars.

It appears from my research that 'culture' is synonymous with 'white English' for many people. It is a term of power, of self-identification, defined by those seeking to reinforce their cultural inclusiveness while excluding others. In the political and religious climate of the late 1990s, 'new nationalisms' were driven by religious identities (Juergensmeyer 2006). Although the examples he gives are generally Islamic and non Euro American, the predominance of Christian Nominalism can also be read as such a phenomenon.

Finally, the act of affiliating to Christianity on the census while not participating in other forms of Christian practice conforms to what Gans (1979) described as 'symbolic ethnicity' where people can (ibid., 8) 'find their identity by "affiliating" with an abstract collectivity which does not exist as an interacting group' (at least in the nominalist experience).

Aspirational identities

Winter and Smart's finding (1993, 648) that non-church attendees were twice as likely as attendees to emphasize and endorse the 'traditional' elements of the church may suggest that the Church of England is conceived by nominalists as reflecting and conferring a certain continuity and respectability. My first inkling that 'Church of England' was linked to respectability amongst my informants came when interviewing Marge, a retired former pub landlady who does not attend church

[9] See also Bäckström et al. (2004).

and does not believe in any form of afterlife. The most important thing to her is her family, she said, and yet, when I asked Marge the census question, she interrupted me before I had listed all the categories and said 'Church of England'. I then asked her if she went to church, and she said no, apart from weddings and funerals: 'But that was where I was christened, Church of England. C of E. I always put that.' She then abruptly switched the topic to something I at first thought was unrelated and told me a long story about her daughter accusing her of not speaking 'proper English'. This suggested to me that Marge clearly made a connection between the Church of England and 'proper English', reflecting, following Skeggs (1997), working-class anxieties about being respectable.

Another person who gave the impression of aspiring was Liam, 21, single, a trainer at a gym, living with parents. In answer to the first question, 'What do you believe in?', he said that he assumed that meant religion, and morals, and as he was not raised with a religious upbringing, he would not be sure whether he believed in that or not. He said he thought he believed in fate, and in 'the things you do coming back to you' in some way or other. For fun, he says, he usually goes out with his friends on the weekends and gets drunk. When it came to the census question, he immediately answered that he would have put Christian. When asked why he said: 'Probably just for the sake of it. Not something I'm into, but it's the category I fall into.' A clue to his desire to affiliate himself with Christianity was his emphasis in the interview on his close relationship with his sister and brother-in-law. He described them as people whom he respects and who often guide him. He positioned them clearly as church-attending Christians who, he said with some wistfulness, had a structure to their lives

Although Liam does not 'believe in' Christianity as a religion, he 'believes in' those Christians he knows and aspires to become as successful, respectable, and happy as they are.

Implications

This chapter explored why apparently non-religious people may sometimes self-identify with Christianity, and argued that while they may be sometimes described as 'nominalist', 'nominalism' is not an empty, vague category. In Table 1 I show how the categories discussed thus far of anthropocentric, theocentric, and godless map onto nominalist identities described above. Christian Nominalism is a form of an anthropocentric belief orientation performed through one's act of

Table 1: Nominalist belief orientations (number of informants)

	Godless		Theists	
	Anthropo-centric	Theo-centric	Anthropo-centric	Theo-centric
Christian				
Natal nominalist	9			
Ethnic nominalist	6			
Aspirational nominalist	4			
Faithful				18
Muslim				1
Buddhist		2		
Other		4		
None	20			
Don't know	4			
Total	43	6		19

self-declaration at specific moments, bringing into being a form of 'doing Christianity' in the social. Anthropocentric, performative Christian Nominalism may be understood partly as the practice of self-identifying as Christian when asked to do so in particular social and temporal contexts, while not necessarily sharing Christian beliefs such as a faith in God or participating in any Christian public acts of worship or ritual observance. Christian Nominalism has inclusive and exclusive functions, often employed to harden religious boundaries.

This has important sociological and political implications. Christian Nominalists may align to an institutional affiliation to strengthen the perception of the UK as a Christian country. Colley, for example, concludes by saying that Protestantism and Christianity as a whole now have only 'limited influence on British culture' (Colley 1992, 374) and are no longer factors which help cement the culture. On the contrary, I have argued: Christianity is an important resource people sometimes use to reinforce their identity and therefore, through public discourse, the 'British culture'. Claiming any identity of Britain as a 'Christian country' should account for those British Christians being similar to the Christian Nominalists described above.

The finding also has theoretical implications. My findings suggest a Durkheimian turn to the social, where the social significance of institutional concepts of religion understood as 'social facts' (Durkheim 1938 [1895]) are not, as Wilson (1966) suggested, decreasing but may be increasing in significance for many people. That such a religious form may be rooted in the social and be independent of beliefs in gods or other conventionally religious forms characterizes what I have explored as performative, anthropocentric Christian Nominalism and somewhat blurs the boundary of what may otherwise be described as religious or secular.

10

Conclusion: Relocating Belief to the Social

This work began with the observation that belief has a discipline-specific genealogy that often remains unspoken and implicit, although recent work in the anthropology of Christianity (Cannell 2005; Day and Coleman 2010; Engelke and Tomlinson 2006; Lindquist and Coleman 2008; Robbins 2003; 2007) attempts to expose how religion and belief are constructed by laying bare, to some extent, the Christian-centric traditions of scholars.

Through tracing belief from Durkheim I explored two main developments that diverged by disciplinary focus: most of early- to mid-twentieth-century social anthropology of religion adopted a Durkheimian analysis where belief was explained in functional rather than substantive terms, shaped by boundaries of time and space. Belief was a social reality. The sociology of religion, alternatively, tended to favour substantive definitions, adopting a Weberian, meaning-centred understanding of belief. Belief was traced to a transcendent universal reality that could not be reduced to other social realities.

Within anthropology and sociology exist two important and different understandings of belief, discussed in this book as the 'pre-formed' and 'performed'. The Durkheimian approach was to put the belonging into belief, by arguing that beliefs were produced (what I would describe as performative) through rituals of belonging. Davies (2008, 12), drawing partly on Csordas (1994) and theories about embodiment, used the evocative phrase 'behaving belief'. Others, notably Geertz, understood ritual as performing already-held beliefs.

Drawing on empirical research, I explored mainstream belief and identity, starting from a case study in northern England and then broadening the data to include other parts of the UK, Europe, and North America. I argued that many people 'believe in belonging', sometimes accepting religious identifications to complement other social and emotional experiences of 'belongings'. I introduced the concept of 'performative Christianity' to explain how otherwise non-religious people can bring into being a Christian identity related to social belongings. Further, I argued that what is often dismissed as 'nominalism' is far from an empty category, but one loaded with cultural 'stuff' and meaning. This contrasts with much established disciplinary theory in both the European and North American schools of the sociology of religion, which asserts that most people are 'unchurched' while privately maintaining beliefs in God and other 'spiritual' phenomena. As this book revealed the complex nature of Christian nominalism, arguably the largest form of Christianity in Euro American countries, my findings complicated theories of modernity.[1]

If belief is different according to places, people, and times, the problem became: how do we identify it, define it, measure it, or compare it cross-culturally? Burridge (1973) argues that the original data examined by the first anthropologists and sociologists were collected from Christian missionaries and colonial administrators, who had a central question about the peoples being encountered: were they human, like us, and if so, in what way are they different from us?[2] In that sense the task became both ethnocentric and comparative, because the criteria of being human emerged from the visitors' experience. Being human would be assessed along lines of morality, religion, customs, rights, obligations, and other features of what the visitors assumed constituted *culture* or *religion*. But this, as Keane (2008, 112) pointed out, provokes a circular route: 'In the history of social and cultural anthropology, the category of "religion" has long stood for the general problem of apparently strange belief.' Once anthropologists could explain such strange beliefs as part of 'culture', then the category of religion itself tends to be subsumed, or at least to slip.

An underlying problem I suggest is that scholars have been too focused on that 'it': the what, the content of belief. To resolve that problem I departed from the arguments by Needham and Ruel summarized in earlier chapters and reclaimed 'belief' as a term for cross-cultural comparison.

---

[1] Significant contributions to this challenge were made by contributors to Day (2008b).
[2] More current post-colonial examples also exist: Graveling (2010) describes the problems that arise when development agencies misconstrue what is meant by religion or belief.

Relocating belief in the social

Belief, like emotion, does not exist pre-formed in the individual but is relationally produced, suggesting resonance with an earlier meaning of belief – 'be loved'. The activity of 'doing belief' is described as an active, reflective orientation towards belief arising from human, emotional interaction and personal reflection.[3] A longing for belonging helps explain aspects of belief which have problematized theories of secularization reliant on divisions between, for example, 'this world' and 'other world' by showing how beliefs in the supernatural can be located in the temporal and social. Questionnaires, for example, that persist in asking if people believe in 'heaven' fail to separate a religious concept of 'heaven' as a place for the godly and good from heaven as a place for continuing adherent relationships.

Relocating belief to the social also illuminates our understanding of people's propensity to sometimes associate causality with supra-human forces such as 'fate'. My research has revealed the extent to which people in the mainstream 'believe in' and want to believe in social values, people, and social institutions that they trust or want to trust – a longing particularly expressed by young people. Belief in 'the social' in this context is an expression of emotion and relatedness through belonging and longing, often arising to draw clear boundaries between 'us' and 'others'. Relocation here reflects the genealogy of belief with which I began this book, tracing the academic understanding of belief as stemming from and then diverging from a Durkheimian perspective that belief arose from social situations. The divergence began with what I have suggested throughout this book was a Tylorian/ Weberian/Geertzian/Bergerist and Luckmann-like tendency to locate belief in some universalist, imagined place of a pre-social yearning for meaning or – as, for example, Evans-Pritchard or Horton argued – for explanation. Although such yearnings, of course, appear in many lives, I located such impulses in the social, and particularly in relatedness. My work explored belief by stressing belief's social location and its role in bringing into being forms of identity that actors strategically create to adapt to and integrate themselves into various social situations. Further, I drew attention to the political, discursive, and ideological influences on constructions and performances of belief. The way belief is resourced and performed in late modern societies may be best

---

[3] Henkel (2005) describes how Turkish Muslims' practice of *salat* (praying five times daily) in different social spaces helps them both bond collectively and also deepen their personal, embodied, religious identity.

explained through multidimensional analysis, where the tendencies discussed above fluctuate according to situation and context.

Performative belief

A process I termed 'performative belief' refers to my neo-Durkheimian construct, where belief is not pre-formed but a lived, embodied performance, brought into being through action and where the object of worship is not an entity such as a god or 'society', but the experience of belonging. Performances, according to Goffman (1959, 36–51), are socialized and idealized: they fit into social expectations and idealize society's values. Within a social context are social relationships: performative belief plays out through the relationships in which people have faith and to which they feel they belong; to which, I suggest, they adhere. Belief in social relationships is performed through social actions of both belonging and excluding. Those 'actions' are not only the ones conventionally measured in social science (church attendance, tithing, prayer, and so on) but other social actions and activities: sharing a 'belief narrative', for example, or filling out a census form, or political activities (see, for example, Lynch 2007). Performative belief, as I am using it, has its own genealogy to which I am indebted and to which I have referred in previous chapters citing, primarily, Austin, Butler, and Bourdieu. The contribution I make is to situate that performance more clearly in the social action of relatedness.

The performative acts I analysed are summarized below.

Claiming cultural identities

People who 'believe in belonging' claim social and cultural identities to reinforce a belief in belonging to specific groups of people, particularly those with whom they have affective, adherent relations or those whom they recognize as having legitimate authority. When those beliefs are performed they create and sustain social identities, such as American, or English, or Christian. Those performances sometimes incorporate other agendas to reinforce social and cultural identities, from American 'crusades' against pornography, to the formation of the Moral Majority in the USA and the relationship of pro-gun lobbying to God. Historical examples from the Catholics of fifteenth-century Spain to the Jews of nineteenth-century Denmark confirm Asad's point that belief needs to be situated in place and time and analysed as not just a religious but also a political force.

One of the main acts I analysed was the production and then response to the religious question on the 2001 Census for England and Wales.[4] My argument was that the reinforcement of the category of 'Christian' and its connection to British identity was necessary for many people at that particular point in history. For example, many people who said they chose 'Christian' as their affiliation on the census also explained that they did not believe in Christianity. They were Christian primarily because they belonged to a family that had raised them as Christian or because they understood 'Christian' as a term coded to colour, country, and culture. It will be interesting to see how that identity changes over time. At the time of writing the 2011 census had just taken place, but preliminary results will not be available until after this book's publication. As a member of the Academic Advisory Board for the Office of National Statistics, I agreed that the question wording – although, as argued elsewhere, flawed – should be retained for comparative purposes.

In his revised version of *Imagined Communities*, Anderson (1991, 163–85) argued that the 'fiction' of the census was that it included everyone and that people had clear, single identities. Although he drew his examples from British colonialism, his remarks remain relevant to all census projects: categories of ethnicity, national identity, religion, and the like are created and change over time by social and political action and expectations. For example, the situated nature of identifying as 'white' was noted by Godreau et al. (2010, 11) in relation to census data in the United States. In the 2000 census, 80.5 per cent of people in Puerto Rico[5] who selected a single racial category self-identified as white, with only 8 per cent identifying as black; 47.2 per cent of Puerto Ricans living in the United States selected 'white'. The authors suggest this contrast is explained by '*blanqueamiento*', or the process of 'whitening': Puerto Rican residents were aspiring to being white, whereas US residents could not pursue this goal on the census because the 'one drop rule' disallowed it.

Although the US census does not contain a question about religion, the political and ideological influence of census questions about language was noted by Leeman (2004), who traced how the development of questions reinforced the assumption that English monolingualism is regarded as a natural and desirable state. For another rich discussion of

---

[4] For comment on the Irish question and its relation to ethnicity, see Walls (2001).

[5] Puerto Rico is a self-governing commonwealth of the United States. Puerto Ricans are American citizens but cannot vote in American presidential elections and have no seats in government.

self-perceptions of ethnicity, see Hiller et al.'s (2009) study about Mayans living in Florida, who claim Mayan identity in preference to others.

Beyond the religious question on the UK census, I drew similar points from the Canadian census and American surveys on religious identification.[6]

Mine is the only study to scrutinize qualitatively the results of the 2001 UK census and in this book I broadened the implications for other industrialized countries with similar apparent contradictions between religious belief and practice. A main implication is the nature of the aging Christian population: De Graaf and Grotenhuis (2008, 595–6) concluded from their study in the Netherlands, with comparisons to the UK (see Crockett and Voas 2006), that religious belief will continue to decline owing to cohort replacement.

Believing through bereaving

The sensuous, social supernatural

By not asking religious questions I was able to draw out beliefs that could only be explained through theories of belonging: atheists who believe in ghosts, for example. Many of my informants often experienced continued belonging with deceased loved ones in what I describe as the sensuous, social supernatural, in contrast to other scholars who would describe such experiences as 'religious'. The everyday, socially situated, non-institutional transcendent experience of continued belonging is brought into being through embodied, physical sensations and emotions and sustained through performative belief rituals where the account is told, re-told, and elaborated.

Covering the cracks in belonging

Just as belonging seems to fuel belief, so, too, does not belonging. Social ruptures in belonging through, for example, isolation, betrayal, tragedy, or loss of control or power may sometimes produce 'cracks in belonging' that people will often attempt to cover through a, usually temporary, belief in fate or supra-human governance. My findings here challenge theories that new forms of spirituality are growing that are subjective and experiential, and suggest different ways of relating to

---

[6] At the time of writing, both the British and Canadian governments are proposing to do away with their censuses altogether.

'the sacred'. On the few occasions in my research when people discussed their relationships to something akin to 'the sacred' (usually expressed as a spirit or higher power) it was, as I argued in Chapter 5 and Chapter 6, more an expression of vulnerability and wishful thinking on the part of those who were bereaved or disappointed in their human relationships. In this case, such beliefs may relate more to an emotive understanding of the word as derived originally from a variation of the term 'beloved' (Lopez 1998; Smith 1967). A quantitative study supporting this point (Norris and Inglehart 2004) argued that socio-economic inequalities sometimes create conditions that threaten human survival and cause people to suffer existential insecurity, which, in turn, leads them to religions that offer reassurance that life has a purpose and will improve, either in this world or in the next. Those ideas conform to a Weberian typology of religious affinities and its application to contemporary social life has been corroborated and critiqued elsewhere.[7] My argument has been that we should consider that explanation situationally, contextually, and holistically within the larger fabric of relatedness.

Doing unto people like us

A further component of my believing-in-belonging thesis is that most of my informants attributed their moral beliefs to human, rather than theistic or religious, sources. I showed, particularly in Chapter 7, how at times this process of attribution countered existing theory connecting religion and Christianity to morality, as if one must be religious to be good. Far from 'doing unto others', most people mark clear boundaries between those to whom they do or do not want to belong. People who are not like themselves are 'others', who are blamed for the ills of society: young people, those perceived to be 'foreign', and mothers who do not behave according to stereotype.

This may be a case of 'symbolic' boundary-making, but with real consequences. As Lamont and Virag (2002, 168) wrote, 'Social boundaries are objectified forms of social differences manifested in unequal access to and unequal distribution of resources (material and nonmaterial) and social opportunities.'

I reviewed informants' moral beliefs using the organic, holistic, multidimensional framework I described in Chapter 8 of content, sources,

---

[7] De Graaf and Grotenhuis (2008, 595) noted that the welfare state in the Netherlands has shrunk as people have become less protected by social security: 'Interestingly, and in contrast to Norris and Inglehart's prediction, secularization is still going on.'

practice, salience, function, time, and place, concluding that the moral beliefs of the anthropocentrics did not differ from the moral beliefs of the theist theocentrics. Both were convinced it was best to treat people as one would like to be treated, and both deplored the behaviours of women, young people, and people from other 'ethnic' groups whom they saw as disrespectful and damaging to society. That tendency to blame others prevailed just as strongly in Yorkshire as it did in Sussex, Tanzania, and Scotland. The legacy of 'Eve' and the motif of the 'fall' seem to pervade Christian-influenced societies over place and time (see, for example, Day 2008a).

Here, I depart from theorists such as Luckmann (1967, 98–9) who argued that people create meanings 'in a relatively autonomous fashion'. Further, my multidimensional framework for understanding belief allows an expansion of the term 'belief' to convey emotional[8] and ideological functions, often serving to strengthen one's sense of identity, where 'the statement "I believe in ...," is sensible only when there are others who do not' (Lopez 1998, 33). Hannah, 35, said she developed ideas about morality 'through talking through things with other people'. This experience of talking through moral questions with friends and family frequently arose. When I asked a class how much of an influence their friends had on them, they said that it was not a deep influence but their friends probably confirmed, through discussion, what they believed anyway. Other sources of affirmation people discussed were mothers and grandparents. Young people, particularly females, often told me about talking with their mothers or grandmothers about problems at school or troubles with friends. Young men talked about talking to their 'mates' or grandparents. Conversations with trusted relatives occurred whether the relative was dead or alive: as I discussed in depth in Chapter 5, many people told me they are still in communication with their dead relatives.

Performing patriarchy

A further implication of this work is to lay bare the 'gender-blindness' in both anthropology and sociology that masks the overarching nature of belief in white patriarchy, raised first in Chapter 8. Bowie (2006) observed that anthropology is constituted of male-constructed theories and definitions, focusing on milieux inhabited by men. Anthropologists thus tend to universalize and marginalize women through

[8] The growing interest in emotion is captured by, for example, Burkitt (1997) and Riis and Woodhead (2010).

ignoring anything specific about women's experience and constructs. This 'gender-blindness' is also a feature of the sociological study of religion, argued Woodhead (2000). She described Weber's idea of the iron cage and Durkheim's concept of anomie as particularly oriented to men because both assume participation in the public realm, a realm from which women were traditionally excluded. I also found it difficult to apply to women Weber's theories on why different groups of people were attracted to different kinds of religions and what their roles may be within those institutions (Weber 1922; 1992 [1930]). Weber's analysis of affinities for a particular type of religion is based on men's economic conditions and occupations: the warrior, the peasant, the artisan, the missionary, the tent-maker, the prince, the capitalist, and so on (Weber 1922: 95–117). He did not suggest female equivalents to help explain the experience of nurses, teachers, low-paid or unpaid domestic labourers such as wives and mothers.

A more recent example of gender-blindness occurs in Wuthnow's (1994, 358) study of small groups, including church-based groups dominated by women, where he concluded that a certain type of wisdom was missing because members did not pay sufficient attention to theological arguments:

> In simplest terms, the sacred comes to be associated with small insights that seem intuitively correct to the small group rather than wisdom accrued over the centuries in hermitages, seminaries, universities, congregations and church councils.

This, I suggest, is a gendered perception of 'wisdom'. With the exception of, for example, convents, such spaces have been male-dominated. Men, not women, have traditionally inhabited hermitages and seminaries, and dominated the universities, congregations, and church councils. Wuthnow expresses concern about what he calls the domestication of the sacred, an implicit reference to women who traditionally occupy the domestic sphere.

Many argue that gender-blindness, or even belief in patriarchy, dominates religious, particularly conservative, groups.[9] Despite apparent progress in the feminist agendas relating to reproduction and employment, women attending the Fourth World Conference on Women in

---

[9] For a sensitive treatment of why women accept the status this implies, see, for example, Ozorak's (1996) study of American Christian women, where she found that their acceptance of the church hierarchy and male domination was partly explained by their sense of having their own space where they felt empowered. Strathern (1984) also discussed how ethnocentric views of women sometimes ignore or denigrate how women value their known positions and labour.

Beijing reported that conservative religious alliances are resisting that progress (Bracke 2003, 345). Further, it has been noted by several scholars that the American response to the apparent increased moral liberalism of the 1960s and 1970s had its roots in religious patriarchal beliefs. Beyer (1994, 124) wrote: 'What the family represents for the New Christian Right is an authority structure beyond the disposition of modern functional reality.'

While I do not disagree with those observations, I found that stereotypic beliefs about women's roles were shared amongst anthropocentrics and theocentrics. Following West and Zimmerman (1987, 145), I suggest my data illustrate how social differentiation assigns everyday personal matters and emotional labour to women in milieux not explicitly dominated by religion: both anthropocentrics and theocentrics believe that women belong to a domestic place. While aware that such terms as 'white' and 'patriarchy' may appear unnecessarily reductionist, I suggest that they necessarily capture both the quality and the intensity of the often emotive expressions imparted in my interviews and convey a sense, as Douglas (1973) might argue, that such concepts reflect a natural order. In reviewing how the use of the term 'patriarchy' has been criticized in the literature, Walby (1990) summarized how feminists and sociologists have been critical of those who use the term 'patriarchy' ahistorically and insensitively to particularities of, for example, culture and class.[10] Bryson (1999) notes similar criticisms and argues it would be wrong to reject 'a handle on the world which can still provoke a powerful sense of recognition' (ibid., 315) by reminding us that men, not women, are the dominant and privileged group.

It is here that I differ from those definitional stances and broaden, for this work, the term 'patriarchy' to include male domination over and oppression of women and young people. By 'young people' I am referring both to men's children and to young people over whom, I argued, they assume inherent authority. The main reason I expand the definition of patriarchy here is because I identified and analysed several recurrent themes in my interviews: a pattern of paternal violence

---

[10] The experience of women of colour was also neglected by early feminists. Recognizing the political, power-based nature of relationships could bring us to consider more often intersectionality as an analytical tool, an approach prompted initially by feminist work (Collins 2000; Crenshaw 1991) pointing to the multiple nature of experience and identity: it is not informative to speak, for example, of 'black women' but, rather, black working-class young urban...Further, an intersectional analysis can uncover how identity is 'performed' as people extract salient parts of their surrounding cultural resources to experiment with their experiences of gender, race, and class (Williams 2009). Intersubjective analysis illuminates inequalities and the hegemonic structures and beliefs supporting them.

towards children; a recurrent theme of males abandoning their children, described by Walby (1990, 106) as a 'flight from fatherhood'; a sense of powerlessness amongst some young males in reference to what they perceive as 'authority'; and a pervasive assumption amongst older males that they have the right to be respected by young people as figures of authority.[11] Making a similar point, Delphy and Leonard (1992, 13) say that feminists agree that the term 'patriarchy' needs to be understood not as 'a series of haphazard, piecemeal oppressions' but as a system of continuous male domination which applies also to young people. Men's physical and economic abuse in family relationships is not, they argue, an occasional event but endemic and systematic. My finding in my work is that a patriarchal system of male dominance over and oppression of women and young people is not only endemic but accepted by many men and women, but not by young people.

This finding is consistent with a theory of discursive patriarchy (Walby 1990), where an apparently natural scheme of gender relations is supported widely within the culture, affecting people's perception of the nature of gender relations, and the way that they act (see also Hochschild and Machung 1989 on women's under-valued labour). That an acceptance of patriarchy is often unarticulated is consistent with the nature of such 'silent' discourses of white superiority (Gilroy 1987). The superiority of white men pervades many of my interviews although, as Gilroy would have predicted, it is not often expressed in precisely those terms but coded in strategic silences. In, particularly, Chapters 3 and 7, I analysed at length how the 'other' in society is often an 'ethnic other' held to be responsible for many problems in society, from street crime to the demise of Christianity. This ethnic exclusivity is not, however, gender-neutral. Discourses of morality intertwined with gender and ethnicity, often demonstrating the patriarchal nature of family life and morality. Fortier (2000) extended the idea of ethnicity to incorporate gender as she analysed how discourses and practices amongst Italian migrants often revolve around themes of family and good mothering, themselves embedded in the sanctification of 'community' and familistic religion.

---

[11] The line between disrespect and revolution may be fine. In her study of how young Iranians are experiencing a sexual revolution linked to their disrespect for current authority structures, Mahdavi (2008, 289) wrote: 'Many young adults do not care about the opinions of the religious leaders, nor do they fear the punishments or sanctions that could be placed on their behaviour by the regime or their parents.'

Belief in belonging

Human or divine orientations

The nature of belief narratives demanded a multidimensional method of analysis that revealed different orientations of being anthropocentric or theocentric towards the human or divine. Conceptually, religion and secularization thus become subsets of 'belief'. Both religion and secularity are released from a temporal dimension: once we stop analysing whether people are more or less religious, we can turn to the proper questions: what do people in a certain place and time believe in and how are those beliefs sourced, valued, practised, and integrated in other parts of social life? In so doing we can reclaim belief as both a religious and a non-religious term. This might help avoid the kinds of alienation that may be provoked by the term 'unbeliever'. As Rudge (1998) poignantly described in her report on how children understand religious beliefs, to say one has no religious belief should not be the same as saying 'I am nothing.' Nevertheless, as I commented earlier in this book, stretching definitions of religion too far may neglect many aspects of what I would describe as social or relational belief.[12]

A main implication then is the necessity to dispense with binary, subsidiary categories of belief, such as 'religious' or secular', and focus instead on multidimensional, interdependent orientations. Although I was not primarily interested in secularization theories, an implication of my work here is that existing theories need to adjust to allow a belief in supernatural entities or events without shifting the locus of power and authority from humans. This conforms to what Shiner (1967, 208) described as a type of secularism proposed in the nineteenth century by G.J. Holyoake as a philosophy to 'interpret and organise life without recourse to the supernatural', or to what Berger described, as discussed in Chapter 1, as subjective secularization, where people regard their world 'without the benefit of religious interpretations', (Berger 1967, 107–8). Allowing for a secular belief in supernatural entities and events would contradict some of the believing-without-belonging argument for the persistence of what has been variously described as common, folk, invisible, or implicit religion. It is rare in the sociology of religion to find research defending secularization, as Swatos and Christiano

---

[12] For example, Clark decided (1982, viii) in his study of a Yorkshire fishing village to 'include in the category of religion, at least for purposes of argument, numerous examples of popular belief, local custom, superstition and ritual'. By casting his net so widely he missed an opportunity to explore what may be more explicitly acts of sociality than 'folk religion'. Rice (2003) notes that religious scholars generally ask questions about supernatural beliefs that are already embedded in religious language.

(1999, 216) noted: 'Virtually no empirical research supports the prediction of a societal slide from the peak of sacrality into a valley of secularity.' As I discussed earlier, that little research supports secularity is not surprising when most research either researches religious people or asks forced religious questions. It would be more instructive, for those concerned with the language of secularism, to set such debates within the historical context of other fictions. Cannell (2010, 86) suggests: 'the meanings of "secular" and "secularism" are constantly shifting in the literature, depending on whether a given author believes that they are real' and how much such terms are linked to equally problematic terms like modernity, religion, and the 'past', and when they are, in fact, 'themselves only a fiction of the historical processes we are examining'. (See also, on that point, Asad 2003 and for other anthropological critiques of 'secular', Day and Coleman 2013a; Kapferer 2001; Pina-Cabral 2001; Stewart 2001.)

Another implication from my research is that it challenges such theories about 'unchurched believers' advanced by, for example Davie (1994) and Stark et al. (2005). I presented a different terminology from 'unchurched' or 'secular', suggesting 'anthropocentric' best describes people who may or may not describe themselves as Christian and may or may not attend church, but believe that human life is social, with meaning, power, and authority located in the social without a divine origin or authority. The categories are not fixed and people may vary, of course, within their lifetimes. Those with an anthropocentric orientation may experience supernatural events but tend to locate transcendence in the social, particularly through their continuing relationships with what they describe as the spirit of their deceased loved ones. As discussed in Chapters 4 and 6, I noticed a distinct gender imbalance (see, also, Goode 2000).

People with a more theocentric orientation believe in a God with whom they have an adherent, emotional, reciprocal relationship. Although some theocentric behaviour might appear to be individualistic, closer examination usually shows a more connected sense of belonging. They also exhibit boundary-marking behaviour, as described in Chapter 7. An American study (Cimino 2005) found boundary-marking increased substantially in Evangelical literature after the events of 9/11, suggesting, as I discuss in relation to 'time', the shifting and responsive nature of collective bonding. A tendency towards 'theological exclusivism' was observed in the United States by Merino (2010), who found that Christians who view the United States as a 'Christian nation' are less likely to include non-Christians in everyday life, perhaps explaining the lack of significant integration of people from other faiths in American society. Christian attitudes to what constitutes authentic religion vary across time, both within and outside any religious community, with various forms of Christianity protected by elites (Stewart and Shaw 1994).

The argument in this book is that my informants have relationship-centred and relationship-guided beliefs, informed by experience and the emotions they (re)produce. That conclusion counters a prevailing fiction in social science that late modernity is characterized by individualism. Although many of my informants pointedly distanced themselves from institutionalized religion, they did not evoke more 'individualized' narratives but, rather, the opposite. This was particularly evident amongst young people, whose sense of what I described as 'belonging to connected selves' spoke to relatedness and sociality, not individuality, with a common theme of belonging to adherent, reciprocal, emotional, legitimate relationships. My findings were compared to and contrasted with other UK, European, and North American examples, some of which concurred with my conclusions and others differed, depending on the context.[13]

My case study data strongly suggested that informants understood themselves as being 'in relation to' something or somebody, often expressing their identity as an expression of belonging. When they discussed what or whom they 'believed in' they were making statements about longing and belonging. I found that narrative discourses and 'glancing tropes' were used to convey connections or disconnections amongst people. This finding problematizes dominant theories in the social sciences relating to individualism and fragmentation. The nature of my informants' belief narratives was indeterminate, open-ended, and often expressed from multiple viewpoints. I argue that this reflects a nature of identity as fluid, malleable, interdependent, multiple, and continuously forming (see, also, Coleman and Collins 2004).

Power, agency, and authority were analysed throughout, leading me to conclude that people differ in how they believe their lives are controlled based primarily on the areas of their lives where they feel most vulnerable and socially disconnected. Unlike theorists who overgeneralize from specific (generally non-empirical) observations, I argued that such disconnections are frequently temporary and not necessarily reason to characterize modernity as a state of anomie.

Close work is required to detect strands of collectivism and institutional belonging in what may appear to be contrary examples. Keenan

---

[13] See Sandberg (2008) for an in-depth discussion of how religion is conceived legally as predominantly a collective rather than individual construct.

(2008) found that the male gay Anglican priests he interviewed often found the institutional space of the church, and its traditions, enabling rather than restricting. In his study of Spring Harvest, the largest annual charismatic-evangelical conference in Britain, Warner (2008) explored how the event's format has changed to allow more individual choice, within a strong collective of a religious group he described as 'bricolage within boundaries'.

In a study of hobby-genealogists in eastern England, Cannell (2011) concluded that tracing one's past through ancestors was not the self-oriented act it is often portrayed as, but a means of caring for the dead. In her discussion of related studies, she notes that many researchers shut down analysis as soon as an informant mentions 'self' and turn to well-worn theories about self-interest and individualism. Her comments remind me of Tom, the young student I have discussed earlier through my interview with him and Gavin. He told me he had his 'own religion'.

> It's like my own religion, it's like I believe in stuff like, I just believe in being good, stuff like that, be grateful for what you get. Others can't get, other people in other countries may not be able to get that. Stuff like that. I always send, you know that shoe box? I've just done one.

It would be a mistake to move from Tom's reference to his 'own religion' to ideas about self-orientation as, for example, did Bellah et al. (1986) when referring to respondent 'Sheila Larson'.

'I believe in God,' Sheila says. 'I am not a religious fanatic. I can't remember the last time I went to church. My faith has carried me a long way. It's Sheilaism. Just my own little voice.'

I suggest that people who believe in their inner voices or capability of working out meaning, destiny, and morality are not individualistic, but reflexive in a highly socialized way. One of the ways people resolve the 'grey' is through talking with other people.

Methods in modernity

This study addressed methodological and intellectual issues relating to belief in the twenty-first century in several original ways. During my study in northern England, I researched religion without asking overtly religious questions or selecting people based on their interest in religion or spirituality. The aim was to probe beliefs amongst three generations of people from a wide cross-section of society. The intellectual scope was then widened beyond sociology to other disciplines, primarily the anthropology of religion. Anthropology, unlike sociology, has had an ongoing debate on how we explore and problematize notions of belief. My findings collapsed distinctions between believing/belonging and private/public, concluding that people 'believe in belonging' to their significant relationships, with religion sometimes signalling such belonging.

Unique to the field of the sociology of religion, I developed an approach for probing and understanding the beliefs of people who were not selected and did not select themselves on the grounds of religious affiliation and without asking them religious questions. Such a method is necessary if we are, as I assume, in an era of late modernity characterized by multiplicity and reflexivity. Converse (1964; 1970) argued that most people answer open-ended questions without really thinking about the issue and their answers, therefore, do not reflect an ideology or belief system. Their responses, Converse concluded, were unstable, and so erratic as not to relate to the instrument or the question. The mood of the respondents, their perceptions about the interviewer (in panel surveys) and desire to please or conform to social norms were major influences on how they answered. Others, a minority of those polled, would have strong and stable opinions. Yet, as Giddens argued, reflexivity is a mark of modernity. Particularly, as I discovered, if people are allowed to recount stories and those stories are deconstructed as holistic, organic belief narratives, then we may well find that when people are being interviewed by a sociologist about ideas, beliefs, and values they are aware that they are not only informing the researcher but are co-agents, constructors of knowledge: see, on ethnographic principles that help inform such accounts, Hammersley and Atkinson (1995).

Organic, multidimensional belief[14]

The seven-part heuristic I developed initially arose inductively from the empirical research I conducted in the UK and then expanded as I drew wider theoretical and cross-cultural comparisons. The model examined not just the content of belief but also sources, practice, salience, function, place, and time. As explained in Chapter 2, while I set out to explore the *content* of informants' beliefs, how their beliefs

---

[14] I use the terms 'model' and 'dimension' broadly: model, here, refers to an interpretive model, a means to interpret evidence, rather than a small-scale representation of a thing. Dimension means both an aspect and a variable, and captures the quality of shape, form, depth, and breadth.

were *sourced*, and how they were *practised*, as the research unfolded I created two more analytical categories: how important beliefs were to informants (*salience*), and what their beliefs did for them (*function*) (Day 2013b). As I moved from the original study to a post-empirical, anthropological review, it became evident that *time* and *place* were two other significant dimensions.[15]

The seven dimensions presented here are neither exclusive nor exhaustive: other researchers may identify new aspects or dispense with some just articulated. What I constructed was a model that moves us well beyond a singular, monodimensional approach and allows us to better understand people's beliefs and compare them cross-culturally. My method, using open-ended questions in semi-structured interviews, produced data that, interpreted through multidimensional belief analysis, led me to conclude that statements of religious affiliation are often expressions of natal, ethnic, and class identity.

My current research, funded by the ESRC, is a qualitative longitudinal study where I return to the field initially discussed in this book to assess if, why, and how people's beliefs may have changed. My preliminary findings indicate that changes that have occurred were provoked not primarily by 'time' or life course, but by changes in social relationships. In conclusion, I hope that by showing how 'belief' does not disappear, but is ever-present in the social, it becomes apparent that belief may be the ultimate 'project' of modernity: always changing and subject to the larger context and social relations that produce it.

---

[15] Although her remit was 'everyday religion' rather than belief, Ammerman's (2007) collection is located overtly in social context, paying attention to the 'social worlds in which religious ideas, practices, groups and experiences make an appearance' (ibid., 6).

References

Abercrombie, N., J. Baker, S. Brett, and J. Foster 1970. Superstition and religion: the God of the gaps. In *A sociological yearbook of religion in Britain*, ed. D. Martin and M. Hill, 93–129. London: S.C.M.

Allport, G.W. 1966. The religious context of prejudice. *Journal for the Scientific Study of Religion*, 5: 447–57.

Amira, M.Z. 2008. Experience beyond belief: the 'strangeness curve' and integral transformative practice. *Social Analysis*, 52, no. 1: 127–43.

Ammerman, N.T. 1997. Golden rule Christianity: Lived religion in the American mainstream. In *Lived Religion in America*, ed. D. Hall, 196–216. Princeton: Princeton University Press.

—— 2007. *Everyday religion: observing modern religious lives*. Oxford and New York: Oxford University Press.

Anderson, B. 1983. *Imagined communities*. London: Verso.

—— 1991. *Imagined communities: Reflections on the origin and spread of Nationalism*. Revised edition. London and New York: Verso.

Archbishops' council. 2006. www.bbc.co.uk/bbctrust/assets/files/pdf/consult/purpose_remits/responses/archbishops_council.pdf, last accessed 3 March 2008.

Asad, T. 1993. *Genealogies of religion: discipline and reasons of power in Christianity and Islam*. Baltimore, Md.: Johns Hopkins University Press.

—— 2003. *Formations of the secular*. Stanford, Calif.: Stanford University Press.

Ashworth, J. and I. Farthing 2007. *Churchgoing in the UK*. Teddington: Tearfund.

Austin, J.L. 1962. *How to do things with words*. Clarendon: Oxford.

Avis, P. (ed.) 2003 *Public faith? The state of religious belief and practice in Britain*. London: SPCK.

Bäckström, A., N.A. Beckman, and P. Pettersson 2004. *Religious change in northern Europe: the case of Sweden*. Stockholm: Verbum.

Bailey, E. 1990. Implicit religion: a bibliographical introduction. *Social Compass*, 37, no. 4: 499–509.

Balzer, M. M. 2008. Healing Failed Faith? Contemporary Siberian Shamanism. *Anthropology and Humanism*, 26, no. 2: 134–49.

Banfield, E.C. 1958. *The moral basis of a backward society*. New York: Free Press.

Barker, E. 1989. And what do you believe? Methods and perspectives in investigating religion. In *Investigating society*, ed. R. Burgess, 32–50. London: Longman.

Barker, J. (ed.) 2007. *The anthropology of morality in Melanesia and beyond.* Aldershot, Hants, England; Burlington, Vt.: Ashgate.

Barker, J. and S. Weller 2003. Is it fun? Developing participatory children centred research methods. *International Journal of Sociology and Social Policy*, 23, no. 1–2: 33–58.

Barth, F. 1969. *Ethnic groups and boundaries.* Bergen: Universitetsforlaget.

Barthes, R. 1988. [1973]. *The semiotic challenge.* Oxford: Basil Blackwell.

BBC   http://news.bbc.co.uk/1/shared/spl/hi/uk/03/census_2001/html/religion.stm (census 2001), retrieved 26 March 2008.

Bauman, Z. 1992. *Intimations of postmodernity.* London: Routledge.

——— 2001. *Community: seeking safety in an insecure world.* Cambridge: Polity.

Beck, U. 1992. *Risk society: towards a new modernity.* London: Newbury Park.

——— and E.Beck-Gernsheim 2002. *Individualization: institutionalized individualism and its social and political consequences.* London: Sage.

Bell, C. 1997. *Ritual, perspectives and dimensions.* New York and Oxford: Oxford University Press.

——— 2000. Acting ritually. In *The Blackwell companion to sociology of religion*, ed. R. Fenn, 371–87. Oxford: Blackwell.

Bellah, R. N. 1964. Religious evolution. *American Sociological Review*, 29: 358–74.

——— 1967. Civil religion in America. *Daedalus*, 96: 1–21.

——— 1970. *Beyond belief: essays on religion in a post-traditional world.* New York: Harper and Row.

——— R. Madsen, W.M. Sullivan, A. Swidler, and S.M. Tipton 1985. *Habits of the heart: individualism and commitment in American life.* Berkeley: University of California Press.

Bengtson, V.L. 2001. Beyond the nuclear family: The increasing importance of multigenerational bonds. *Journal of Marriage and Family*, 63: 1–16.

——— T.J. Biblarz, and R.E.L. Roberts 2002. *How families still matter: a longitudinal study of youth in two generations.* Cambridge: Cambridge University Press.

Bennett, G. 1999. *Alas, poor ghost! Traditions of belief in story and discourse.* Logan, Utah: Utah State University Press.

Berger, H.A. and D. Ezzy 2007. *Teenage witches: magical youth and the search for the self.* New Brunswick, N.J.: Rutgers.

Berger, P.L. 1967. *The sacred canopy: elements of a sociological theory of religion.* New York: Doubleday.

——— and T. Luckmann 1966. *The social construction of reality: a treatise in the sociology of knowledge.* Garden City, N.Y.: Anchor Books.

Berger, P. 2002. Postscript. In *Peter Berger and the Study of Religion*, ed. L. Woodhead with P. Heelas and D. Martin, 189–98. London and New York: Routledge.

Berliner, D. and R. Sarró (eds) 2007. *Learning religion, anthropological approaches.* New York and Oxford: Berghahn Books.

Beyer, P. 1994. *Religion and globalization.* New York: Sage.

Bialecki, J. 2008. Between stewardship and sacrifice: agency and economy in a Southern California Charismatic church. *Journal of the Royal Anthropological Institute* 14: 372–90.

Bielo, J. 2008. Cultivating intimacy: Interactive frames for Evangelical Bible study. *Fieldwork in Religion*, 3, no. 1: 51–69.

Blanes, R.L. 2006. The atheist anthropologist: believers and non-believers in anthropological fieldwork. *Social Anthropology*, 14: 223–34.

Bloch, M. 1986. *From blessings to violence*. Cambridge: Cambridge University Press.

—— 1992. *Prey into hunter*. Cambridge: Cambridge University Press.

Borhek, J.T. and R.F. Curtis 1975. *A sociology of belief*. New York: John Wiley and Sons.

Bourdieu, P. 1991. *Language and symbolic power*. Cambridge: Polity Press.

Bowie, F. 2006. *The anthropology of religion*. Oxford: Blackwell.

Bracke, S. 2003. Author(iz)ing Agency: Feminist Scholars Making Sense of Women's Involvement in Religious 'Fundamentalist' Movements. *European Journal of Women's Studies*, 10, no. 335: 335–46.

Brierley, P. 1999. Numbering the Nominals. In *They call themselves Christian*, ed. H. Wraight, 69–88. London: Christian Research.

—— 2000. *The tide is running out*. London: Christian Research.

—— 2003. 'Good news for the church!' http://www.christianresearch.org.uk/2001census.htmago, last accessed 21 March 2008.

—— 2006. *Pulling out of the nose dive: a contemporary picture of churchgoing; what the 2005 English church census reveals*. London: Christian Research.

Brown, C. 2001. *The death of Christian Britain*. London: Routledge.

Bruce, S. 1988. *The rise and fall of the new Christian right: Conservative Protestant politics in America*. Oxford: Clarendon.

—— 1995. *Religion in modern Britain*. Oxford: Oxford University Press.

—— 2001. Christianity in Britain, r.i.p. *Sociology of Religion*, 62, no. 2: 191–203.

—— 2002. *God is dead*. Oxford: Blackwell.

—— and T. Glendinning 2003. Religious beliefs and differences. In *Devolution: Scottish answers to Scottish questions*, ed. C. Bromley et al., 86–115. Edinburgh: Edinburgh University Press.

Bruner, J. 1987. Life as narrative. *Social Research*, 54, no. 1: 11–32.

Bryson, V. 1999. Patriarchy: a concept too useful to lose. *Contemporary Politics*, 5, no. 4: 311–25.

Buckser, A. 2008. Cultural change and the meanings of belief in Jewish Copenhagen. *Social Analysis*, 52, no.1: 39–55.

Burkitt, I. 1997. Social relationships and emotions. *Sociology*, 31, no.1: 37–55.

Burns, R.B. 2000. *Introduction to research methods*. London: Sage.

Burridge, K. 1973. *Encountering aborigines: a case study; anthropology and the Australian aboriginal*. New York: Pergamon Press.

—— 2004. Mambu: A Melanesian millennium. London: Routledge.

Butler, J. 1990. *Gender trouble: feminism and the subversion of identity*. New York: Routledge.

—— 1993. *Bodies that matter: on the discursive limits of 'sex'*. New York and London: Routledge.

Caldwell, J.C., O. Orubuloye, and P. Caldwell 1992. Underreaction to aids in sub-saharan Africa. *Sc. Sci. Med*, 34, no 1.: 1169–82.

Cannell, F. 2005. The Christianity of anthropology. *Journal of the Royal Anthropological Institute*, 11, no. 2: 191–400.

—— (ed.) 2007. *The anthropology of Christianity*. Durham and London: Duke University Press.

—— 2010. The anthropology of secularism. *Annual Review of Anthropology*, 39: 85–100.

—— (2011) English ancestors; the moral possibilities of popular genealogy. *Journal of the Royal Anthropological Institute*, 17, no. 3.

Campbell, C.D. 1971. *Towards a sociology of irreligion*. London: Macmillan.

Çarkoğlu, A. 2008. Social vs. spiritual capital in explaining philanthropic giving in a Muslim setting: The case of Turkey. In *Religion and the individual*, ed. A. Day, 111–26. Aldershot: Ashgate.

Carrithers, M. 1992. *Why humans have cultures: explaining anthropology and social diversity*. Oxford: Oxford University Press.

Carsten, J. (ed.) 2007. *Ghosts of memory: essays on remembrance and relatedness*. Oxford: Blackwell.

Carter, G.L. 1997. *The gun control movement*. New York: Simon and Schuster Macmillan.

Casanova, J. 1994. *Public religions in the modern world*. Chicago: University of Chicago Press.

Castañeda, Q.E. 2006. Ethnography in the forest: an analysis of ethics in the morals of anthropology. *Cultural Anthropology*, 21, no. 1: 121–45.

Chapple, E.E.D. and C.S. Coon 1947. *Principles of Anthropology*. London: Cape.

Chong, K.H. 1998. What it means to be Christian: the role of religion in the construction of ethnic identity and boundary among second-generation Korean Americans. *Sociology of Religion*, 59, no. 3: 259–86.

Christopher, K., P. England, T.M. Smeeding, and K.R. Philips 2002. The gender gap in poverty in modern nations: single motherhood, the market, and the state. *Sociological Perspectives*, 45, no. 3: 219–42.

Cimino, R. 2005. No God in common: American evangelical discourse on Islam after 9/11. *Review of Religious Research*, 47, no.2: 162–74.

Clark, D. 1982. *Between pulpit and pew: folk religion in a North Yorkshire fishing village*. Cambridge: Cambridge University Press.

Clydesdale, T. 2007. *The first year out, understanding American teens*. Chicago: University of Chicago Press.

Cohen, A.P. 1982. *Belonging: identity and social organization in British rural cultures*. Manchester: Manchester University Press.

—— 1985. *The symbolic construction of community*. London: Routledge.

Cohen, S. 1972. *Folk devils and moral panics: the creation of the mods and rockers*. London: Macgibbon and Kee.

Coleman, S. and P. Collins (eds) 2004. *Religion, identity and change: perspectives on global transformations.* Aldershot: Ashgate.

Colley, L. 1992. *Britons: forging the nation 1707–1837.* New Haven, Conn.: Yale University Press.

Collins, P. 2008a. Accommodating the individual and the social, the religious and the secular: Modelling the parameters of discourse in 'religious' contexts. In *Religion and the individual*, ed. A. Day, 143–56. Aldershot: Ashgate.

—— 2008b. Hospital chaplains: sustaining religious identity in a hostile environment? Presented at *Belief and identity in late modernity: transcending disciplinary boundaries*, University of Sussex, 8 November 2008.

Collins, P.H. 2000. Gender, black feminism, and black political economy. *Annuals of the American Academy of Political and Social Science*, 568: 41–53.

Collins-Mayo, S. 2008. Young people's spirituality and the meaning of prayer. In *Religion and the individual*, ed. A. Day, 33–46. Aldershot: Ashgate.

Converse, P.E. 1964. The nature of belief systems in mass publics. In *Ideology and discontent*, ed. D.P. Apter, 206–61. New York: Free Press.

—— 1970. Attitudes and non-attitudes: combination of a dialogue. In *The quantitative analysis of social problems*, ed. E. Tufte, 168–89. Reading, Mass.: Addison-Wesley.

Copen, C.E. and M. Silverstein 2008. The transmission of religious beliefs across generations: do grandparents matter? *Journal of Comparative Family Studies*, 38: 497–510.

Cornelio, J.S. 2008. New Paradigm Christianity and commitment-formation: the case of Hope Filipino (Singapore). In *Religion and the individual*, ed. A. Day, 65–78. Aldershot: Ashgate.

Crenshaw, K.W. 1991. Mapping the margins: intersectionality, identity politics, and violence against women of color. *Stanford Law Review*, 43, no. 6: 1241–99.

Crockett, A., and D. Voas 2006. Generations of decline: religious change in twentieth-century Britain. *Journal for the Scientific Study of Religion*, 45: 567–84.

Csordas, Thomas J. 1994. *Embodiment and experience: The existential ground of culture and self.* Cambridge: Cambridge University Press.

Cush, D. 2010. Teenage witchcraft in Britain. In *Religion and youth*, ed. S. Collins-Mayo and P. Dandelion, 74–81. Aldershot: Ashgate.

Davidman, L. 2007. The new voluntarism and the case of unsynagogued Jews. In *Everyday religion: observing modern religious lives*, ed. N.T. Ammerman, 51–67. Oxford and New York: Oxford University Press.

Davie, G. 1990. 'An ordinary god': the paradox of religion in contemporary Britain. *The British Journal of Sociology*, 41, no. 3: 395–421.

—— 1994. *Religion in Britain since 1945: believing without belonging.* Oxford: Blackwell.

—— 2002. *Europe: the exceptional case.* London: Darton, Longman and Todd.

—— 2004a. New approaches in the sociology of religion: A Western perspective. *Social Compass*, 51, no. 1: 73–84.

—— 2004b. 2003 Presidential Address: Creating an agenda in the sociology of religion: common sources/different pathways. *Sociology of Religion*, 65, no. 4: 323–40.

—— 2007. Vicarious religion: A methodological challenge. In *Everyday religion: observing modern religious lives*, ed. N.T. Ammerman, 21–36. Oxford and New York: Oxford University Press.

Davies, D. J. 2008. Cultural intensification: a theory for religion. In *Religion and the individual*, ed. A. Day, 7–18. Aldershot: Ashgate.

Dawson, A. 2008. Religious identity and millenarian belief in Santo Daime. In *Religion and the individual*, ed. A. Day, 183–96. Aldershot: Ashgate.

Day, A. 2005. Doing theodicy: an empirical study of a women's prayer group. *Journal of Contemporary Religion*, 20, no. 3: 343–56.

—— 2006. Believing in belonging: a case study from Yorkshire. Ph.D. thesis, Lancaster University, Lancaster, UK.

—— 2008a. Wilfully disempowered: a gendered response to a fallen world. *European Journal of Women's Studies*, 15, no. 3: 261–76.

—— (ed.) 2008b. *Religion and the individual*. Aldershot: Ashgate.

—— 2009a. Researching belief without asking religious questions. *Fieldwork in Religion*, 4, no. 1: 89–106.

—— 2009b. Believing in belonging: an ethnography of young people's constructions of belief. *Culture and Religion*, 10, no. 3: 263.

—— 2010a. Believing in belonging: an exploration of young people's social contexts and constructions of belief. In *Religion and youth*, ed. S. Collins-Mayo and P. Dandelion, 97–104. Aldershot: Ashgate.

—— 2010b. Propositions and performativity: relocating belief to the social. *Culture and Religion*, 11, no.1: 9–30.

—— and S. Coleman (eds) 2010. *Broadening the boundaries of belief*. Special issue of *Culture and Religion*, 11, no. 1.

Day, A. and S. Coleman 2013a. forthcoming "Secularization" In *Oxford Bibliographies Online: Anthropology*. New York: Oxford University Press.

Day, A. 2013b. forthcoming, 'Doing Qualitative Longitudinal Religious Research' in Linda Woodhead, ed., 'How to Research Religion: Putting Methods into Practice', Oxford: Oxford University Press.

Day, A. 2013c. forthcoming 'Understanding Generation A' in Nicola Slee, ed. *The Faith Lives of Girls and Women*, Aldershot, Ashgate.

Day, G. 2006. *Community and everyday life*. London and New York: Routledge.

Day, J.M. 1993. Speaking of belief: language, performance, and narrative in the psychology of religion. *International Journal for the Psychology of Religion*, 3, no. 4: 213–29.

De Graaf, N.D. and M. Te Grotenhuis 2008. Traditional Christian belief and belief in the supernatural: diverging trends in the Netherlands between 1979 and 2005. *Journal for the Scientific Study of Religion*, 47: 585–98.

Delanty, G. 2010 [2003]. *Community*. London and New York: Routledge.

Delphy, C. and D. Leonard 1992. *Familiar exploitation: a new analysis of marriage in contemporary western societies*. Cambridge: Polity Press.

Demerath, N.J., III. 1965. *Social class in American Protestantism*. Chicago: Rand McNally.

—— 1992. The sacred as surrogate: notes on implicit a-religion. *The Alister Hardy Trust Occasional Papers 1*. Westminster College: Oxford.

Demerath, N.J., III. 2000. The rise of 'cultural religion' in European Christianity: learning from Poland, Northern Ireland, and Sweden. *Social Compass*, 47, no.1: 127–39.

Demerath, N.J., III. 2001. *Crossing the Gods: World religions and worldly politics.* New Brunswick, N.J.: Rutgers University Press.

Demircioğlu, M. 2010. The rhetoric of belief and identity making in the experience of infertility. In *Broadening the boundaries of belief*, ed. A. Day and S. Coleman, 51–67. Special issue of *Culture and Religion*, 11, no. 1.

Dilger, H. 2008. We are all going to die: kinship, belonging, and the morality of hiv/aids related illnesses and deaths in rural Tanzania. *Anthropological Quarterly*, 81, no.1: 207–32.

Douglas, M. 1966. *Purity and danger: an analysis of pollution and taboo.* London: Routledge.

—— 1973. *Natural symbols: explorations in cosmology.* London: Barrie and Jenkins.

—— (ed.) 2004 [1970]. *Witchcraft confessions and accusations.* London: Routledge.

du Boulay, J. and R. Williams 1987. Amoral familism and the image of limited good: a critique from a European perspective. *Anthropological Quarterly*, 60, no. 1: 12–24.

Dudley, R.L. 1999. Youth religious commitment over time: a longitudinal study of retention. *Review of Religious Research*, 41, no. 1: 110–21.

Durkheim, E. 1915. *The elementary forms of the religious life.* London: George Allen and Unwin.

—— 1938 [1895]. *Rules of sociological method.* Trans. S.A. Solovay and J.H. Mueller. New York: The Free Press.

—— and M. Mauss 1963 [1902]. *Primitive classification.* Translated from the French and edited with an introduction by Rodney Needham. London: Cohen.

Eccles, J. 2008. Speaking personally: Women making meaning through subjectivised belief. In *Religion and the individual*, ed. A. Day, 19–32. Aldershot: Ashgate.

Edgell, P. and E. Tranby 2007. Religious influences on understandings of racial inequality in the united states. *Social Problems*, 54, no. 2: 263–88.

Elisha, O. 2008. Moral ambitions of grace: The paradox of compassion and accountability in Evangelical faith-based activism. *Cultural Anthropology*, 23: 154–89.

Elliot, N. 2008. It's special but is it spiritual? Presented at *Belief and identity in late modernity: transcending disciplinary boundaries*, University of Sussex, 8 November 2008.

Ellison, C. 1992. Are religious people nice people? Evidence from the National Survey of Black Americans. *Social Forces*, 71 no. 2: 411–30.

Engelke, M. 2002. The problem of belief: Evans-Pritchard and Victor Turner on 'the inner life'. *Anthropology Today*, 18, no.6: 3–8.

—— and M. Tomlinson (eds) 2006. The limits of meaning: case studies in the anthropology of Christianity. Oxford: Berghahn Books.

Evans-Pritchard, E.E. 1940. *The Nuer: a description of the modes of livelihood and political institutions of a nilotic people.* London: Oxford University Press.

—— 1976 [1937]. *Witchcraft, oracles, and magic among the Azande.* Oxford: Clarendon Press.

Fackre, G. 1982. *The religious right and Christian faith*. Grand Rapids, Mich.: William B Eerdmans.

Favret-Saada, J. 1980. *Deadly words: witchcraft in the Bocage*. Cambridge: Cambridge University Press.

Fenn, R.K. 2001. Religion and the secular; the sacred and the profane: the scope of the argument. In *The Blackwell companion to sociology of religion*, ed. R.K. Fenn, 3–22. Oxford: Blackwell.

Field, C.F. 2001. The haemorrhage of faith? Opinion polls as sources for religious practices, beliefs and attitudes in Scotland since the 1970s. *Journal of Contemporary Religion*, 16, no. 2: 157–75.

Firth, R. 1948. Religious belief and personal adjustment. *The Journal of the Royal Anthropological Institute of Great Britain and Ireland* 78, no. 1/2: 25–43.

Flick, U. 2002. *An introduction to qualitative research*. London: Sage Publications.

Ford, R. 2008. Is racial prejudice declining in Britain?. *British Journal of Sociology*, 59, no. 4: 609–36.

Fortes, M. 1983 [1959]. *Oedipus and Job in West African religion*. Cambridge: Cambridge University Press.

Fortier, A. 2000. *Migrant belongings, memory, space, identity*. Oxford: Berg.

Foucault, M. 1972. *The archeology of knowledge*. London: Tavistock.

—— 1980. *Power/knowledge: selected interviews and other writings 1972–1977*. Ed. C. Gordon. Brighton: Harvester Press.

Francis, L. 2003. The flaw in the 2001 census in England and Wales. In *Public faith? The state of religious practice in Britain*, ed. P. Avis, 45–64. London: SPCK.

Frazer, W.J. 1996 [1922]. *The golden bough*. London: Penguin.

Garnett, J., M. Grimley, A. Harris, W. Whyte, and S. Williams (eds) 2006. *Redefining Christian Britain: post 1945 perspectives*. London: SCM.

Gallup, G. and S. Jones 1989. *100 questions and answers*. Princeton: Princeton Research Centre.

Gans, H.J. 1979. *Deciding what's news: a study of CBS evening news, NBC nightly news, Newsweek, and Time*. New York: Pantheon.

Geertz, C. 1973. *The interpretation of cultures: selected essays*. New York: Basic Books.

Gellner, E. 1970. Concepts and society. In *Rationality*, ed. B.R. Wilson, 18–49. New York: Harper and Row.

Geyer, A.L. and R.F. Baumeister 2005. Religion, morality, and self-control: values, virtues, and vices. In *Handbook of the psychology of religion and spirituality*, ed. R.F. Paloutzian, and C.L. Park. New York: Guilford Press.

Giddens, A. 1990. *The consequences of modernity*. Stanford, Calif.: Stanford University Press.

—— 1991. *Modernity and self-identity: self and society in the late modern age*. Cambridge: Polity.

Gill, R. 1999. *Churchgoing and Christian ethics*. Cambridge: Cambridge University Press.

—— 2001. Future of religious participation and belief. In *The Blackwell companion to sociology of religion*, ed. R.K. Fenn, 279–91. Oxford: Blackwell.

Gill, R., C. Hadaway, and P. Marler 1998. Is religious belief declining in Britain? *Journal for the Scientific Study of Religion,* 37, no. 3: 507–16.

Gilroy, P. 1987. *There ain't no black in the Union Jack.* London: Hutchinson.

Glock, C. and R. Stark 1965. *Religion and society in tension.* Chicago: Rand McNally.

Godreau, I., H. Lloréns, and C. Vargas-Ramos 2010. Colonial incongruence at work: employing US census racial categories in Puerto Rico. *Anthropology News,* 51, no. 5: 11–12.

Goffman, E. 1959. *The presentation of self in everyday life.* New York: Doubleday.

Good, B.J. 1994. *Medicine, rationality, and experience.* Cambridge: Cambridge University Press.

Goode, E. 2000. *Paranormal beliefs: a sociological introduction.* Prospect heights, Ill.: Waveland Press, Inc.

Graveling, E. 2010. That is not religion, that is the gods: Ways of conceiving religious practices in rural Ghana. In *Broadening the boundaries of belief,* ed. A. Day and S. Coleman, 31–50. Special issue of *Culture and Religion,* 11, no. 1.

Grillo, R. 2005. Saltdean can't cope: protests against asylum-seekers in an English seaside suburb. *Ethnic and Racial studies,* 28, no. 2: 235–60.

Gusfield, J. 1963. Symbolic crusade: Status politics and the American Temperance Movement. Champaign, Ill.: University of Illinois Press.

Hadaway C.K. and P.L. Marler 2005. How many Americans attend worship each week? An alternative approach to measurement. *Journal for the Scientific Study of Religion,* 44, no. 3: 307–22.

—— —— and M. Chaves 1993. What the polls don't show: a closer look at U.S. church attendance. *American Sociological Review,* 58, no. 6: 741–52.

Hall, S. 1996. Introduction: who needs 'identity'? In *Questions of cultural identity,* ed. S. Hall and P. du Gay, 3–11. London: Sage.

Halman, L. and O. Riis (eds) 2003. *Religion in secularizing society: the Europeans' religion at the end of the 20th century.* Leiden and Boston: Brill.

Hammersley, M. and P. Atkinson 1995. *Ethnography: principles in practice.* London: Routledge.

Hardy, A.C. 1979. *The spiritual nature of man: a study of religious experience.* Oxford: Clarendon Press.

Harris, A. 2010. 'A place to grow spiritually and socially': the experiences of young pilgrims to Lourdes. In *Religion and youth,* ed. S. Collins-Mayo and P. Dandelion, 139–48. Aldershot: Ashgate.

Harrison, F.V. 1995. The persistent power of 'race' in the cultural and political economy of racism. *Annual Review of Anthropology,* 24: 47–74.

Hay, D. 1982. *Exploring inner space: scientists and experience.* Harmondsworth: Penguin Books.

—— and K. Hunt 2000. *Understanding the spirituality of people who don't go to church.* Nottingham: Nottingham University.

Hayes, D. and A. Hudson 2001. *Basildon: the mood of the nation.* London: Demos.

Heelas, P. 1996. *The new age movement.* Oxford: Blackwell.

—— and L. Woodhead 2005 (with B. Seel, B. Szersynski, and K. Tusting). *The spiritual revolution: why religion is giving way to spirituality.* Oxford: Blackwell.

Heintz, M. (ed.) 2009. *The anthropologies of morality*. Oxford: Bergahn.

Henkel, H. 2005. Between belief and unbelief lies the performance of salat: meaning and efficacy of a muslim ritual. *The Journal of the Royal Anthropological Institute*, 11, no. 3: 487–507.

Hervieu-Léger, D. 2000. *Religion as a chain of memory*. Cambridge: Polity Press.

Hill, P.C. and R.W. Hood 1999. *Measures of religiosity*. Birmingham, Ala.: Religious Education Press.

Hiller, P.T., J.P. Linstroth, and P. Ayala 2009. 'I am Maya, not Guatemalan, nor Hispanic': the belongingness of Mayas in Southern Florida. *Forum qualitative sozialforschung/Forum: Qualitative Social Research*, 10, no. 3.

Himmelstein, J.L. 1983. The new Christian right. In *The New Christian Right*, ed. R.C. Liebman and R. Withnow, 15–30. New York: Aldine.

Hochschild, A. and A. Machung 1989. *The second shift: working parents and the revolution at home*. Berkeley and London: University of California Press.

Hoge, D.R, G.H. Petrillo, and E.I. Smith 1982. Transmission of religious and social values from parents to teenage children. *Journal of Marriage and Family*, 44, no. 3: 569–80.

Hubbard, P. 2005. Accommodating otherness: anti-asylum centre protest and the maintenance of white privilege. *Transactions of the Institute of British Geographers*, 30, no.1: 52–65.

Hunt, A. 1997. 'Moral panic' and moral language in the media. *British Journal of Sociology*, 48, no. 4: 629–48.

Hunt, S. 2002. *Religion in Western society*. Basingstoke: Palgrave.

—— 2005. *Religion in everyday life*. Abingdon. Routledge.

Hunter, J.D. 1983. The Liberal reaction. In *The New Christian Right*, ed. R.C. Liebman and R. Withnow, 150–67. New York: Aldine.

Inglis, T. 2007. Catholic identity in contemporary Ireland: belief and belonging to tradition. *Journal of Contemporary Religion*, 22, no. 2: 205–20.

Jackall, R. 1988. *Moral mazes*. New York and Oxford: Oxford University Press.

James, W. 1982 [1903]. *The varieties of religious experience*. New York: Penguin.

Jenkins, R. 1997. *Rethinking ethnicity*. London: Sage.

Johnstone, R.L. 1975. *Religion and society in interaction: the sociology of religion*. New Jersey: Prentice Hall.

Jordan, B., M. Edley, and S. James 1994. *Putting the family first*. London: University College London Press.

Juergensmeyer, M. 2006. Nationalism and religion. In *The Blackwell companion to the study of religion*, ed. R. Segal, 357–68. Oxford: Blackwell.

Kadushin, C. 2007. Theologically correct survey questions. Paper delivered to *2007 conference of the Society for the Scientific Study of Religion, Tampa, Florida*, 4 November 2007.

Kapferer, B. 2001. Anthropology: the paradox of the secular. *Social Anthropology*, 9: 341–4.

Keane, W. 2002. Sincerity, modernity and the protestants. *Cultural Anthropology*, 17, no. 1: 65–92.

Keane, W. 2007. *Christian moderns.* Berkeley and Los Angeles: University of California Press.

—— 2008. The evidence of the senses and the materiality of religion. *Journal of the Royal Anthropological Institute,* 14: 110–27.

Keenan, M. 2008. Freedom in chains: Religion as enabler and constraint in the lives of gay male Anglican clergy. In *Religion and the individual,* ed. A. Day, 169–82. Aldershot: Ashgate.

Kirsch, T.G. 2004. Restaging the will to believe: religious pluralism, anti-syncretism, and the problem of belief. *American Anthropologist,* 106, no. 4: 699–709.

Kuper, A. 1973. *Anthropology and anthropologist.* London and New York: Routledge.

—— 2008. Changing the subject: about cousin marriage, among other things. *Journal of the Royal Anthropological Institute,* 14: 717–35.

Lambeck, M. (ed.) 2002. *A reader in the anthropology of religion.* Malden, Mass.: Blackwell.

Lambert, Y. 2004. A turning point in religious evolution in Europe. *Journal of Contemporary Religion,* 19, no. 1: 29–45.

Lamont, M. and M. Virag 2002. The study of boundaries in the social sciences. *Annual Review of Sociology,* 28: 167–95.

Larner, C. 1984. *Witchcraft and religion: the politics of popular belief.* Oxford: Blackwell.

Leeman, J. 2004. Racializing language: a history of linguistic ideologies in the US census. *The Journal of Language and Politics,* 3, no. 3: 507–34.

Levi-Strauss, C. 1966 [1922]. *The savage mind.* Chicago: University of Chicago Press.

Levitt, P. 2007. Redefining the boundaries of belonging: the transnationalization of religious life. In *Everyday religion: observing modern religious lives,* ed. N.T. Ammerman, 103–20. Oxford and New York: Oxford University Press.

Lévy-Bruhl, L. 1926. *How natives think.* London: George Allen and Unwin, Ltd.

Liebman, R.C. and R. Wuthnow (eds) 1983. *The New Christian Right.* New York: Aldine.

Lindquist, G. and S. Coleman 2008. Introduction: against belief? *Social Analysis,* 52, no. 1: 1–18.

Lopez, D. 1998. 'Belief'. In *Critical terms for religious studies,* ed. M.C. Taylor, 21–35. Chicago: University of Chicago Press.

Lüchau, P. 2007. By faith alone? Church attendance and Christian faith in three European countries. *Journal of contemporary religion,* 22, no. 1: 35–48.

Luckmann, T. 1967. *The invisible religion.* London: Collier-Macmillan.

Luhrmann, T.M. 1989. *Persuasions of the witch's craft.* Cambridge: Harvard University Press.

—— 2007. How do you learn to know that it is God who speaks? In *Learning religion, anthropological approaches,* ed. D. Berliner and R. Sarró, 83–102. New York and Oxford: Berghahn Books.

Lukes, S. 2005. *Power: a radical view.* Basingstoke: Palgrave Macmillan.

Lynch, G. 2002. *After religion: 'generation x' and the search for meaning.* London: Darton, Longman, and Todd Ltd.

—— 2007. *The New Spirituality: An Introduction to Progressive Belief in the Twenty-First Century.* London: IB Tauris.

Macfarlane, A. 1970. *Witchcraft in Tudor and Stuart England: a regional and comparative study.* London: Routledge and Kegan Paul.

Mahdavi, P. 2008. *Passionate uprisings: Iran's sexual revolution.* Stanford, Calif.: Stanford University Press.

Malinowski, B. 1961 [1922]. *Argonauts of the Western Pacific.* New York: E.P. Dutton.

—— 2002 [1935]. *Coral gardens and their magic: a study of the methods of tilling the soil.* London: Routledge.

Mannheim, K. 1952. *The problem of generations, in the sociology of knowledge.* London: Routledge.

Margo, J. 2008. *Make me a criminal: preventing youth crime.* London: IPPR.

Martin, D. 1978. *A general theory of secularization.* Oxford: Blackwell.

Mason, D. 1995. *Race and ethnicity in modern Britain.* Oxford: Oxford University Press.

Mason, M., A. Singleton, and R. Webber 2007. *The spirit of Generation Y.* Melbourne: John Garratt.

Mcleod, H. and U. Ustorf (eds) 2003. *The decline of Christendom in western Europe 1750–2000.* Cambridge: Cambridge University Press.

Merino, S.M. 2010. Religious diversity in a 'Christian nation': the effects of theological exclusivity and interreligious contact on the acceptance of religious diversity. *Journal for the Scientific Study of Religion,* 49: 231–46.

Middleton, R. and S. Putney 1962. Religion, normative standards, and behavior. *Sociometry,* 25, no. 2: 141–52.

Mitchell, C. 2005. Beyond the ethnic marker: religion and social identification in northern Ireland. *Sociology of Religion,* 66, no. 1: 3–21.

—— and J. Todd 2007. Between the devil and the deep blue sea: nationality, power and symbolic trade-offs among Evangelical Protestants in contemporary northern Ireland. *Nations and Nationalism,* 13, no. 4: 637–55.

Mitchell, J.P. 1997. A moment with Christ: the importance of feelings in the analysis of belief. *Journal of the Royal Anthropological Institute,* 3: 79–94.

—— and H. Mitchell. 2008. For belief: embodiment and immanence in Catholicism and Mormonism. *Social Analysis: the international journal of cultural and social practice,* 52: 9–94.

Mol, H. 1976. *Identity and the sacred: A sketch for a new social-scientific theory of religion.* New York: Free Press.

Morgan, B. 2003. 'Church enthrones new archbishop'. http://news.bbc.co.uk/1/hi/wales/3060347.stm, last accessed 23 March 2008.

Morgan, S.P. 1983. A research note on religion and morality: Are religious people nice people? *Social Forces,* 61, no. 3: 683–92.

Needham, R. 1972. *Belief, language and experience.* Chicago: Chicago University Press.

Niemelä, K. 2008. *Does confirmation training really matter?* Tampere: Church Research Institute.

Norris, P. and R. Inglehart 2004. *Sacred and secular: religion and politics worldwide.* Cambridge: Cambridge University Press.

Nussbaum, M. 1999. *Sex and social justice.* Oxford: Oxford University Press.

Ozorak, E.J. 1996. The power, but not the glory: how women empower themselves through religion. *Journal for the Scientific Study of Religion*, 35, no.1: 17–29.

Pace, E. 2007. Religion as communication: The changing shape of Catholicism in Europe. In *Everyday religion: observing modern religious lives*, ed. N.T. Ammerman, 37–50. Oxford and New York: Oxford University Press.

Peacock, J.L. and R.W. Tyson 1989. *Pilgrims of paradox: Calvinism and experience among the primitive Baptists of the Blue Ridge.* Washington and London: Smithsonian Series in Ethnographic Inquiry.

Percy, M. 2004. Losing our space, finding our place. In *Religion, identity and change*, ed. S. Coleman and P. Collins, 26–41. Aldershot: Ashgate.

Pina-Cabral, J. 2001. Three points on secularism and anthropology. *Social Anthropology*, 9: 329–33.

Pollack, D. 2008. Religious change in Europe: theoretical considerations and empirical findings. *Social Compass*, 55, no. 2: 168–86.

Putnam, R.D. and D.E.Campbell 2010. 'Walking away from church'. http://articles. latimes.com/2010/oct/17/opinion/la-oe-1017-putnam-religion-20101017, last accessed 25 March 2011.

Quarles, C.L. 2004. *Christian identity: the Aryan American bloodline religion.* Jefferson, N.C.: MacFarlane & Company.

Ray, L. and D. Smith 2004. Racist offending, policing and community conflict. *Sociology*, 38, no. 4: 681–99.

Regnerus, M.D., C. Smith, and B. Smith. 2004. Social context in the development of adolescent religiosity. *Applied Development Science*, 8, no. 1: 27–38.

Reimer, K.S., A.C. Dueck, J.P. Morgan, and D.E. Kessel 2008. *A Peaceable Common: Gathered Wisdom from Exemplar Muslim & Christian Peacemakers.* In *Religion and the individual*, ed. A. Day, 79–94. Aldershot: Ashgate.

Reinharz, S. 1992. *Feminist methods in social research.* New York and Oxford: Oxford University Press.

Rice, T.W. 2003. Believe it or not: religious and other paranormal beliefs in the United States. *Journal for the Scientific Study of Religion*, 42: 95–106.

Riis, O. and L. Woodhead 2010. *A sociology of religious emotion.* Oxford: Oxford University Press.

Robbins, J. 2003. What is a Christian? Notes toward an anthropology of Christianity. *Religion*, 33, no. 3: 191–9.

—— 2007. Continuity thinking and the problem of Christian culture. *Current Anthropology*, 48, no. 1: 5–17.

—— 2006. Afterword: on limits, ruptures, meaning and meaninglessness. In *The limits of meaning: case studies in the anthropology of Christianity*, ed. M. Engelke and M. Tomlinson, 211–24. Oxford: Berghahn Books.

—— 2009. Morality, value and radical cultural change. In *The anthropologies of morality*, ed. M. Heintz, 62–80. Oxford: Bergahn.

Robertson Smith, W. 1912. *Lectures and essays of William Robertson Smith*. London: Adam and Charles Black.

Roof, W.C. 1993. A generation of seekers: the spiritual journeys of the baby boom generation. San Francisco: Harper.

—— and W. McKinney 1987. *American mainline religion: its changing shape and future*. New Brunswick, N.J.: Rutgers University Press.

Rudge, L. 1998. 'I am nothing' – does it matter? A critique of current religious education policy and practice in England on behalf of the silent majority. *British Journal of Religious Education*, 20, no. 3: 155–65.

Rudiak-Gould, P. 2010. Being Marshallese and Christian: A case of multiple identities and contradictory beliefs. In *Broadening the boundaries of belief*, ed. A. Day and S. Coleman, 69–87. Special issue of *Culture and Religion*, 11, no. 1.

Ruel, M. 1982. Christians as believers. In *Religious organization and religious experience*, ed. J. Davis, 9–32. Asa Monograph 21. London and New York: Academic Press.

—— 1997. *Belief, ritual and the securing of life: reflexive essays on a Bantu religion*. Leiden: Brill.

Sammet, K. 2009. Religious and non-religious worldviews in precarious conditions of life. Paper presented to ISSR/SISR Spain, July 2009.

—— 2011. Fate, Luck or God's Will: Religious and Secularized Interpretations of the Contingent. Paper presented to BSA, London, April 2011.

Sandberg, R. 2008. Religion and the individual: A socio-legal perspective. In *Religion and the individual*, ed. A. Day, 157–68. Aldershot: Ashgate.

Savage, S., S. Collins-Mayo, B. Mayo, and B. Cray 2006. *Making sense of generation y: the worldview of 15–25-year-olds*. London: Church House Publishing.

Schnapper, D. 1994. The debate on immigration and the crisis of national identity. *West European Politics*, 17: 127–39.

Schofield-Clark, L. 2007. Religion, twice removed: Exploring the role of media in religious understandings among 'secular' young people. In *Everyday Religion, observing modern religious lives*, ed. N.T. Ammerman, 69–82. Oxford and New York: Oxford University Press.

Shiner, L. 1967. The concept of secularization in empirical research. *Journal for the Scientific Study of Religion*, 6, no. 2: 207–20.

Singh, J. 2010. British Sikh youth: identity, hair and the turban. In *Religion and youth*, ed. S. Collins-Mayo and P. Dandelion, 131–8. Aldershot: Ashgate.

Skeggs, B. (ed.) 1995. *Feminist cultural theory: process and production*. Manchester: Manchester University Press.

—— 1997. *Formations of class and gender: becoming respectable*. London: Sage.

Smart, N. 1998. *The world's religions*. Cambridge: Cambridge University Press.

Smith, C. and M. Denton 2005. *Soul searching: the religious and spiritual lives of American teenagers*. Oxford: Oxford University Press.

Smith, W.C. 1967. *Problems of religious truth*. New York: Scribner's.

—— 1977. *Belief and history*. Charlottesville: University of Virginia Press.

Smith, W.C. 1978. *The meaning and end of religion*. London: SPCK.

—— 1979. *Faith and belief*. Princeton: Princeton University Press.

Southworth, J.R. 2005. 'Religion' in the 2001 census for England and Wales. *Population, Space and Place*, 11: 75–88.

Speer, S.A. and I. Hutchby 2003. From ethics to analytics: aspects of participants' orientations to the presence and relevance of recording devices. *Sociology*, 37, no. 2: 315–38.

Stark, R. 1999. Secularization, R.I.P. *Sociology of Religion*, 60, no. 3: 249–73.

—— E. Hamberg, and A.S. Miller 2005. Exploring spirituality and unchurched religions in America, Sweden, and Japan. *Journal of Contemporary Religion*, 20, no. 1: 3–23.

—— and L.R. Iannaccone 1993. Rational choice propositions about religious movements. *Religion and the Social Order*, 3A: 241–61.

Stewart, C. 2001. Secularism as an impediment to anthropological research. *Social Anthropology*, 9: 325–8.

—— and R. Shaw (eds) 1994. *Syncretism/anti-syncretism: the politics of religious synthesis*. London: Routledge.

Strathern, M. 1984. Domesticity and the denigration of women. In *Rethinking women's roles: perspectives from the pacific*, ed. D. O'Brien and S.W. Tiffany, 13–31. Berkeley: University of California Press.

Street, A. 2010. Belief as relational action: Christianity and cultural change in Papua New Guinea. *Journal of the Royal Anthropological Institute*, 16: 260–78.

Stringer, M.D. 1996. Towards a situational theory of belief. *Journal of the Anthropological Society of Oxford*, 27, no. 3: 217–34.

Sutcliffe, S. (ed.) 2004. *Religion: empirical studies*. Aldershot: Ashgate.

Swatos, W.H. and K.J. Christiano 1999. Secularization theory: the course of a concept. *Sociology of Religion*, 60, no.3: 209–28.

Swidler, A. 1986. Culture in Action: Symbols and Strategies. *American Sociological Review*, 51, no. 2: 273–86.

Tajfel, H. and J.C. Turner 1986. The social identity theory of inter-group behavior. In *Psychology of intergroup relations*, ed. S. Worchel and L.W. Austin, 2–24. Chigago: Nelson-Hall.

Tambiah, S.J. 1985. *Culture, thought, and social action: an anthropological perspective*. Cambridge, Mass.: Harvard University Press.

—— 1990. *Magic, science, religion, and the scope of rationality: the Lewis Henry Morgan lectures, 1984*. Cambridge: Cambridge University Press.

Tilley, J. and A. Heath 2007. The decline of British national pride. *The British Journal of Sociology*, 58, no. 4: 661–78.

Tipton, S. 1982. *Getting saved from the sixties: moral meaning in conversion and cultural change*. Berkeley: University of California Press.

Towler, R. 1974. *Homo Religious: Sociological problems in the study of religion*. New York: St. Martin's Press.

Tylor, E. 1958 [1871]. *Primitive culture*. New York: Harper.

Van Gennep, A. 1960. *The rites of passage*. Chicago: Chicago University Press.

Vitebsky, P. 2006. *The reindeer people: living with animals and spirits in Siberia.* New York: Houghton Mifflin Harcourt.

Voas, D. 2009. The rise and fall of fuzzy fidelity in Europe. *European Sociological Review* 25, no. 2: 155–68.

—— 2010. Explaining change over time in religious involvement. In *Religion and youth,* ed. S. Collins-Mayo and P. Dandelion, 25–32. Aldershot: Ashgate.

—— and S. Bruce 2004. The 2001 census and Christian identification in Britain. *Journal of Contemporary Religion,* 10, no 1: 23–8.

—— and A. Crockett. 2005. Religion in Britain: neither believing nor belonging. *Sociology,* 39, no. 1: 11–28.

—— and A. Day 2007. Secularity in Great Britain. In *Secularism and secularity: contemporary international perspectives,* ed. B.A. Kosmin and A. Keysar, 95–112. Hartford, Conn.: Institute for the study of secularism in society and culture.

—— —— 2010. Recognizing secular Christians: toward an unexcluded middle in the study of religion. *The Association of Religion Data Archives.* http://www.thearda.com/rrh/papers/guidingpapers.asp.

—— D.V.A. Olson, and A. Crockett 2002. Religious pluralism and participation: why previous research is wrong. American Sociological Review, 67, no. 2: 212–30.

Walby, S. 1990. *Theorizing patriarchy.* Oxford: Blackwell.

Walls, P. 2001. Religion, ethnicity and nation in the census: some thoughts on the inclusion of Irish ethnicity and Catholic religion. *Radical Statistics,* 78: 48–62.

Walter, T. and G. Davie 1998. The religiosity of women in the modern west. *The British Journal of Sociology,* 49, no. 4: 640–60.

Ward, K. 1992. *In defence of the soul.* Oxford: Oneworld Publications.

Warner, R. 2008. Autonomous conformism: the paradox of entrepreneurial protestantism (spring harvest: a case study). In *Religion and the individual,* ed. A. Day, 151–78. Aldershot: Ashgate.

Warner, R.S. 1993. Work in progress towards a new paradigm for the sociological study of religion in the United States. *The American Journal of Sociology,* 98, no. 5: 1044–93.

—— and R.H. Williams 2010. The role of families and religious institutions in transmitting faith among Christians, Muslims and Hindus in the USA. In *Religion and youth,* ed. S. Collins-Mayo and P. Dandelion, 159–66. Aldershot: Ashgate.

Weber, M. 1922. *The sociology of religion.* Boston: Beacon Press.

—— 1978. *Economy and society.* Ed. G. Roth and C. Wittich. Berkeley: University of California Press.

—— 1992 [1930]. *The protestant ethic and the spirit of capitalism.* London: Routledge.

Weller, P. 2004. Identity, politics and the future(s) of religion in the UK: the case of the religion questions in the 2001 decennial census. *Journal of Contemporary Religion,* 19, no. 1: 3–21.

West, C. and D.H. Zimmerman 1987. Doing Gender. *Gender and Society,* 1: 125–51.

Williams, S.L. 2009. Doing culture with girls like me: why trying on gender and intersectionality matters. *Sociology Compass*, 3, no. 2: 217–33.

Wilson, B. 1966. *Religion in secular society*. London: C.A. Watts & Co. Ltd.

—— (ed.) 1974. *Rationality*. Oxford: Blackwell.

—— 2001. Salvation, secularization, and de-moralization. In *The Blackwell companion to sociology of religion*, ed. R.K. Fenn, 39–51. Oxford: Blackwell.

Winter, M. and C. Smart 1993. Believing and belonging in rural England. *British Journal of Sociology*, 44, no. 4: 635–51.

Wood, M. 2004. Kinship identity and nonformative spiritual seekership. In *Religion, identity and change: perspectives on global transformations*, ed. S. Coleman and P. Collins, 191–206. Aldershot: Ashgate.

Woodhead, L. 2000. Feminism and the sociology of religion: from gender-blindness to gendered difference. In *The Blackwell companion to sociology of religion*, ed. R. Fenn, 67–84. Oxford: Blackwell.

Wraight, H. (ed.) 1999. They call themselves Christian. London: Christian Research.

Wulff, D. 1999. Beyond belief and unbelief. *Research in the Social Scientific Study of Religion*, 10: 1–15.

Wuthnow, R. 1994. *Sharing the journey: support groups and America's new quest for community*. New York: Free Press.

—— 1998. *After Heaven: Spirituality in America Since the 1950s*. Berkeley and Los Angeles: University of California Press.

—— 2001. Spirituality and spiritual practice. In *The Blackwell companion to sociology of religion*, ed. R.K. Fenn, 306–20. Oxford: Blackwell.

Xiaowen, L., R. O'Leary, and L. Yaojun 2008. Who are the believers in religion in China? In *Religion and the individual*, ed. A. Day, 47–64. Aldershot: Ashgate.

Yin, R.K. 2003. Case study research design and methods. Thousand Oaks, Calif. and London: Sage.

Young, J. 1999. *The exclusive society*. London: Sage.

Zinnbauer, B.J., K.L. Pargament, B. Cole, M. Rye, E.M. Butter, T.J. Belavich, K.M. Hipp, A.B. Scott, and L. Kadar 1997. Religion and spirituality: unfuzzying the fuzzy. *Journal for the Scientific Study of Religion*, 36, no. 4: 549–64.

Zuckerman, P. 2008. *Society without God*. New York and London: New York University Press.

Zurcher, L.A. and R.G. Kirkpatrick 1971. The anti-pornography campaign: A symbolic crusade. *Social Problems*, 19, no. 2: 217–38.

Index

Index

5T Durkheim – key = how belief upholds society
6T Davie – belief is propositional – functional 21
8T Weber – meaning understood subjectively – individualistic – Substantive 21

Jago – belief propositional, individualistic universalising
8R ∟ also individualistic – private
– fair to define belief

9R read (2014)   cf 191 *
⌐ Anthropology = belief functional
∟ Sociology = belief substantive – meaning centred

∟T⌐ Durkheim – Society determinstic
Belief pre-formed.
∟ Belief performed – Weber
Beliefs
Produced through rituals of belonging 16
* the emotional experience of belonging being celebrated *

11B Contradiction in 'belief' overcome by the *
need to preserve relationships
13T and pragmatic – to achieve a sense of coherence
13B Religion a subset to the Social – Faith
14T Cultural patterns make human when they are driven by the problem of meaning – Weber
14 Influence of symbols and values

16T Belief in – believing
Belief that – knowing – propositional
17T Medieval Europe – belief = a form of knowledge
Post Enlightenment – belief = believing
[Protestant]
230 [Re – its truth lies in whether it creates a communal world.]

19 B Boyer - most important distributary
~ Sacred ~ others - not sacred ~ profane
(Durkheim)

[Re = Naughter - communise ~ non communal]
   their religious institutions
   conversive to this

[Ok ~ what matters is how belief
   shapes society = re-formed &
   but also have then performed
   so to know in what aims first
   preceded the communion was out]

20 Is the search for meaning a religious concern.°

25 B Community bathe free *

26 T Religion a source of strong identity

27 B Belief is an expression of how they belong

_____

29 V.K Jordan - a 'Christian' who doesn't   cf. 167 B
                    believe anything

38 [no membering 3Ss or 4Es]
53 'Community' as boundary of relationships
   54 signifies a cultural identity
   Cohen on symbols
   community & core religious 'precepts' *
53 Believing in belonging better than
   the religious/secular concepts *
68 Vital aspect of anthropocentric beliefs
   ~ to nurture of sense & belonging (to *
   their own group).
            L From exclusive community]
[this concept of 'belief' very sociological
   as my 3Ss = can feste of very
   exclusive collective]
[56 T Seven dimensions of belief 158f
   [Apples and oranges]
[Sure derives function from belief
   ~ no vice versa] &

_____

174 Self-identification with Xtianity — 'nominalism'

177 ~~Side-steps~~ what is 'a true Christian'

└ 177 A sense of cultural belonging
— she wants to cash 'cultural' out
└ 177 doesn't attend church

189 ⊓ [He claim is that self-identifying as
'Christian' = 'belief in belonging' to a
culture which embraces Christian
history and rituals and symbols (still)]
— but the person has no 'belief' of
a traditional Christian kind.

[I think this is the same as my belonging
without believing]   * *

182 then narrative Christian identity * *
anchored with —
family (love) — natal / odds 207
where English Protestant — ethnic   class 207
* affirmation with an abstract collectivity
                                            187

187 Association with a Church
which is absent community and
expectational ———→ aspirational

189 this leads to 'doing Christianity' in the
sense — performative Christian nominalism
Durkheimian in character
Been the religious — secular divide.

193 The power of 'longing for belonging'   *
— strengthens My need to reinforce
relative boundaries
Religion located in the social — to strengthen
~~belief~~   identity
194 'performative belief' ——— believers,
embodied performance where the object   *
of worship is the experience of belonging
'involves belonging and excluding'

Performative act ———
claiming social and cultural identities
— in space and time — a positive face
└ of imagined communities, 1950

26 Belonging focused on decased latter area?

27 People turn to 'religion' when vulnerable
   Belief in doing - unto others - but only to ✱
   those under whom they wish to belong

30 [Importance of patriarchy & faith   ✱
      clericalism —
         not just priest & people
            but male & female and the young]

32 The widening of the religious - secular
                                      debate

33 Her anthropocentric refusal
       theocentric

04 She challenges the assumption that
      individualism is growing

[Still not quite sure what she means by
   'belief' — commitment to,
      investment in, value system,
         conviction ?]

Lightning Source UK Ltd.
Milton Keynes UK
UKOW04f0623020314

227404UK00002B/2/P